Why Modern Society Invented UFOs

To my dad, who during my psychotic breakdown, told me whatever you want out of life you can achieve it. By golly, it stuck!

Why Modern Society Invented UFOs

Albert Ramos

Self-published through Createspace.com, a subsidiary of Amazon.com

Ramos, Albert, 1970 –

Why Modern Society Invented UFOs/ by Albert Ramos

Includes bibliographical references and index.

ISBN-13: 978-1512337174

Cover Image: Maggie Cousins, *Why Modern Society Invented UFOs.*

Acknowledgements

I would like to thank my mentor and good friend, Frank Montanez, who inspired me to write an updated edition for this book. As far as my proofreaders, Andrew Fleishman and A.B. Lugo, did a superb job correcting my mistakes. And without Orlando Plaza introducing me to Lugo, I would not be able to meet a very talented man.

Table of Contents

Foreword

Whenever I tell people I published a book about UFOs with a skeptical approach, they often ask how I got involved in such a topic. It was in the 1990s, during the alien abduction craze that intrigued me.

The unusual thing I that noticed was that the large majority of those abducted were white. I couldn' t help to realize the typical description of the aliens. They were short, often less than five feet tall, grey-skinned extraterrestrials. But I soon realized how the nearest and possible inhabitable planet, most especially if it had intelligent life, was just so damn far away. Thus, I concluded that the alien abduction narrative had to be some form of delusion.

Of pertinence was how these grey-skinned aliens had slanted, oversized eyes that smacked of East Asian culture; if that was the case, the alien abduction hysteria had to be Earthbound. It became obvious to me that these aliens represented the fear of Japanese invasion. I also noticed how these abduction accounts coincided with the rise of the immigration of ethnic groups from Third World, non-white societies.

It took some time to learn about UFOs. I dove into learning about alien abductions before I could formulate my thesis. Earning a degree in sociology and fascinated with social theory, it was reasonable to apply these tools into my study. After seven years of writing, *How Modern Society Invented UFOs* was born. I was still learning to write - finding my voice, learning about transition, and discovering flow in my craft. I decided to update *Modern Society* with more information and a more readable text. I now bring you, *Why Modern Society Invented UFOs*.

Introduction

Unidentified Flying Objects (UFOs) have been alluring since 1947. In this book, we will explore this modern myth in the making, where whoever have been flying such aircrafts must be from outer space. Although we will discuss nuts and bolts, we do so in passing. Thus, a reader, who firmly believes we are being visited from space aliens, and is looking for the meat and bones of UFOs, will not find it here. Our approach will be *socio-skeptical*; that is, the belief in UFOs will be treated as a myth – and we will explain why this is the case. While the skeptical aspect is partly nuts and bolts, it complements the sociological approach with the attempt to show that Earth has not been nor is being visited by beings from another galaxy, nor from another dimension. For example, UFO motifs will be explained as reflections of culture and time period.

The thesis of this book is twofold. First, it will be argued that the myth of Earth-visiting aliens is a result of terrestrial conditions, namely the anxiety-filled era of the Cold War. Scoondly, a religious crisis in the second part of the twentieth century called for something novel, even if experimenting with new religious beliefs was welcomed in order to fill the void. Bear in mind, many Americans believed they were living in the end of times. A multitude claimed they directly communicated with aliens and later, starting in the 1960s, many would claim abduction by aliens for religious or spiritual reasons. Not everyone believed aliens were benevolent, but the belief in evil aliens would become more pervasive by the 1980s and onwards.

Since our investigation pinpoints the Cold War, we should briefly look at what led to the animosity between the United States and the Soviet Union. In 1943, the American-Soviet alignment soared, an alignment built during the World War II. After the war, circumstances changed. Border disputes erupted between the West and the Soviets as the latter annexed territories in Eastern Europe. Like the American public, their politicians were displeased. The President of the U.S. at the time, Harry S Truman, put pressure on the Soviets to relinquish the territories. Despite the tough policy of Truman, the Soviets did not budge. The Soviets' excuse was to keep Germany in check since, through Poland, they were invaded.

Additionally, Americans feared communism. In 1917, the Soviets violently overthrew their capitalistic system and were bent on spreading it beyond their borders. The escalation between both countries vastly increased right after World War II. Both countries, not just the U.S., now had atom bombs. There were mutual feelings of distrust at a time when both countries emerged as superpowers.[1]

Indeed, the militaries of the U.S. and the Soviet Union had great size and strength; missiles were stationed, pointing at each other, in their respective allies. Due to the outbreak of the Korean War, Korea became divided between North and South. The Koreans in the North became Communists and were supported by the Soviets, while those in the South stayed democratic and capitalistic and were backed by the U.S. As an ally of the Soviets, Cubans (themselves Communist), allowed their much larger supporters to bring nuclear missiles to be stationed on their land since Cuba was much, much closer to the U.S. The Soviets, however, were not successful in their mission, thwarted by the American military. This became known as the Cuban Missile Crisis. Both

---

[1] John Lewis Gaddis, *The U.S. and the Origins of the Cold War: 1943-1946*. The University of Texas at Austin, University Microfilms, Ann Arbor, MI, 1968.

countries spied on each other, and because of espionage the Americans were able to counter since they had foreknowledge of the move made by the Soviet military. Similarly like the Korean War, the Vietnam War broke out as the American government was hell-bent on stopping the spread of communism. Finally, with the collapse of the Berlin Wall - due to the tough politics of Ronald Reagan - the Soviet Union was no more. [2]

The golden age of UFOs occurred in the 1950s, right at the time the Cold War began. Communism was greatly feared by the U.S., its politicians not happy at all to see China change to this hated economic and political system in the 1950s. Paranoia of the spread of communism, even domestically, was the reaction. Could there be spies and Communists secretly hiding among us? McCarthyism was in full swing, as Republican Senator McCarthy accused many Americans of being Communists. It was a witch hunt as there were no evidence those accused were subscribers of this ideology, with the exception of a very small minority. This paranoia included many Americans believing outer space satellites launched by the Soviets contained nuclear missiles. [3]

Even this belief has religious dimensions, the angry Almighty bent on punishing Earthly sinners. This fear of the end of the world reminds one of the Biblical story of Sodom and Gomorrah. The Genesis story explains God's rage towards the Earth-dwellers of these cities for their unspeakable sins. From the heavens fell brimstone and fire, scorching both evil cities. Only the hero Lot and his daughters were

[2] Robert Cowley, *The Cold War: A Military History*. Random House, New York, 2005.
[3] Robert Nagel, Project Editor, *Space Exploration: Almanac: Volume I*. Thompson Gale, Farmington Hills, MI., 2005, p. 85-105.

saved. [4] There have been proponents who have used the Bible to argue that therein are accounts of ancient aliens. For now, we revert to our argument that the Cold War had a lot to do with fueling the belief in Earth-visiting aliens.

It was in the 1950s that the Cold War was alive and well and the thirst for knowledge of outer space was infectious. More importantly, the Space Race between the U. S. and the Soviet Union was a known fact, both eager to spend plenty of money and outdo each other. Hollywood seized the opportunity to create movies of Earth-invading aliens. Enthusiasm for space travel also influenced engineers and other experts. Wernher von Braun was a leading expert. He tried and succeeded in convincing the government and the American public of what he believed to be the importance of space travel. Sputnik had already been launched by the Soviets, and by 1957, Sputnik II was also launched; the Soviets had satellites orbiting in space, while the U. S. had none. This was the official beginning of the space age. Other Sputniks were launched, where small animals, such as mice, were inside. Sputnik II had a dog named Laika. These animals, and poor Laika, were guinea pigs to measure how humans could withstand the pressure of outer space. Obviously, America had fallen behind the Soviets and became eager to catch up. Unfortunately, two rockets that were launched exploded. The third rocket, however, was a success. After Vanguard I, in June of 1958, Explorer I became the first American satellite to reach above the Earth's atmosphere. Satellites would be used as espionage tools, to spy on America's counterpart by mapping out Soviet territories. As a result of the aggression of the American government's space program, more than one hundred satellites were in orbit by the early 1970s.

---

[4] "Genesis 19:24-26", *The Holy Bible: Old and New Testaments*, King James Version. Thomas Nelson Bibles, city not available, 2003.

President Eisenhower, in 1958, founded NASA who had been integral for the U.S.'s space program.[5]

UFOlogists, and believers in general, tend to down play the direct relationship between the UFO phenomenon (which we are arguing is not a phenomenon at all since it is a complete myth) and the Cold War. Many government activities during the Cold War were classified. For example, the "Skyhook Program" was top secret. Weather balloons were sent up into the highest reaches of the sky to spy on the Soviets, where radiation from Soviet atomic tests would be measured. Weather balloons were highly top-secret missions, and not coincidently, aerial sightings from the ground were often reported by civilians.[6]

The sheer power of the American military, but most importantly the constant cover-ups of these secretive activities, alienated many. And because the Space Race had begun, where science and the military were closely tied together, many believed the Air Force was withholding public information that extraterrestrials had colonized the air space.

These social conditions ought to be taken into account. It was the Cold War, and with the possibility of atomic extinction, anxiety abounded. It is a given that some believed UFOs might have been extraterrestrials, but others were concerned that these sightings might have been spy aerials from the Communists of Eastern Europe. UFOs might have been secret weapons. Besides arguing that UFOs are not from outer space or another dimension, our position is that the belief of alien visitations reflect Earthly anxieties and frustrations. For the reader who believes in aliens, if you want to argue nuts and bolts, skeptics concentrating on these areas can be

---

[5] Nagel, *Space Exploration*, p. 106 to the end.
[6] B.D. Gildenberg, "The Cold War's Classified Skyhook Program". www.csicop.org/si/2004-05/skyhook.html. Accessed in June, 2007.

consulted. The heart of our argument involves mythological and folkloric elements. In other words, there is a social-psychological need to believe in beings that were once gods. This has to do with the religious crisis that was already present, but took on a different meaning in the post-Hiroshima era.

Since this book focuses on the *psycho-social hypothesis*, it makes sense to point to anxiety and hysteria as the best answers, although it is our contention that the hypothesis should be reverted to the "social-psychological model," [7] given that the collective jitters stem from the social conditions. Throughout the chapters, themes have been picked to argue why belief in UFOs became necessary. All of the themes, we stress, have religious dimensions. This reflects the second part of our thesis, mentioned above, revolutionary social change in the form of the decline of old time religion and the rise of secularism best explains the need for supernatural connection. Since the cosmos was declared as completely material, corporal aliens came from the skies, to save humanity, although many Christians claimed such beings are demonic. What replaced supernatural angels and demons were technological aliens.

We do not have enough writing space to explain the human need for a higher order to worship. It is well known among scholars how mythology can repeat itself, returning in rehashed forms to fit the time and culture. The belief in UFOs and aliens are a product of modern society, shaped spontaneously and on various occasions deliberately, like the charlatans who published books to become rich. The

---

[7] The online encyclopedia, Wikipedia, discusses the French origins of tying UFOs to folklore and the supernatural, suggesting such a myth stems from the imagination, not objective reality. Plug in "psycho-social hypothesis". Accessed September 8, 2014.

purpose of the title of this book is to make it clear that the belief in alien encounters is strictly a modern, social construct.

A relative subject includes alien abductions. From a believer's standpoint, the kidnapping of humans can be interpreted depending upon religious views. Some abductees have claimed aliens are spiritual beings, while others, largely looking in from the outside, are convinced aliens are evil. Be that as it may, whether it was the 1950s or the late twentieth century and early twenty-first, what has been pervasive is anxiety about the end times.

Brief History of UFOs

It is only fair to discuss the history of UFOs. For more in-depth information, one can consult *The UFO Controversy in America* by historian David Jacobs or *Watch the Skies!* by Curtis Peebles. The mythology of UFOs began in June of 1947, when business man and pilot, Kenneth Arnold, was flying his plane in search of a downed aircraft. According to his testimony, he spotted nine unusual objects, aerially moving, weaving in and out of their positions. Arnold flew his plane to get a closer look and realized these strange bodies were traveling at the high speed of 1200 miles per hour. Upon landing his aircraft, Arnold told a news reporter of what he saw during his flight, describing the items as skipping in saucer-like fashion. Within forty-eight hours, newspapers all over the country sensationalized his eyewitness account, writing, "Kenneth Arnold saw a Flying Saucer." Apparently, the news reached other parts of the globe, since people all over the world also reported seeing flying saucers. The American public believed flying saucers were either weather balloons, hoaxes, or secret Soviet weapons.

What really made belief in UFOs blow up was when writer and retired Marine, Donald Keyhoe, published an article in *True*, a men's magazine, entitled "Flying Saucers are Real." Keyhoe accused the United States Air Force of covering up the reality that flying saucers were from outer space, coming to Earth out of concern of the buildup of atomic weapons between the U.S. and the Soviet Union. These interplanetary beings, declared Keyhoe, arrived from outer space to watch, from above, the most technologically advanced countries since the nineteenth century. What developed throughout the 1950s, subsequent to Keyhoe's article, were cults of "contactees." They were referred to as such, since they claimed to have direct communication with the aliens. The contactees claimed the visitors were angelic beings that had come to save Earth from its own destruction. These beings were described as not unlike the northern Europeans, considering the accounts depicted them as Caucasian with blond hair and blue eyes.

Throughout the 1950s, scores reported seeing flying saucers. The government debunked the sightings as the planet Venus or weather balloons. The government set up Project Blue Book, although reports of flying saucers continued. The American government became concerned that these flying saucers might be national threats. Understandably, the Soviets were feared for being possible invaders. But in 1958, it changed the language from flying saucers to any form of unknown aerial sightings, referring them as Unidentified Flying Objects, or simply UFOs. The U.S. Air Force tried to calm the collective nerves, debunking UFO reports, not as space crafts but more likely as Earthly phenomenon. Of course, the public began to distrust the government, many individuals feeling their elected officials were not telling the truth. Civilian UFOlogists, referred to as such for investigating UFOs, put constant pressure on the government to divulge what they were hiding. It became a widespread belief that the Air Force, and the government in general, were hiding the fact that UFOs were vehicles from other planets.

In the late 1960s, the Air Force hired scientists from the University of Colorado to research UFOs, with the hope of settling the matter of their origin once and for all. This body of scientists were later called the Condon Committee. By 1969, the committee decided they collected enough information, making it public there was no evidence of extraterrestrial visitations. The public, as expected, were not pleased. Below is a gist of what the Committee reported. [8]

Most UFOs were man-made. They were satellite re-entries, weather balloons, aircrafts, kites, or hoaxes. UFOs were also of natural origin, misidentifying Saturn and Venus, insects, birds, meteors, and even clouds. The Committee labeled about ten percent of the sightings as unknown, simply since not enough information was available to make determinations. These cases are not necessarily considered closed according to UFOlogists – because in their minds, the unknown sightings might be alien space crafts. Mysteries should not be unknown; they ought to be considered possibilities. But the Condon Committee were trained scientists, but to many UFOlogists this did not matter. Seemingly, because they were authority figures, UFOlogists barked they made mistakes or were deliberately deceptive.

The Committee also reported that perceptions could be optical illusions. Witnesses overestimated the speeds of UFOs, flying in great velocity, yet

---

[8] University of Colorado, *Final Report of the Scientific Study of Unidentified Flying Objects*. E.P. Dutton and Colorado University Press, New York, 1969.

without accompanying sonic booms. As far as colors, when the sun shines at given angles to weather balloons, the perceptions tend to be pinkish hues. Particular types of weather can also affect perception. No matter what the object, smog, mist, rain, and smoke can distort visual contacts. Lastly, photos of UFOs were often clouds, a negative defect, and very often were hoaxes. Different types of UFOs, though, were recognized.

Dr. Allen Hynek, a skeptic who converted, created a taxonomy of alien encounters. He classified UFO sightings as Close Encounters of the First Kind. Close Encounters of the Second Kind describe landing traces. Supposedly, UFOs leave burned circular marks. What the Committee concluded was that landing traces were humanly made. In one instance, lighter fluid was found near the burned area. [9] In subsequent decades, apart from the Committee, a paper was published arguing for natural causes of the so-called landing traces. In effect, circular areas of dead grass can be caused by lightning, insects, or fungus growth. What was once circles made by dancing fairies, according to European folklore, changed to UFO landing traces. [10] By the 1990s, crop circles would be believed to be alien landing traces. However, drinking buddies, Doug and Dave, working under the cover of darkness, were artist pranksters. [11]

Close Encounters of the Third Kind are alleged reports of actual alien beings standing near the landed UFO. Popular in the 1950s, were claims by contactees of seeing aliens land their crafts and step out into the environment. There were contactees

---

[9] University of Colorado, p. 87-9.

[10] Angel M. Nieves-Rivers, "The Fellowship of the Rings: UFO Rings versus Fairy Rings," *Skeptical Inquirer*, Volume 27, no. 6, November/December, 2003.

[11] Jim Schnabel, *Round in Circles: Poltergeists, Pranksters, and the Secret History of Cropwatchers*. Prometheus Books, Amherst, NY, (2003) 2004.

who also claimed they rode inside the UFOs. Even UFOlogists at the time scoffed at these claims as these contactees were attention-seeking hoaxers. The Committee paid little attention to the Third Kind since their main focus was aerial sightings. There have been reports of aliens outside of their crafts, walking and exploring while taking soil samples. Whether these sightings were hoaxes or hallucinations is difficult to decipher. But as history has shown, including in the case of religions, that as society changes, so will the motifs. Thus, UFOs say more about us - us humans - not Earth-visiting aliens. Even contactees who were not hoaxers may have imagined seeing aliens. In some circles, such as England's George King, claimed to have contacted aliens through channeling. Channeling is a form of altered state of consciousness, which could be called *psycho-cultural drama*.[12]

UFO mythology is a field of wild speculation. Taking on science fiction qualities, the Ancient Astronaut Theory became very popular, and infamous, from the late 1960s, throughout the 70s, 80s, and on. Dutch layman, Erich von Däniken, with his book, *Chariots of the Gods?*, created an overwhelming buzz. With other subsequent books, von Däniken made a fortune. Many believed his theory that aliens made a big difference in humanity's existence. The "evidence" pointed to the ruins of ancient civilizations and works of art of those periods. The aliens' arrival in the ancient past, in a sort of Garden of Eden, propelled humanity to acquire civilization. Adherents of the Ancient Astronaut

---

[12] *Psycho-cultural drama* is a term I use to describe purported psychic activity or some form of possession. The phrase can simply be broken down according to its semantics. The altered state is cued by theatre. Besides alien abductions, different forms of possession, whether interpreted as benign or malevolent, are dramas dependent on specific cultural circumstances.

Theory say ancient humans considered these sky visitors as gods, perceiving their advanced technology as magic. Believers of ancient aliens say these gods were actually extraterrestrials. But for what it is worth, these otherworldly beings — with their sophisticated intelligence and far superior technology — are still magical and might as well be gods anyway.

It should be clear how the religious dimensions of UFOs are unraveling as we move forward. After the 1950s, UFO sightings significantly died down, yet not entirely went away during the latter 1960s. Von Däniken's timing was perfect. Instead of the imagination looking upwards, where aliens were believed to originate from somewhere in the heavens, the present was projected into the past. Although ancient astronauts, Gods to von Däniken and others, came from the skies to build civilizations, it shows the need to believe (or to dabble with) religious pluralism. That ancient peoples, no matter what part of the world, came from one source. Such ancient aliens were not only technologically savvy, they were the originators of religion.

As the new millennium drew nearer, two UFO themes came to the fore — alien abductions and the UFO Conspiracy Theory. In first turning to alien abductions, Bud Hopkins published a best seller in 1981, *Missing Time*. What made his book controversial was his claim that humans were being abducted by aliens and subjected to medical experiments. This was done without the abductees' knowledge nor with their consent. The floodgates were widely open once Whitney Strieber published *Communion* six years later. After some readers finished reading it, they came forward to claim that they were also kidnapped. It is difficult to determine the exact number of abductees in the U.S., let alone around the world. It does seem that the numbers were quite substantial; it could be in the thousands; it could be much more. Unlike the contactees, however, abductees were not attention-seekers. Proponents of alien abductions have used this feature to support the "authenticity" of the experiences, arguing how embarrassing they tend to be because of their sexual nature.

Some conspiracy theorists would argue the government was allowing these nefarious things to occur, quarreling that the aliens were not benevolent at all, but were simply ill-intentioned and determined to conquer Earth. This was when UFO mythology became sinister, although Harvard University professor, John E. Mack, claimed the abductees were experiencing some form of transformative experience via an alternate consciousness. Seemingly, this matrix coincides with the world on the internet. Therein, UFO conspiracies (and other government conspiracies) found a home in cyberspace.

Our attempt is to show why belief in UFOs and alien abductions is mythological. We will show what social and psychological needs they address, in light of elusive evidence. The reason evidence is lacking, according to UFO conspiracy theorists, is that the government is covering up the presence of aliens. From this point of view, the U.S. government, and authority in general, is the antagonist. It is a corrupt bureaucracy and is in the way of great knowledge and wisdom. *The U.S. government is hiding the truth.* In comparison, there was a time when the Catholic Church was in the way of connecting with God. In the midst of becoming secular, modern society has conquered what was once divine territory; the new frontier is outer space. As a product of the Space Race, a myth developed where aliens come to us. The key phrase is *connecting with God*. The messianic promise of science and technology seems to be one of deception. Because secularism rose, but more so because of materialism's insistence the universe is strictly natural, the divine was debased. Seemingly, with all the technological advancements what was really ushered in was degradation. Science and old time religion were not the answers. Undeniably, something was amiss.

Part 1

From Supernatural to Natural

1

Tracing Ancient Aliens

Pre − 1947

The Ancient Astronaut Theory and this particular chapter have similar themes. As we discuss in chapter two, the theory of ancient aliens is a doctrine purporting that space aliens have been visiting Earth since the days of Adam and Eve − attempting to "scientifically prove" that they arrived long ago by interpreting the mathematical precision of ancient ruins, and arguing that aliens were depicted in ancient works of art.

Instead, this book wants to show that omens, folklore, and the supernatural are predecessors of the belief of the modern and postmodern belief of extraterrestrials. While the Ancient Astronaut Theory claims that supernatural entities and anomalous aerial sightings are possible alien visitations, we are claiming this is not the case whatsoever. Aliens, themselves, are social constructs − just like fairies, ghosts, goblins, demons, and celestial omens − are all misidentifications.

Ancient Sky Gods

The UFO myth can be traced back to ancient gods, deities that existed in the imaginations of ancient worshippers. Before 1947, hundreds of years before Kenneth Arnold's flying saucer sighting, Greek and

Roman gods were dismissed by Europeans. This was the Christian age - when modernity ushered in - as science started eroding Christianity - doubts about the existence of the Judeo-Christian God became more perceptible. The supernatural, in itself, did not entirely disappear. Among the educated elite, magic, the supernatural, and religion as well were discredited. It makes sense that the UFO and alien abduction myths stepped in as a sort of marriage between, magic, religion, and modern technology. Rather than non-corporal beings, aliens are physical humanoids which coincides with scientific materialism. Further, aliens are magical beings who are capable of remarkable abilities humans wish they had. With the need to believe in something higher than the mundane, today's aliens have been cross-referenced with ancient gods, where ancient sky gods might have been extraterrestrials after all.

In today's times, ancient sky gods coincide with interplanetary beings, as much as ghosts coincide with today's belief in alternate realities and parallel universes. The underworld was once believed in, though in today's Christian terms, this translates to hell where Satan and his demons reside. [13] Indeed, souls of the dead went to the

---

[13] By the Latter Middle Ages (1200-1400) creative people, such as artists and playwrights, updated notions of the underworld from Classical and Norse mythology, and legendary trips to Fairyland. It became for mystics and the laity who emulated them to report their visions of traveling to purgatory, heaven, and hell. See Alice K. Turner, *History of Hell*. Harcourt Brace & Co., New York, 1993, p. 89-91; In addition, the word "hell" was derived from Hel, the Scandinavian death goddess. Sent by Pope Gregory the Great, Christian missionaries learned how northern Europeans believed in various gods who ruled their underworlds. In ancient Greek culture, the underworld goddess was Hades. Among the German tribes, Hellia was Hel's name. Legendary heroes have been reported to travel to the underworld for special purposes. As for the Celts and Germans, they believed a supernatural world parallel to that of living humans. Mythological encounters included giants, elves,

underworld. When the underworld was Christianized, souls of evil people were sent to hell for eternal punishment. In today's times, aliens are believed to occupy secretive, underground bases.

There were various ways ancient cultures interpreted the sky gods' activities. Lightning, comets, even visions of descending angels were manifestations of celestial lords. Such signs, no matter what they were, were always interpreted based upon the dominant religious thought. Greek culture and the Near East in general would have different content and different interpretations. In the Middle Ages, western Europe interpreted signs and omens based on the type of Christianity at the time. In the nineteenth century, as the West secularized more than ever, phantom ships reflected the rapid technological change. When the Cold War began, flying saucers (or UFOs) were witnessed by many. It goes to show the human need to view things in terms of magic. [14]

From a skeptic's secularized view, UFO sightings are stripped away, when a strict methodology is employed to come up with the best explanation. Even science is a product of culture, as is the debunking of UFOs. Yet, the scientific method has been the best way to measure phenomena. We have a better understanding of historical research, sociology, and psychology. It ought to be understood that perception, including memory of what was witnessed, is not reliable in measuring objective truth. Though we will not arrive at absolute truths, we have tools that can aid us – helping us comprehend ourselves. Therefore, reasonable conjecture must reflect its context.

---

dwarfs, goblins, fairies, leprechauns, werewolves, and all types of magical beings. See Turner, *History of Hell*, p. 105-08.
[14] Otto Billing, *Flying Saucers: Magic in the Skies: A Psychohistory*. Schenkman Publishing, Cambridge, MA., 1982.

There was once a fear of comets. They were omens, and whenever comets were witnessed an overwhelming feeling of doom resulted. By looking at the tails of comets, its structure was interpreted as specific messages sent by gods. If the tail looked like a mournful woman, this indicated the gods were disenchanted. Seeing a sword across the sky indicated war and death. Comets were also omens, and it was feared cataclysms would soon follow. In the Middle Ages, for example, Halley's comet was blamed for bringing the Black Death. In today's language, however, these kinds of interpretations are discouraged.[15] UFO sightings do reflect the collective fear of the impending end of times. Although the motif changes the theme remains the same.

Omens were not necessarily associated with the end of the world. They could also mean a promising and successful future. When Roman emperor Constantine mobilized his military before a major battle, he saw in the sky a cross-shaped image. To him this was a sign that the Christian god was on his side. This event inspired the emperor to convert to Christianity. After what may have been a solar visual effect, Constantine declared Christianity as the official religion of the entire Roman Empire.[16]

The material conditions, therefore, have a lot to do with structures of belief systems. The belief of ethereal beings, no less sky gods, are dependent upon the human relationship with its environment. Since we live in the space age, it makes sense for those to believe in aliens from outer space or from an alternative dimension, not to just say hello but to leave a lasting impression – to provide the

---

[15] Calvin J. Hamilton, "Comets in Ancient Cultures". www.solarviews.com/eng/cometancient.htpl. Accessed July, 2007.
[16] Noel Lenski, ed., *The Cambridge Campion to the Age of Constantine*. Cambridge University Press, New York, 2006, p. 113-6.

meaning of life and spell out its purpose. Ever since tribal cultures transformed into more sophisticated organisms the earliest civilizations' emerged Earth spirits changed into sky gods. [17] City-states and empires had their own pantheons, though not mutually exclusive. The ancient air was filled with deities. Not only can these deities can be found in the annals of the Near East and the Mediterranean, but also in the Far East and among Native American cultures. Such beings were held in awe, although there were those who were feared because they were evil. [18] Adad, as a Mesopotamian rain god, was supplicated by Syrians and Palestinians (1900 BCE - 200 BCE) to destroy their enemies, sending fierce winds, dangerous lightning, and copious rains. When crops were in danger of drought, Adad's rainfall provided agricultural fertilization. [19] Worshippers of Adad did fear this celestial being, but the enemies of Adad must have considered him evil since his representation was to rival foreign cultures.

Ancient Egypt has fascinating myths. Since the Egyptians believed in the afterlife, they believed their gods could resurrect. According to one version of the creation myth, gods and humans lived together on Earth until humans rebelled, prompting the gods to ascend to the heavens. In fact, the main deity – Ra, the sun god – had a daily combat with a giant snake in the underworld. He was always victorious, but it was important that he did so, since the world depended on him to emerge from the underworld, lighting up the sky anew, arising from the eastern

---

[17] Bruce Lerro, *From Earth Spirits to Sky Gods: The Socioecological Origins of Monotheism, Individualism, and Hyperabstract Reasoning from the Stone Age to the Axial Iron Age*, Lexington Books, New York and Oxford, 2000.

[18] Tamra Andrews. *Legends of the Earth, Sea, and Sky: An Encyclopedia of Nature Myths*. ABC-CLIO, Santa Barbara & Denver, 1998, p. 7.

[19] Ibid., p. 2.

horizon. The symbolism that light defeats darkness should be clear. This dichotomy reflected the human hierarchy of ancient Egypt. Ra was the highest-ranking god as Seth, who was an evil god, had no choice but to live in the harsh desert. As Ra traveled the skies in his aerial boat, he descended into the underworld upon dusk. In his place were Geb and Nut, the stars replacing Ra for the night. Ra's councilman, Thoth, appeared as the moon – the dim light in the sky remindful of Ra's eminence. Priests and the Pharaoh had to conduct rituals to assure that Ra remerged into the sky. And since it was the goal to join Ra in his glorious boat in the afterlife, sophisticated prayers and rituals were conducted to assure the lifeless body ascends into heaven as well.[20]

In the 1950s, contactees who claimed they rode on flying saucers expressed how privileged they were to do so. The more sinister type of experience would come some years later with the alien abduction narrative, where purportedly embarrassing medical procedures were done to the abducted by aliens. The UFOs motifs of ascendance have similar characteristics to ancient Egyptian mythology we just described.

Ancient astronomy may have been pseudoscience, but the ancient sky watchers accurately related celestial behavior in relation to the order of nature, such as the change of the seasons and the rising and setting of the sun – actions attributed to the sky gods.[21] These inflight beings, not just the sun god, but also including the deity of the moon, proudly rode in their chariots. During solar and

---

[20] Dimitri Meeks and Christian Favard-Meeks. *Daily Life of the Egyptian Gods*. Translated from the French by Cornell University Press, Ithaca, NY, 1996.
[21] Andrews, 1998, p. 17-8.

lunar eclipses, the ancients believed the gods were being attacked by evil monsters since the sources of light were obscured. [22] UFO conspiracy theorists believe the U.S. government (and other governments as well) are covering up the alleged fact of extraterrestrial visitations, deliberately to obstruct the cosmic enlightenment of the human race.

From Supernatural Beings to Space Aliens

In the Middle Ages, the British believed in dragons. The savior of humanity became a saint when he slayed these beasts. Dragons were also ominous. They were strange lights - misidentified as dragons - similar to UFOs of today. In the year 793, monks witnessed flying dragons. As an omen itself, the self-fulfilling prophecy came true when Vikings raided the monastery, killing every single monk. In 1222, dragons were seen over London. Thereafter, a fierce thunderstorm caused widespread flooding. Dragons, like aliens, are a part of mythology that reflect human fear. [23] There is no doubt the "dragons" were lightning, seen from a distance as a storm was headed toward London. Despite our scientific advances, lightning is still feared. Thor was a god who was feared because whenever there was lightning, it was Thor's angry doing.

One can point to the belief of the supernatural in medieval Europe as the forerunner of today's aliens. The type of magical being depends on the type of culture and era. Ghostly visitations, demonic possessions, shamanic visions all fall under the

---

[22] Ibid., p. 71-2.
[23] www.dragonfire.com/dragon2/reddragonlady/dragon.html. Accessed July, 2007.

supernatural.[24] The kidnappings of humans by fairies, like the abduction of Earthlings by aliens, are striking. In pre-modern northern Europe, fairies came from Fairyland into the human realm, sometimes resulting in hybrid babies. The alien abduction motif is amazingly similar, but instead of Fairyland, Earthling and alien interaction takes place, presumably in a spaceship. Fairy folklore of old returned as technological beings from outer space.[25] Also in the Middle Ages, it was believed humans copulated with demons. Debate was heated back then with many theorists struggling to come to terms with how supernatural beings could have sex with humans made of flesh. Lasting from 1400–1700, the controversy was a buildup for today's heated debates of whether aliens are actually abducting humans or if it reflects more as pervasive hysteria.[26]

Whether demon-human copulation is indication of a crisis of belief is hard to prove. Notice how this phenomenon between evil beings and humans emerged during drastic social change. In the Middle Ages and throughout the postmodern world, many truly believe human history will come to a close. Fairies and demons described above are not the same beings, even if they do have similar functions. It is also wiser not to assume that pre-modern gods were aliens, because they were not. One could argue the ancients did not understand what they saw in their skies. This is a fair argument, yet the lack of understanding of what they saw does not confirm they were aliens. When ghosts were popular in the Victorian era, it was

---

[24] Barbara Walter, ed., *Out of the Ordinary: Folklore and the Supernatural*. Utah University Press, Logan, 1995.
[25] Thomas E. Bullard, "UFO Abduction Reports: The Supernatural Kidnap Narrative Returns in Technological Guise. *Journal of American Folklore*. April, 1989. Volume 102, Iss 104, p. 147.
[26] Walter Stephens, *Demon Lovers: Witchcraft, Sex, and the Crisis of Belief*. University of Chicago Press, Chicago, 2002.

hoped that scientific materialism was wrong about no afterlife. In our current times, however, cosmic consciousness has changed. As we became aware of outer space, the vast distance from one point to another overwhelmed many. Since outer space is very dark, with the exception of the stars, its blackness seemed to have served as an unconscious metaphor for emptiness. In a post-Freudian world, the depth of the unconscious and the cosmic mystery of outer space need intense probing to unveil its secrets.

In the 1950s, outer space replaced the supernatural, while aliens replaced ghosts and demons. The vampire was an additional motif of the Victorian age and a forerunner (although not an exclusive one) of alien abduction. The vampire originally came from Eastern Europe, becoming popular in the West later. Vampires, as believed in folklore, attacked their victims to draw blood from them. This points to the dreaded fear of death, sucking the life out. Many believed vampires haunted the living as restless spirits, which not uncommonly attacked their victims by sexual molestation. A common practice was digging corpses of those who recently died and were suspected of being vampires. The bodies were then mutilated or burned. [27]

The connection of one myth to another is very clear since, "there is a similarity between alien abduction narratives motifs from vampire films. Like space aliens, vampires manifest themselves in their victim's bedroom in the middle of the night. They have the power to walk through locked doors and windows, and have hypnotic eyes that compel humans to do their bidding. Vampires extract bodily fluids from their victims (who, like abductees, are predominantly women) during quasi-sexual episodes, and leave

---

[27] Rosemary Ellen Guiley, *The Complete Vampire Companion: Legend and Lore of the Living Dead.* Macmillan, New York, 1994.

strange marks on their bodies afterwards." [28] As we will discuss later, aliens kidnap humans and perform embarrassing medical experiments of a highly sexual nature.

The vampire motif and the alien abduction narrative point to the continuation of life, where sexual interactions lead to reproduction. It was during the Cold War when UFOs, and later alien abduction, were expressions directly related to the end of the world. Likewise, the belief in vampires, mostly particularly when this myth arrived in the West, was also a product of the end of times, albeit in secular expression. It was the late nineteenth century and the expectation of a new century was viewed pessimistically. Referred to as the *Fin de Siècle*, signs and omens created unease. [29]

There is something to the attraction of believing in magical beings, inhabitants of a world that is dictated by different rules. As Western Civilization changed, the supernatural had to change as well. Even from the Renaissance to the nineteenth century (c. 1300–1900), the method of contacting ethereal worlds did not go away. Rather, it became updated.

In the late nineteenth century, Anton Mesmer stroked his hands over his patients' bodies in order to restore their health. This was called mesmerism (and subsequently developed into hypnosis). Mesmer believed his diseased patients had magnetic fluids. By stroking his hands, often with a magnet across their bodies, Mesmer believed he could transfer healthy fluids to his patients. As expected, skeptics

---

[28] Paul Meehan, *Saucer Movies: A UFological History of the Cinema*. Scarecrow Press, Lanham, MD, 1998, p. 11.
[29] Hannu Salmi, *Nineteenth-Century Europe: A Cultural History*. Polity Press, Cambridge & Malden, MA, 2008, Ch. 9.

cried fraud. His patients, though, were purported to show clairvoyant abilities. [30]

Trance states have had enormous consequences in the history of the paranormal, whether it is possession or contacting the spirit world. The contactees in the 1950s, as much as abductees during the 1980s and onwards, would make claims regarding intergalactic connections. The problem is the contactees described their aliens as beautiful, with blond hair and blue eyes. The abductees, although not exclusively, described their aliens as blue greyish with bulbous heads and large wrap-around eyes, and short, less than five feet tall. The contactees had their aliens; the abductees had theirs; northern Europeans once had their fairies; and the Victorians had their ghosts and spirits. All of these beings are social constructs and all come from imaginary worlds. Thus, in contacting alternate, non-physical reality that reality is not an external experience, it is an internal one. Because once in a dream world, a realm where natural laws are suspended, delusion takes over as a remedy and hopefully the answers to the mysteries of life.

This leads us to Emmanuel Swedenborg (1688–1772). He exemplifies the search for common ground between magic and science. Swedenborg was born into a wealthy Swedish family during the rise of science. He is recognized for being a scientist, inventor, and philosopher. [31] Swedenborg set the stage for the contactees of the 1950s and beyond. He claimed to have communicated with beings in our solar system, describing them as having different nations and being family-oriented. They were non-violent creatures.

---

[30] John Beloff, *Parapsychology: A Concise History*. St. Martin's Press, New York, 1993, p. 16-37.
[31] Erland J. Brock, General Editor, *Swedenborg and His Influence*. The Academy of New Church, Bryn Athen, PA, 1988.

According to Swedenborg, they are wise and beautiful and frown upon Earthlings for not leading spiritual lives.[32] Swedenborg deepened his spiritual search when he reached his 50s. A devout student of the Bible and curious about the spiritual world, he sought to confirm the soul's existence through the study of anatomy. In his self-absorption, this creative thinker left recorded history of travels to all kinds of realms. Swedenborg wrote about his dreams, spoke to invisible figures, engaged in trances, went to heaven and hell, and meditated. Swedenborg was convinced that spirits could interact with humans.[33]

It goes without saying how imaginative he was. Besides a thinker, he was also a mystic. Mystics are known to contact otherworldly realms. Even if Swedenborg was an eccentric man, his historical importance is significant when it comes to UFOlore – although symptoms of his mental illness are more than obvious. We are not insinuating that UFO eyewitnesses and alien abductees are schizophrenic. But we are signifying that certain parties might be prone to suggestibility. The space for this discussion is limited, though we can say that Swedenborg was influential with his vivid imagination. It was not just contactees, alien abductees – after role-playing with hypnotists – developed false memories that they were abducted. In Swedenborg's case, he applied some form of self-hypnosis. The fact that even licensed therapists use hypnosis as a path to

---

[32] Rev. John Faulkner Potts, B.A., ed. *Arcana Coeletica, The Heavenly Arcana: Contained in the Holy Scriptures or Word of the Lord Unfolded Here Those Which Are In Exodus Together With Wonderful Things Seen in the World of Spirits and in the Heaven of Angels. Vol X.* Translated from the Latin of Emmanuel Swedenborg. Swedenborg Foundation, Inc. New York, NY 1951 (organized in 1850 as the American Swedenborg Printing and Publishing Society).
[33] Wilson Van Dusen. *The Presence of Other Worlds: The Psychological/Spiritual Findings of Emmanuel Swedenborg*. Chrysalis Books. West Chester, P.A. (1974) 2004.

mental stability does not make them crazy or insane. Even educated people have shown to be highly suggestible. Swedenborg was no doubt fantasy-prone.

Still in Swedenborg's lifetime, Europe was battling demons, while astronomers, philosophers, and thinkers began speculating on the plurality of worlds and the possibility of extraterrestrials occupying those worlds. We can thank the Greeks for starting this debate. Speculation of otherworldly beings reached a crescendo throughout the 1700s until the present day. [34]

The world during Swedenborg's time was already in the process of modernizing. Europeans came into contact with all kinds of cultures, from Africa, Asia, and of course, the Americas. In the eyes of the European, such exotic peoples were, shall we say, "alien." As such, the notion that Columbus "discovered America" is well-known, opening the floodgates that allowed not only Europeans, but also allowed people from all over the world. Indeed, such peoples, in a sense, are all aliens. They were not natives of North or South America, first arriving in boat and later by airplanes. The extraterrestrial myth, therefore, is enveloped as a projection.

Because of rapid social change, namely revolutionary technological change, [35] it struck many as a form of alienation, alienation from God and alienation from oneself. [36] The industrial revolution

---

[34] Michael J. Crowe. *The Extraterrestrial Life Debate: 1750 – 1900: The Idea of Plurality of Worlds From Kant to Lowell.* Cambridge University Press. New York, NY, 1986.

[35] T.K. Derry and Trevor I Williams, *A Short History of Technology: From the Earliest Times to A.D. 1900.* Dover Publications, New York, (1960) 1993, see Part II.

[36] Although the word "God" is used, our emphasis is alienation due to the overwhelming machinery of the industrial revolution. See Amy E. Wendling, *Karl Marx and Technology.* Palgrave Macmillan, New York, 2009.

made great headway, but Karl Marx bitterly complained how commodities became fetishes, greatly admired as magical in worship-like idolatrous way.[37] No matter what it was, the exotic drew multitudes to endless possibilities.

Life on other planets was one possibility, with the moon being no exception. In the summer of 1835, the now defunct *New York Sun* concocted a wild story that life on the moon was discovered. The discoverer was identified as Sir John Hershel, a leading astronomer of his time. According to the *Sun,* the moon's content contained forests, inland seas, and animals resembling those of Earth. As far as intelligent life, the moon had biped beavers and winged humanoids. Yet, Hershel did not even know he was given credit for these discoveries. This did not matter, because newspaper sales soared like never before. Skeptics, however, did not find these articles amusing. They preferred that the *Sun* admit these stories were totally fictional, although the newspaper never admitted to what would be known as "the great moon hoax."[38]

The lure of "the other" in this newspaper story was infectious. It reflected seeing another race as freaks of nature. The lure of the other was also expressed in supernatural terms.

Thus, thirteen years later, in 1848 was when the Fox sisters, teenagers at the time, claimed they could communicate with a dead person's spirit, an individual who lived in the same house before he was murdered. The Fox sisters said their spirit-friend was contacting them through rapping sounds. From Upstate New York, spiritualism spread across the

---

[37] Ibid, p. 51, 54.
[38] www.museumofhoaxes.com/moonhoax.html. Accessed on July 2007.

Atlantic.[39] As expected, skeptics scoffed at the Fox sisters. Others claimed they could also contact the dead. The primary method of contacting the spirit world was through séances. Attendees held hands in dimly lit rooms. Indications spirits were contacted occurred whenever the table tilted, chairs moved, or if the medium levitated. Musical instruments were alleged to play by themselves. Clairvoyant capabilities were even attempted. Mesmerism was also applied. One could also speak to extraterrestrials. Objects as well as spirits materialized. The Society for Psychical Research jumped on the opportunity to measure if it really was scientifically possible to prove the afterlife. The evidence presented was photos of ghosts. Bad exposures there were, many more photos were fraudulent, however.

Dishonest mediums (and there were many) were exposed. This did not slow down the movement. However, a huge admittance of falsity arose when the Fox sisters came forward and explained how they used their toe joints to make the rapping sounds of dead spirits. Skeptics were not surprised, but believers found it hard to accept it as true. The movement continued, only to seriously be challenged by various skeptics, of which Harry Houdini, the famous escape artist, was the most effective. In the 1920s, Houdini, who was so close to his mother who had recently died, desperately sought to contact her. He wanted to believe that getting in touch with her was possible and that the afterlife was true. In a fit of rage because of their deceptions, Houdini demonstrated how mediums were duping the public. They were exposed for what they were, charlatans trying to make a fast buck.

---

[39] Ruth Brandon. *The Spiritualists: The Passion for the Occult in the Nineteenth and twentieth Centuries*. Alfred A. Knopf, Inc. New York, NY 1983.

When it came to "true" mediums, there was a still a catch. Indeed, there were mediators who were authentically in trance states. But for the skeptic, this did not provide proof of an afterlife. Trance states are manifestations of altered states of consciousness. True, voices may change during the sessions, similar to how voices change during "demonic possessions." The best explanation of this type of phenomenon is the natural one. So-called supernatural communications have been observed in natural states. What has to be taken into account, if one is a believer, are psychological components triggered by specific social circumstances.

The social-psychological component is extremely vital in our argument that Earth-visiting extraterrestrials are entirely mythological. UFOs have their roots in the occult; the fascination with the hidden and magical and the method of contacting beings, i.e. demons, from another reality is infectious. Are demons real? Absolutely not, for they are also social constructs. The same is true of space aliens. Thus, as society changes, the occult does the same – the newer occult emerging from its previous structure. [40]

The craze of the spiritualism movement of the nineteenth century and early twentieth century influenced the mythology of intergalactic beings. Many believers raised the issue that there is no way Earthlings are the only intelligent beings in the entire universe. That is not an argument for this book. What is being conveyed is that there is no evidence we are being visited, just there like there is no proof of supernatural beings interacting with humans.

---

[40] Dan Burton and David Grandy. *Magic, Mystery, and Science: The Occult in Western Civilization*. Indiana University Press. Bloomington, IN, 2004

Both Spiritualism and UFO lore emerged in times of crisis, developing as religion withdrew from everyday life. Here are some components UFO lore borrowed from spiritualism:

A) Belief in otherworldly beings – ghosts were non-corporal entities from the afterlife. As outer space replaced the supernatural, aliens were perceived as coming from other worlds made of physical matter.

B) Pseudoscience – Parapsychology developed to prove the existence of the afterlife, which they failed to do. UFOlogy and the alien abduction narrative also failed to prove we are being visited by intelligent creatures. All three methods have been scorned as illegitimate disciplines. They are not scientific at any level, though they have, admittedly, provided foundations to understanding other aspects of their respective beliefs. This is being demonstrated with this book.

C) Gendered Trance State versus gendered alien abductees – Many mediums of the spiritualist movement were women and the majority of those mesmerized were also women. Mesmerists were overwhelmingly men. Later, as alien abduction claims took off, hypnotists were mostly men. Women were instilled with the false belief that they were kidnapped by aliens were hypnotized subjects. Further, contactees, although not necessarily the domain of men, also claimed they could communicate with celestial beings. Many were obviously fraudulent. The "authentic" types simply believed aliens picked them as representatives to bring messages of peace and love.

D) <u>Photos of ghosts versus photos of UFOs</u> – The purported photographic capture of ghosts, of spiritualism, and UFOs, were either misidentifications of objects that may look like items of its relevant subject. However, photos of ghosts and UFOs have been largely faked, often done so through special effects.

The structure of culture can have influence on social optics. In the late nineteenth century (as fans of spiritualism were being flimflammed during dimly lighted rooms), debate between astronomers entailed if there was a dying civilization on Mars. This debate was sparked after a mistake in translation. Italy's Giovanni Schiaparelli made a public announcement that Mars had a system of "canali." The translation of canali, which means "channels," was translated to "canals." Thus, rumors spread. The excitement of life on Mars, as indicated by intelligently built canals, amazed many. Other astronomers, observing Mars with their telescopes, also reported seeing these canals. At last, there must be intelligent life on Mars and we are not alone. Critics suggested these canals were not canals at all; they were simply optical illusions. This information would not slow down the enthusiasm for life on Mars. Instead of an empty planet, it was a dying one. Some astronomers said they saw flashing lights to flag down Earthly observers as signs that their Martian civilization was dying. By the early twentieth century, the canals of Mars were dead since the view prevailed the canals were optical illusions.[41]

---

[41] Michael J. Crowe. *The Extraterrestrial Life Debate: 1750 – 1900: The Idea of Plurality of Worlds From Kant to Lowell*. Cambridge University Press. New York, 1986, p. 480-586.

The UFO Myth Finally Emerges

Celestial sightings, as they were explained earlier, are reflections of their times. Sociologist Robert Bartholomew and psychologist George Howard teamed up in order to explain the social-psychology of UFOs. Before June of 1947, when Kenneth Arnold sparked the world with his flying saucer sighting, there were already developments involving UFOs long before. Anomalous aerial sightings decades beforehand had everything to do with perception, not what was being perceived. [42]

In the anticipation of inventing heavier than air flying machines, people across continental America reported seeing airships. A revolutionary invention, although not yet invented, the possibility swept Americans off their feet. These airships were described as looking like modern-day blimps with propellers and wings, some even saying these machines flapped like a bird. Some of the vessels were also described as cigar-shaped. The sightings took place between November of 1896 and May of 1897. Technology took over as the most influential social fact and its progress was highly welcomed, with all types of inventions made one after another – the telephone, gramophone, filament, lamp, motorcar, steam turbine, diesel engine, x-rays, the radio, etc. – dramatically changing people's lives.

There was enthusiasm and the atmosphere was collectively positive. Many could not wait to see the air conquered. In December of 1903, the Wright Brothers flew their plane in brief hops. The race, therefore, to be the first to invent the first flying machine, either in Europe or America, was on. News coverage spread public knowledge of these trends. No

---

[42] Robert E. Bartholomew and George S. Howard. *UFOs & Alien Contact: Two Centuries of Mystery*. Prometheus Books. Amherst, NY, 1998.

doubt influenced by what was written in the newspapers, two men on horseback claimed they saw three seven-feet-tall Martians. This claim might have been a hoax as a ploy to sell more newspapers. The sensationalism of flying machines was aided by pyrotechnics and fire balloons, balloons made of paper with candles attached.

There were occasions witnesses reported seeing human occupants and hearing their faint voices as these objects flew across the sky. The reports say Martians. How can this be explained? According to Bartholomew and Howard, "a person' s mental state or frame of reference has a strong influence on how external events are interpreted and internalized as reality." [43] The anticipation of the revolutionary airships were "seen" by a multitude across North America. To say the least, human perception is fallible. We saw how the anomalous Martians lines were optical illusions. It is often that we misperceive objects based on what we would like to see or often times what we fear. As such, Mars became part of popular culture. It is no wonder why H. G. Wells seized this opportunity to publish *War of the Worlds* in 1898.

Social stress can possess the collective imagination, more than we realize or are willing to admit; optics reflect the cultural and historical settings. The fear of impending war serves as a great example. In 1908, the concern of the British rose when the Germans were expanding their military, including zeppelins in their arsenals. Rather than attacking directly, the British believed they might attack a faraway colony, New Zealand. As expected, New Zealanders saw zeppelins, sightings that were unfounded. Between 1912 and 1913, the British also saw zeppelins, none of which were confirmed. The

---

[43] Bartholomew and Howard, p. 57.

Canadians were also distrustful towards Germans, becoming paranoid that German-Americans would cross the border in an invasion. Canadians reported seeing UFOs (not yet called as such) by mistaking their sightings as German fighter planes. In America, German-Americans were blamed for the spread of influenza. The residents of Delaware mistook Venus and Jupiter as German war planes. The Swedes also held grudges, distrusting Russia for centuries. In 1946, they believed their sightings were World War II-confiscated, German V-rockets launched by Russia. Since rumors of Russian nuclear tests spread, the Swedes were seeing meteors under unorthodox atmospheric conditions. Finally, it was a year later, when in June of 1947, Kenneth Arnold reported seeing his infamous flying saucer.

But even before Arnold's sighting, Ray Palmer, writing for *Amazing Stories*, wrote fictional accounts as though they were true. In 1945, two years before Arnold's sighting, in a short story called, "I Remember Lemuria by Richard Shaver," Palmer hired artists to draw disc-shaped objects. Palmer had also written about Deros, beings who lived underground. Palmer, who disguised himself as Shaver and other pseudonyms, received lots of letters from readers demanding the authenticity of such stories. [44] Because of Palmer's creative writing, the sales of *Amazing Stories* went through the roof. On the front page of this pulp fiction magazine were flying disks from outer space.

---

[44] John A. Keel, "The Man who Invented Flying Saucers." greyfalcon.us/The%20Man%20who%20Invented%20Flying%20saucers.htm. Accessed September 11, 2014.

2

UFOs and their Religious Dimensions

1949 - 1979

The search for new religious experiences became apparent in the 1950s, a decade of religious and spiritual experimenting. [45] Celestial apparitions emerged at a time of need. This would continue through the new millennium when the anticipation of a new era arrived in conjunction with the arrival of messianic extraterrestrials. The Space age, as a revolutionary era, called for new religion or at the very least updated religious perspectives – even if dressed in secular garb. Iconography of extraterrestrials became the new angels. This was a moment where old-time religion needed to be updated. Therefore, a new framework was ushered in to fit into the new time of cosmic consciousness.

The search for a religious experience began with Kenneth Arnold's sighting in 1947. It was not necessarily a religious experience, but a mystical event. Since the media sensationalized his sighting, others were inspired to view objects in flight and misidentified them as UFOs. At first they were seen as possible secret weapons, Soviet or American. However, when Donald Keyhoe asserted UFOs were being

---

[45] Robert S. Ellwood, *The Fifties Spiritual Marketplace: American Religion in a Decade of Conflict*. Rutgers University Press, New Brusnwick, NJ, 1997.

covered up, the origins of flying saucers were construed as interplanetary. [46] In other words, the inability to recognize aerial sightings (because of their mysterious nature) often led to the assumption of their outer space origins. Therefore, these strange crafts were believed to be piloted by more advanced and wiser beings from other worlds.

Contactees and their Intergalactic Angels

Individuals came forward and publicly claimed they were in communication with extraterrestrials. Such claims were met with skepticism, yet believers flocked to the contactees' side. George Adamski was the first contactee when, in November of 1952, he said he met an alien in a California desert. He told his story with Desmond Leslie in *Flying Saucers Have Landed*. Leslie, like Keyhoe, believed flying saucers have been around since ancient times. Leslie was in awe of these sightings, yet he found worth in being critical of scientists. Leslie compares the spirit world and extraterrestrials that can manipulate life. Aliens may explain supernatural beliefs. One of the things aliens can do is read minds. It was asserted they were using the moon as a space station. Since they were advanced, they were referred to as gods by Leslie. They can be found in different religious texts, including the Bible. These elder brothers, as Leslie refers to them, have come to provide teachings of love.

Adamski's alien is an angelic being with shoulder-length hair. He is a warm fellow from Venus and full of wisdom. This alien became concerned about atomic weapons acquired by powerful nations. This messianic alien's message is that we need to

---

[46] Donald E. Keyhoe. *The Flying Saucers Are Real*. Fawcett Publications, New York, NY, 1950.

understand the creator instead of the "laws of materialism." Six witnesses, including Adamski's secretary, Lucy McGinnis, and contactee George H. Williamson, all signed affidavits swearing to the incident of witnessing the otherworldly encounter between Adamski and the alien.[47] Clearly, Adamski used this position to take advantage of the economic boom of the 1950s, and one can assume to amuse himself through media hype.

Other contactees took the flying saucer religiosity much more seriously. George Hunt Williamson accords aliens should not be worshipped as gods, but respected as our brothers. Communication with aliens was done through radio and through telepathy. To Williamson, science and religion are one, although old-time religion and materialism are not sufficient. A new radical era called for something novel. The new wisdom of the space age shall set man free (we are assuming free from the materialist shell). The creation of the atomic bomb, as materialism's downfall, does not escape Williamson's criticism. God sent the brothers since they are spiritually more developed. Their ancient wisdom found in the Bible are the prophets who spoke to the space people. The contactees of today are simply the modern prophets of the Bible.[48] We get a glimpse of the Ancient Astronaut Theory, the belief in ancient aliens which would not take off until 1968, thanks to Erich von Däniken.

In the meantime, different contactees had different aliens. These inconsistencies bring the entire movement into question. Daniel Fry's alien revealed himself as Alan. He spoke to Fry in a voice

---

[47] Desmond Leslie and George Adamski. *Flying Saucers Have Landed*. The British Book Centre, New York, 1953.

[48] George Hunt Williamson. *"Other Tongues-Other Flesh"*, Amherst Press, Amherst, WI, 1953.

in the desert by telepathy. Fry entered Alan's ship and rode in it. He and his companion extraterrestrials originally came to Earth where there were the great empires of Mu and Atlantis. These so-called lost civilizations were believed to be more spiritually developed, [49] but saw their own destructions which the current nostalgia reflects the rampant pessimism including that postmodern civilization could also be destroyed.

Contactees tended to have their own personal space alien, taking on roles of angels rather than ancient gods. Truman Bethurum's alien was called Captain Aurora Rhanes. She was from the planet Clarion, located on the other side of the moon. Rhanes was in command of men no taller than five feet. They also spoke in English. She used her mind to telepathically communicate with Bethurum to meet her at the landing spot. Rhanes explained that there were no troubles on Clarion. Clarionites are Christians and believers in God. They do not suffer from poverty, enjoy education, and fill up churches. Bethurum alleged he went to see this for himself when he went to Clarion. [50]

The message of Bethurum's contacteeism is obvious, and it is similar to Fry's encounter. Living in a world where it could be blown up, civilizations with high spiritual developments and the perfection of life are superior alternatives, but more so as fantasies in the volatile era of the 1950s. Adamski, like other contactees, felt illuminated with evolved spiritual wisdom. What the aliens actually provided, as proclaimed by George Adamski, was a sense of connection with the universe. The Space age brought a new sense of aloneness. The

---

[49] Daniel W. Fry. *The White Sands Incident*, publisher unknown, 1952.
[50] Truman Bethurum. *Aboard A Flying Saucer*, Devors & Co., Los Angeles, 1954.

universe is a vast area where one can feel small. A connection with wise and beautiful aliens attempted to fill that void in a seemingly godless world. A trip to utopian planets is like a trip to heaven, where somewhere above is paradise. "On Venus there is true equality in all respects…" was Adamski's contention, using a Marxian bent of heaven on Earth. Contacteeism, like different forms of Christianity, and the embracing of democracy while denouncing Communism, did not stop some from dabbling with exotic ideologies and philosophies. In short, the 1950s was a decade of religious and spiritual experimentation.[51]

In communicating with aliens, in what used to be communing with supernatural beings, is done through scientific means, but not necessarily replacing the paranormal technique either. George Williamson and John McCoy tried communicating with the aliens through radiotelegraphy and by telepathy. They both felt that there was a UFO cover up controlled by a silence group (a contention of Donald Keyhoe's, which we will cover in the last chapter). The government was viewed as the Antichrist, the antithesis of the benevolent aliens. In anticipation of atomic disaster, aliens will assist the people of Earth to other worlds.[52] This is the story of Exodus; rather than fleeing Egypt and freeing themselves from slavery, Earthlings will flee their planet that at any moment can be destroyed. Undeniably, the end of the world was a pervasive and frightening theme in the 1950s.

Marian Keech was a writer who believed she could contact the dead, particularly her dead father.

---

[51] Robert S. Ellwood, *The Fifties Spiritual Marketplace: American Religion in a Decade of Conflict*. Rutgers University Press, New Brusnwick, 1997.
[52] George Hunt Williamson and John McCoy. *UFO's Confidential! The Meaning Behind the Most Closely Guarded Secret of All Time*. Publisher Unknown, 1955.

Interested in theosophy, she began receiving messages from spiritual beings from planets Clarion and Gus. The messages contained the imminent destruction of Earth. Placing trust in these wise beings will result in enlightenment and joy from these immortal aliens, Keech was their Earthly representative. She and her followers believed the aliens would arrive in space landings to rescue them. Although the landings never took place, Keech's followers were still faithful. Keech also believed Lucifer was leading scientists in the construction of bombs to destroy the world, also believing a flood will take place and flying saucers will land to save the chosen ones. Even if her prophecy failed, she and her followers maintained faith in their wise and beautiful aliens. [53]

Who were these contactees? They believed the world was going to end from atomic war, simply because they believed Earth people were uncivilized and barbaric, unlike the aliens who gave up violence a long time ago. Some also believed and promoted the scriptures came from them. The aliens arrived to provide harmony of space, science, and religion. They were also God's angelic beings and were here to help mankind. They came to Earth to show how to live without disease, poverty, sickness, and even death. There was more to know about the aliens; believing cosmic knowledge is endless but the government created a mystery with a cover-up. [54]

The 1950s witnessed several contactee cults, although the zany George King and his Aetherius Society was one the most successful ones. This was a sect that believed one can acquire wisdom from the aliens who are more spiritually advanced. Among the

---

[53] Leon Festinger, Henry W. Reicken and Stanley Schachter, *When Prophecy Fails*. University of Minnesota Press, Minneapolis, 1956.
[54] <u>Farewell, Good Brothers</u>. Video, Discovery Channel's Collector's edition. 1992.

spiritually advanced leaders are Shri Krishna, Lord Buddha, and the Master Jesus. They came from advanced worlds with sophisticated civilizations and made themselves available to help mankind. One of the most important doctrines of the Aetherius Society is reincarnation. Lessons will be learned in millions of years through bodies transferred into future lives. Heaven and hell were included within this belief system.

George King believed the goal was to reach higher classrooms, an advanced state of consciousness located on other planets with cosmic masters. Part of the cosmic philosophy is to respect planet Earth. As such, cosmic spirituality was favored over material science. A leader is needed to save Earthlings from the peril of atomic destruction. The arrival of the next master was expected by George King in 1958, because humans and their science created a catastrophic mess. Thereby, global healing became necessary. Poverty and pollution and other global ills must be dealt with head on. The goal was to be selfless and not selfish since – according to George King – materialism promotes selfishness. [55]

The Aetherius Society would be one of the well-known contactee organizations. They actually became a UFO religion. During the early 1960s, Indian astrologers, based on weird alignments of the planets, feared the end of the world. Aetherius Society members went to the English hilltops to pray. [56] Of course, nothing happened. But the Aetherius Society did not believe in established facts. The flight to the moon in 1969 did not impress this UFO religion. They believed there was already life on the moon thanks to the aliens colonizing it. According to

---

[55] www.aetherius.org.

[56] United Press International. Feared 'Doom Weekend' off to Wild Start. Los Angeles Times, February 4, 1962.

Atherius dogma, humans were prohibited to land on the alien-occupied moon. [57]

Even before the 1970s rolled in, the UFO myth took a different path. Massive sightings, referred to as UFO waves, were a thing of the past. In 1973, like in the 60s and 50s, there were UFO waves. This could explain the fizzling out of the contactee movement. Not all contactee sects folded. Towards the new millennium, contacteeism became a relevant issue, although we will not discuss this subject in our current chapter. Next up, are UFOs themselves as aerial religious experiences, apparitions that are directly related to materialism.

Jung on UFOs

The 1950s is considered the golden age of UFO mythology. Many claimed they saw UFOs. Controversy was abound since skeptics and believers were at each other's throats. One would come forward to provide a different bent on the subject, Carl Gustav Jung. Jung's psychology is difficult to deal with yet we will do our best to understand it.

To begin with, Carl Jung was a psychoanalyst and a contemporary of Sigmund Freud. Breaking away from Freud, Jung started his own school of thought. Freud had the personal unconscious while Jung developed the theory of the Collective Unconscious. He applied this school of psychoanalytic thought to the UFO phenomenon. Jung was fascinated with UFOs and was the first to write extensively about it. Although Jung considered massive sightings as mythological, he was not sure what to make of flying saucers. He was writing at a time when the UFO myth was young. Of no

---

[57] Jerry M. Flint. "Moon Flight Is Only A Hop to Space-Age Religion." *New York Times*, July 14, 1969.

less importance, though, was Jung's intrigue by the mystery. Jung entertained the possibility of a mass hallucination, but he also understood times were changing. The astrological epoch, as Jung saw it, the New Age of Aquarius was upon us. This is manifested in the UFO myth, taking on characteristics of symbols. UFOs, rather than humanoid encounters, including contactees, Jung considered to be science fiction. Therefore, he considered the U.S. as a science fiction oriented society.

In times of stress, signs are seen. For our sake they are UFOs. Jung (writing in the late 1950s) attributed the social anxiety due to the souring relationship between the Soviet Union and the West, when the Cold War began. In addition, the possibility of human space travel became projected through the alleged extraterrestrials visiting Earth. To Jung this is the unconscious seeping through, "a psychic disturbance." The materialization of the unconscious is the archetype, the flying saucer. As its technological representation, UFOs represent wholeness and they are projections of the collective fear of death. Aliens are the new messiahs, "technological angels" who came to Earth to save humankind from its own suicide.[58]

Jung was right to consider UFOs a modern myth in the making. Due to the Cold War, society was looking for answers in an ever-increasing secular society, with the new Space age having an impact. Where heaven was above for millennia, the nearby planets became the new heaven. Extraterrestrials came from utopian worlds where their mission was to save Earth. This was the desire of some, craving and hoping there was something left in the religious tank, given that the West was going through a

---

[58] Carl Gustav Jung. *Flying Saucers: A Modern Myth of Things Seen in the Skies*. Princeton University Press, (1958) 1978.

spiritual crisis. Based upon comments from contactees, this crisis was not subconscious or unconscious. People in the 1950s knew (whether they believed in UFOs or not) something was amiss. Jung, as an astute thinker, knew this was the case.

Our proper conclusion, however, is to evaluate Jung's ideas as having shortcomings. He professed that the new astrological era was taking place as one was replacing another. History does not work this way. Labeling with astrological signs is a pseudoscience, although it cannot be denied the West was in a new era. We entered the atomic age where it was believed that wars had the potential to be more destructive than ever before. And, perhaps, this was why Jung was so fascinated with flying saucers. Because unlike other theorists, Jung lived in an unprecedented position to psychoanalyze UFOs, yet this is the wrong approach.

Jung believed the UFO myth was a product of the unconscious. But after Kenneth Arnold's sighting, many others began to see flying saucers. This was the influence of the media, not to mention the nervous times in which the West was living. Consequently, we must disagree with Jung's analysis. The UFO myth was born out of a *collective consciousness*; many were fearful as there was a sense of listlessness and malaise. Since there was the need for higher forms of celestial beings, many started seeing apparitions in the skies. Even if these sky watchers did not understand what they were reporting, these events were conscious acts – rather than originating from the reservoir of the Collective Unconscious. The air space, due to its militaristic presence, created collective anxiety. Jung was correct in attributing flying saucers as ominous signs which aroused the collective. Venus, clouds, weather balloons, even satellite reentries were collective misidentifications – and their descriptions as cigar shape or discs coincided with what was consciously culturally available.

The best aspect of Jung's analysis is considering UFOs as religious experiences. This is an interesting argument. UFOs are actually unrecognized objects in flight that perplexed many. What made it a religious experience was its mystification. The contactee was the more obvious, but there were individuals such as Donald Keyhoe who speculated that the aliens were far advance than humans. This influenced the religious movement, namely the contactees believing the aliens were messiahs.

No less is the desire to turn to mysticism, and to experience transcendence in a new age of collective death. Jacques Vallée wrote an essay called, "Consciousness, Culture, and UFOs." Therein, he explains the need to demystify UFOs by "supernaturalizing" Newtonian physics. [59] Vallée mentions Jung and his Collective Unconscious concept, [60] using Jung's idea that it is innate and universal. This is terrible logic. It has not been demonstrated whether there is a Collective Unconscious. [61] Jung tells us the UFO is an archetype of the Collective Unconscious. This cannot apply since for Jung archetypes are universal, and it so happens symbols ought not to be universalized because symbols may not mean the same thing from one culture to another – let alone from different time periods. As UFOs have been sighted, initial reactions have been not recognizing the aerial objects being witnessed at those very moments. Howard and

---

[59] Jacques Vallée, "Consciousness, Culture, and UFOs." In Diana G. Tumminia, ed., *Alien Worlds: Social and Religious Dimensions of Extraterrestrial Contact*, Syracuse University Press, Syracuse, 2007, p. 193-209.

[60] Ibid, p. 197-9.

[61] Don McGowan, *What Is Wrong with Jung*. Prometheus Books, Buffalo, 1994.

Bartholomew teamed up and demonstrated the psychology and sociology of the reference of mind that may influence what is observed, [62] as misidentifications. There was a time when flying dragons were misinterpreted lighting. Since dragons are not believed in anymore, it is very rare to hear about such sightings. Though, the closest thing has been the Loch Ness monster. According to Vallée, "belief in UFOs provides a back door to manipulating the unconscious." [63] The question is, "How is this so?" Vallée, in doing damage to his theory, does not provide any evidence.

There are others, namely Bryan Sentes and Susan Palmer, who say Jung's Collective Unconscious does not go far enough. [64] Rather than simply attributing Jung's concern with UFOs as a product of the Cold War, UFOs serve as antithesis to scientific materialism – the major blow being that God is not included. [65] We could use this framework to supplement our thesis, considering the spiritual crisis at the time. Concerning Sentes and Palmer, however, their assessment has more weight if they completely dispute Jung's Collective Unconscious. In fairness to them, they are not in the position to do so. Besides Vallée being influenced by Jung, folklorist Thomas Bullard, also believed there might be a psychoanalytic connection. When it comes to alien abductions the folkloric link (i.e. fairy sightings) does carry weight, but attributing alien encounters of any form

[62] Robert E. Bartholomew and George S. Howard. *UFOs & Alien Contact: Two Centuries of Mystery*. Prometheus Books, Amherst, NY, 1998, p. 57.
[63] Vallée in Tumminia, p. 198.
[64] Bryan Sentes and Susan Palmer, "Presumed Immanent: The Rëlians, UFO Religions, and the Postmodern Condition." In Diana G. Tumminia, *Alien Worlds*, Ch.4.
[65] Ibid, p. 61-2.

to Jungian psychology has not been backed up by scientific evidence. [66]

In sum, according to Richard Landes, UFOs fall into the millennial category. The ever-changing technology makes this a possibility, because the future will likely be improved. The reason for the current turmoil has everything to do with technology's destructive capability – technology belonging to advanced civilizations, but not to Third World societies. When it comes to far superior alien technology, humans are no match. However, Earth will not be destroyed since the aliens are friendly. In this divine order, belief in God may not be the answer. [67]

---

[66] Stuart Appelle, Steven Jay Lynn, Leonard Newman, and Anne Malaktaris, "Alien Abduction Experiences", Ch.8. In Etzel Cardeña, Steven Jay Lynn, and Stanley Krippner, Eds., *Varieties of Anomalous Experience: Examining the Scientific Evidence*, second edition. American Psychological Association, Washington D.C., 2014, page cited 226.
[67] Richard Landes, *Heaven on Earth: The Varieties of the Millennial Experience*. Oxford University Press, Oxford and New York, 2011, p. 393-5.

3

The Ancient Astronaut Theory
1968 - c. 2000

The belief that space aliens are not new and had visited Earth eons ago, has its roots not in science but more so through science fiction. Many writers jumped on the bandwagon to make money and would stamp their publications as non-fiction. The heart of the Ancient Astronaut Theory (AAT) is the claim that humanity could not have advanced if it were not for the ancient aliens and their superior technology.

There are two things that give away the falsity of these claims. The word astronaut, a modern term, is projected back into the past. No matter how scientifically advanced we have become, there were beings who have already beat us in this game. In other words, as modern society became "sophisticated" what was needed was its measurement. How advanced are we compared to another race from another galaxy? Wondering if we have "arrived" does not sit well for many, the notion that humankind became its own god.

Technology, our second point, is also projected into the past. The result is the rewriting of history. Since technology and secularism undermined the sacred, technology became spiritualized. UFO enthusiasts believe our human roots are in debt to technological beings. What were once angels or demons, transformed into extraterrestrials.

It is more comfortable to believe this, rather than believing we come from monkeys. Indeed, the AAT subscribes to this form of creationism. There are three basic models of the AAT. Firstly, certain passages in the Bible are argued to be events of extraterrestrial visitations. Admired archaeological sites had to have been built by space aliens as according to the AAT, such ruins were built with remarkable mathematical precision. Lastly, accounts of gods written in mythologies from all over the world were proof of aliens.

Strangely, once Christianity was significantly undermined, those believing in the AAT projected today are aliens into the ancient past, superimposing the gods of old. Building on the past, even if it is antithetical, is common in many cultures. In the case of UFOs, and later alien abductions, religion and technology synthesized.

Before Erich von Däniken

Erich von Däniken is a household name. He and the AAT are one and the same. He rose to stardom, as well as infamy, during the very late 1960s, in the heyday of the counterculture. But von Däniken was not the first to employ the AAT; there were others before him.

Donald Keyhoe, who accused the government of covering up the presence of Earth-visiting aliens who from their UFOs had been watching humanity since the nineteenth century. Sightings of UFOs, say Keyhoe, returned in his era (1950s) out of concern of the buildup of atomic weapons. The government knew full well about UFOs and was selfishly hiding this information from the public. [68] Keyhoe made the aliens

---

[68] Keyhoe, Donald. *The Flying Saucers Are Real*. New York, Fawcett Publications, Inc., 1950

the guardians of technology, except that humans were stockpiling evil forms of technology. The storyline was structured as the following: the government was the antagonist, while the aliens were the protagonists. As for Keyhoe, he was the hero. He was a modern-day Prometheus, enlightening the public with knowledge only a privileged few wished they had and more precisely, information Keyhoe believed he had.

As Keyhoe and others, pursued cosmic, inaccessible knowledge, the Bible was used as a source that flying saucers were actual flying objects intelligently flown. Howard Menzel describes this phenomenon:

> When, in 1953, I pointed out that flying saucers are mentioned in the Holy Bible, I inadvertently opened up a Pandora's box. Most of the leading writers of UFOlogy got into the act and similar claims, without credit to me, of course. Their UFO's were manned machines from a super civilization, intruding into the affairs of ignorant men. I pointed out that two famous visions of the prophet Ezekiel, recounted by him in chapters 1 and 10 of Ezekiel, were in fact singularly accurate descriptions, albeit in symbolic and picturesque language, of a phenomenon well known to meteorologists, technically called "Parhelia."[69]

Parhelia is a mock sun with rainbow hues. Menzel attributed the strange atmospheric conditions contributed to misidentifying aerial events. For those living in biblical times, these occurrences would be religious experiences. As for today's UFO sightings, these experiences are not completely secular experiences since there is the sense of mystique when spotting a UFO. The awesome feeling of apparitions presumably supplies transcendence. UFOs, therefore, have religious dimensions. The ancient sky gods were greatly admired and even feared by their

---

[69] Carl Sagan and Thornton Page eds. *UFO's – A Scientific Debate*. Cornell University Press, 1972, p. 177.

worshippers. Egyptians, for example, imagined their sun god trekking across the sky in an aerial barque. The Nile River, an important life source for the Egyptians, was once sailed by barques. When it comes to UFOs, they have looked like objects that are culturally relevant.

When Menzel visited the Brussels Museum of Ancient Art, he noticed how religious paintings had objects that looked like UFOs. Once more, Menzel anticipated that UFO buffs would argue, as they would do so by the late twentieth century, that hundreds of years ago artists constructed religious paintings and deliberately painted UFOs on them. [70]

While Menzel was the first to see the connection between the Bible and UFOs, the AAT has its direct roots in H. P. Lovecraft, a science fiction writer. In the 1920s, this creative American wrote short stories about how space beings were the originators of extraordinary archaeological ruins. Lovecraft was influenced by H. G. Wells, author of *War of the Worlds*. It was one science fiction writer influencing another. In turn, Lovecraft would inspire French writers. [71]

Several others before von Däniken's time had already written their versions of the AAT during the 1950s, the golden age of UFOs. UFOlogist Morris Ketchum Jessup, speculated that South American ruins were built by aliens[72] – as would George Adamski, the leader of the contactee movement at the time. In *Flying Saucers Have Landed*, Adamski says the "fiery

---

[70] Cuoghi, Diego. "The Art of Imagining UFO's" , *Skeptic Magazine*, Volume 11 No.1, 2004.

[71] Colavito, Jason. "Charioteer of the God", *Skeptic Magazine*, Volume 10, number 4, 2004, p.36 .

[72] Jerome Clark, *The UFO Encyclopedia: The Phenomenon from the Beginning: Volume 1: A-K, 2nd Ed. Omnigraphics,* Inc. Detroit, 1998, see Morris Ketchum Jessup, p. 39-42.

chariots" have been around for hundreds of years and have returned to provide humanity wisdom, a similar storyline to Keyhoe's. Adamski made it clear and boldly said what the ancients saw in their skies were flying saucers. Egyptian and South American ruins were built by extraterrestrials, and Adamski furthers UFOs are described in sacred Indian texts. [73]

The Bible, as the most important book of religion in the West, began to be used as an ancient reference book to identify angelic beings from God. Surely, in an age of scientific and technological progress this was a way to spiritualize secular, modern and postmodern society. For example, the 1960s produced *Flying Saucers and the Scriptures*, as well as *The Bible and Flying Saucers*, both authors believing the Bible made references [74] to these mysterious, quasi-supernatural aerial machines. Decades later, many would believe that some form of technology (if not all of it) were bequeathed to us by space aliens. Sentiment of the 1960s reflects the cynicism of that decade. In prior decades, criticism against the Bible led some to conclude its invalidity. Like any other mythology in the world, the Bible is also mythological. The radical 60s produced radical theology; a number of books – echoing Frederick Nietzsche, the late nineteenth-century philosopher – proclaimed "God is Dead." [75] The craving of some form of religious resurrection was a result.

---

[73] George Adamski and Desmond Leslie. Flying *Saucers Have Landed*. The British Book Centre, N.Y. 1953.
[74] Dean, John W., *Flying Saucers and the Scriptures*. Vantage Press, Inc. New York, NY, 1964; Downing, Barry H. *The Bible and Flying Saucers*. J.B. Lippincott & Co. Philadelphia and New York, 1968.
[75] Patrick Allit. *Religion in American Since 1945: A History*. Columbia University Press. New York, NY, 2003, see Radical Theology in chapter 4, pgs, 72-79.

Indeed, it was not just Americans, but also the French that were delighted with the AAT. Thomas Paul published *Flying Saucers through the Ages.*[76] This book was translated into English, arguing extraterrestrials have been around since the beginning of history. Though unbeknownst to Louis Pauwels and Jacque Bergier, their co-written book, *The Morning of the Magicians,* would have an indirect impact on the AAT movement that would explode onto the Western and world scene.[77] These French authors, attracted to the esoteric and alternative history, speculated that ancient ruins may have been built (or helped being built) by ancient extraterrestrials. *Magicians,* despite the authors' enthusiasm for ancient archaeology, was a mild success. Erich von Däniken picked up a translated copy, and inspired by the French authors wrote his own book, proclaiming that the marvelous ruins of antiquity were built by far-more advanced intergalactic beings. Some skeptics, as a result of investigative work, realized that von Däniken plagiarized *Magicians* since he did not give it any credit. That notwithstanding, 1968 became a pivotal year in UFO history when von Däniken published *Chariots of the Gods?*

Von Däniken Rides Lovecraft's Coattail

The reasons for the Ancient Astronaut Theory's small impact before 1968 was that the contactee movement, UFOlogists, and the government's debunking of UFOs were headline stories. The ideal past was not as

---

[76] Paul Thomas. *Flying Saucers Through the Ages.* Translated from the French by Gavin Gibbons. Neville Spearman. London, U.K. (1962) 1965.
[77] Louis Pauwels and Jacques Bergier. *The Morning of the Magicians.* Eds. Gallimad, 1960. English translation by Souvenir Press, London, U.K. 2001.

important. What was important and nerve-racking in the 1950s, was the here and now. The Cold War signaled to many that there may not be a future due to a nuclear Apocalypse. Although the counter-culture movement's seeding was the flying-saucer craze of the 1950s (of which many historians and critics overlooked), it was in full swing in the 1960s. Even if UFO sightings did not entirely disappear, UFO reports dropped significantly once the Condon Committee presented their scientific findings in 1969.

There was still a need to believe in the otherworldly. The contactee movement and UFO waves transformed into the alien abduction narrative, which we will discuss later. Contact with space aliens changed by swooping into people's bedrooms and taking them against their will. Once the contactees faded from media exposure, von Däniken stepped in to change things, providing faith that the aliens arrived on Earth eons ago and will return as promised to clean up the degraded mess. As a result, Erich von Däniken became the new guru. As our quasi-religious language implies, von Däniken was accepted as a larger than life figurehead.

The premier authority of the history of the AAT is Jason Colavito. Once a believer in ancient aliens, he dug deeper into archaeology and realized this theory did not add up, even if he could not pinpoint its shortcomings. Colavito, furthermore, was a voracious reader. Becoming familiar with science fiction, especially H.P. Lovecraft's work, Colavito realized there was a connection between what was supposed to be scientific fact and science fiction. In other words, the AAT is a complete myth. Colavito goes further, insisting in his thesis that the AAT was publically embraced as Western civilization reached its apex and began going downhill very quickly. A glorious past was invented to deal with the distrust of institutional authority, namely science, the government, and the military – all of which have played major roles in the postmodern discontent. [78] We are arguing that the UFO and alien abduction phenomenon are mythological elements that emerged as science rose to its prominence and debased religion in the middle of the twentieth century.

Colavito eloquently shows how Lovecraft influenced theorists promoting the AAT. Lovecraft himself wrote his science fiction stories as a way to channel his rage and his own discontent. Howard Phillips Lovecraft (1890–1937) was born in Rhode Island of British descent and came from a relatively wealthy family. Unfortunately, his father died when H.P. was a child, leaving his mother and his aunts to raise him. His mother is described as an anxiety-filled individual, who would have a nervous breakdown worrying about the family's dwindling finances. Furthermore, H.P. was brought up by his mother's strict, emotionally withdrawn, oppressive Victorian values. Lovecraft as a young man was influenced by the Gothic Horror that exemplified the Victorian discontent, many of which were British writers – although American writer of horror, Edgar Allen Poe – was H.P.'s idol. Thus, the loss of faith, mostly within elitist circles, was already occurring in the nineteenth century. Influential agnostics and atheists made inroads with their ideas. [79]

H.P. was an atheist and a materialist. Well-versed in the archaeology of late nineteenth-century pseudoscience, H.P. created his own form of science fiction and horror genre. Whether it was Atlantis, Lemuria, or Mu, such legendary lost civilizations

---

[78] Jason Colavito, *The Cult of Alien Gods: H.P. Lovecraft and Extraterrestrial Pop Culture*. Prometheus Books, Amherst, NY, 2005.
[79] No specific authors are referenced here. However, some atheists were more known than others. Thomas Hobbes and Karl Marx are two examples.

were part of the Victorian Romantic consciousness, a movement rebelling against materialism and the Darwinian notion that humans came from apes. The progress of science and technology were actually signs that society had morally regressed. Many Victorian writers used Gothic Horror as expressions of their gloominess.

H. P. expressed his own discontent, as it would be later known in his writing career, through "The Cthulhu Mythos." This new genre would become popular in pulp fiction magazines of the 1930s (no doubt read by many readers escaping the Great Depression), years before Arnold' s flying saucer sighting. As we noted in the last chapter, Ray Palmer published "I Remember Lemuria by Richard Shaver" in *Amazing Stories* in March of 1945. The reader may recall Palmer hired artists to draw discs that would become flying saucers a little over two years later.[80] In the 1950s, Hollywood began showing the cinema version of the evil aliens from the pulps, science fiction converted from the pen to the silver screen. This would have interesting consequences later. But for now, H. P.' s work subsequently reached the French, of which, *Morning of the Magicians* was published. The co-writers, Bergier and Pauwles, Colavito informs us, were big fans of Lovecraft and his work, calling their own work non-fiction, rather than fiction in 1960. In 1962, *Morning* was translated from French into German, and a copy picked up by a Swiss hotelier.[81]

It is obvious that this Swiss hotel clerk was Erich von Däniken. Von Däniken, however, would be convicted of embezzlement, sentenced for three and a

[80] John A. Keel, "The Man who Invented Flying Saucers." greyfalcon.us/the%20Man%20who%20Invented%20Flying%20saucers.htm. Accessed 9/11/2014.
[81] Colavito, *The Cult of Alien Gods*, p. 133-8.

half years for stealing money from the very hotel he worked for. This fraudulent guru claimed he needed the money for traveling expenses to investigate marvelous archaeological sites around the world. [82] Von Däniken, while heroic for standing up against the status quo, inflamed archaeologists and historians when he published *Chariots of the Gods?* Placing the AAT at the forefront of the late 1960s and throughout the 1970s, and with his Catholic upbringing and understanding of the Bible, von Däniken cross-referenced the Christian book with archaeological speculation. However, we have already seen his capability for dishonesty. Von Däniken will go down in history as a phony. To be sure, gurus of all types have been known to be fakes upon exposure.

However, von Däniken, the folk hero, championed the idea that humanity's origins came from the stars. If it was not for the intervention of space aliens, the ancients would not be able to have advanced. The large majority of his readers accepted the romantic necessity of aliens imposing upon native Earthlings. Technology of ancient native Earthlings, says von Däniken, was primitive and there was no way marvelous structures, such as the Egyptian or Mayan pyramids, could have been built given the technology at the time. [83] Was von Däniken really onto to

---

[82] Ibid., p. 141-2.

[83] Erich Von Däniken, *Chariots of the Gods?: Memories of the Future_ Unsolved Mysteries of the Past*. G.P. Putnam's Sons, New York, NY (1968) 1969.

_____. Gods *From Outer Space: Return to the Stars or Evidence for the Impossible*, G.P. Putnam's Sons, New York, NY (1968) 1970.

_____. *Gold of the Gods*. Souvenir Press. London, U.K. (1972) 1973.

_____. *In Search of Ancient Gods: My Pictorial Evidence for the Impossible*, Michael Heron and Souvenir Press, Toronto, CA. 1973.

_____. *According to the Evidence: My Proof of Man's Extraterrestrial Origins*, Michael Heron and Souvenir Press, New York, N.Y., (1981) 1982.

something, even If he had no professional background as an archaeologist? Such notions are eerily familiar; it sounds like a science fiction spoof of actual history, when the white man began colonizing "colored" peoples all over the world.

According to von Däniken, an advanced extraterrestrial race arrived eight thousand years ago, landing in the ancient Middle East near the ancient civilization of Sumer. The semi-savages mistook these visitors as gods. The advanced visitors made a Sumerian citizen king. As an Earthly representative, he was given a radio device in order to communicate with his superiors before they took off to outer space. Before the gods left they chose several women for fertilization. This improvement made humans smarter and consequently a stage in evolution was skipped. Watching from a distance, the gods became displeased with the impurity of the human race. Something drastic, a complete change, had to be made. Thus, the biblical story of Noah's Flood was the result of angry gods destroying the Earth. Even the giants mentioned in the Bible might have been cosmonauts.

According to the Swiss Catholic, mythology may not be fantastic accounts after all. They may be real references, actual historical records of extraterrestrial visitations. The "evidence" is in various sacred texts of all religions. Other types of

_____. *Pathways to the Gods: The Stones of Kiribati*, Michael Heron and Souvenir Press, New York, N.Y., (1981) 1982.
_____. *The Gods and Their Grand Design*, Michael Heron and Souvenir Press, London, U.K., (1982) 1984.
_____. *The Eyes of the Sphinx*, Berkeley Books, New York, NY, 1996.
_____. *The Return of the Gods: Evidence of Extraterrestrial Visitations*, Element Books, Ltd., Rockport, Ma, (1995) 1997.
Erich Von Daniken, *Miracles of the Gods: A Hard Look at the Supernatural*. Souvenir Press, London, U.K., (1974) 1975.

evidence was drawn in ancient art, in cave drawings, in Egyptian and Mayan hieroglyphics, and other forms of tribal art that depict "aliens." Von Däniken was also impressed with other incredibly well-constructed items that could not have been built by humans, at least not by themselves. The Native American calendar, England's Stonehenge, ancient Egyptian pyramids, Mesoamerican and South American ruins, the large heads at Easter Island, and ancient Chinese ruins were all made by the technologically sophisticated gods. In addition, the Nazca Lines of Peru, drawings of animals only seen in the air, was an airport for the gods to land on. In short, without the intervention of the gods, human civilizations could not have evolved on its own.

Von Däniken's speculation also led him to believe that pre-historic peoples would not be able to become intelligent if it was not for genetic manipulation. After extraterrestrials enhanced human genes, [84] it was then possible for the aliens to have sex with Earthlings, as described in the Old Testament when the angels (aliens, according to von Däniken) meddled with human women. Humans were made through cloning and the different races were intentionally designed by extraterrestrials. [85] Von Däniken asks, "Was the black race a failure and did the extraterrestrials change the genetic code by gene surgery and then programme a white or yellow race?" [86] According to him, Caucasians are on the top of the racial pecking order, followed by Asians, but those of African heritage are dead last.

Archaeologist Kenneth Feder, rightly considers von Däniken's ideas racist. Feder demonstrates the

---

[84]Von Daniken, *Gods From Outer Space: Return to the Stars or Evidence of the Impossible* .

[85] *Signs of the Gods?* Michael Heron and Souvenir Press, London, U.K., (1979) 1980.

[86] Ibid, p. 66.

biases von Däniken presents. Ancient Roman and ancient Greek civilizations are overlooked, while non-European ruins are given emphasis and needed help from extraterrestrials because the inhabitants were "less intelligent." Considering how the West has perceived non-whites as having backward societies, it was hard to believe that non-Westerners – with their current impoverished conditions – once had great civilizations. [87] We are reminded of Jason Colavito's thesis: the Ancient Astronaut Theory became ripe as Western Civilization began descending from its apex, [88] but we think it is more appropriate as a result of decolonization. [89]

Von Däniken, continuing throughout the 1970's until the late 1990's, focused on non-Western ancient civilizations up until he published *Odyssey of the Gods* in 2000, arguing ancient Greek myths are also tales of extraterrestrial visitations. [90] The lost continent of Atlantis he placed near the Caribbean rather than the Mediterranean. Atlantis was invented by the Greek philosopher Plato. [91] But according to von Däniken, the aliens landed in Atlantis where they would influence the natives of the Lesser Antilles, the Greater Antilles, Mesoamerica, and South America. As the new millennium was ushered in, von Däniken

---

[87] Kenneth L. Feder, See Chapter 9, "Prehistoric E.T. The Fantasy of Ancient Astronauts" in *Frauds Myths, and Mysteries: Science and Pseudoscience in Archaeology*, 2nd edition, Mayfield Publishing Company, Mountain View, Ca., 1996, p. 165-193.

[88] Jason Colavito, *The Cult of Alien Gods*.

[89] By decolonization, we are arguing the withdrawal of European powers from their colonies does not exactly equate to a down-hill slide of Western hegemony. Western Europe and especially the United States are still influential (one could also say dominant) in various matters, from the political to the arena to popular culture. However, one could make a good argument that the West did reach its climax.

[90] Erich Von Däniken, *Odyssey of the Gods: An alien History of Ancient Greece*, Element Books, Boston, 2000.

[91] See chapter 8, "Lost: One Continent-Reward" in *Frauds, Myths and Mysteries: Science and Pseudoscience in Archaeology*, p. 141-164.

made somewhat of comeback by the 1990s and 2000s, even though his ideas were more accepted in Europe.

Many readers, in accepting the AAT theory popularized by a layman, identified with its anti-authority sentiment. Even as a pseudoscientist, von Däniken was a heretic. In the 1970s, supernaturalism made a return. The rebellious youth, including university students, embraced occultism. The AAT was already on the rise, so were alien abductions, and intriguingly demonic possessions – otherworldly experiences inspired by Hollywood and television shows.[92] The power of suggestion is more powerful than imagined. The counter-culture involved the Civil Rights movement, anti-Vietnam war sentiment, the sexual revolution, women's liberation, the rise of Satanism, and other forms of occultism. The AAT, therefore, was a political movement, tied with neo-romanticism and the search for new philosophy.

Von Däniken's AAT influenced popular culture in different facets:

1. *Chariots of the Gods?* was the second highest selling book of the 1970s.[93]
2. Tourists were inspired to visit the Peruvian Nazca Lines.[94]
3. He inspired motion picture plots. There was the television series *Battle Star Galactica,*[95] *X-Files: The Movie,* and

---

[92] Colavito, *The Cult of Alien Gods*, p. 177-8.

[93] Ray Walters, "Ten Years of Best Sellers; Best Sellers." *New York Times*, New York, N.Y., December 30, 1979.

[94] William R. Long, "Culture Dry Spell Hits Town of Ancient Dessert Designs Shortage of Tourists and Water Plague Nazca. And its Devoted 'lady lines' is now disabled." *Los Angeles Times*, Los Angeles, Ca. December 15, 1992, p.3.

[95] www.dtl.org/dtl/article/sci-fiets.htm.

notably the television series, *Out on a Limb.* [96]

4. Interest in ancient civilizations soared.

5. The book market became flooded with other authors discussing their versions of the AAT.

6. As an indirect influence of the AAT, the fascination with the Mayan calendar led to the hysteria that by the end of 2012, the end of the world would ensue or there would be a new beginning. Although UFOs and alien abductions were tied into these expectations, the 2012 movement overlapped more so with New Age. [97]

As the 1970s matured, von Däniken's ideas faded in popularity. However, the AAT would not, with other writers stepping in to offer more exotic explanations of the outer space origins of admired ancient ruins.

While the skeptical argument has correctly exposed the racism of the AAT, there is more to the story. Wonders of the world have intrigued many throughout history. Undeniably, these marvels include the Peruvian, pre-Hispanic, Nazca Lines. They are massively drawn lines of birds, a monkey and its elongated tail, among other lines that are only viewable from afar, riding on an airplane, helicopter, or seen from a mountain. It has attracted many visitors, including romantic-exotic theorists trying to explain the purpose of these iconic,

[96] Feder, *Frauds, Myths, and Mysteries: Science and Pseudoscience in Archaeology*, p. 193.

[97] Mathew Restall and Amari Solari, *2012 and the End of the World: The Western Roots of the Mayan Apocalypse*. Rowan and Littlefield Publishers, Inc., New York and Toronto, 2011.

seemingly human-made lines. [98] If it sounds like there are religious dimensions to these art forms, it is because there are. By publishing *Chariots?*, von Däniken took advantage of a movement that was already in place. The *Age of Aquarius* was the anticipation of a New Age to come. Due to von Däniken's first publication many flocked to Peru, in Nazca, in search of intellectual or spiritual inspiration. This was a 1970s pilgrimage in search of the divine since interest in psychic phenomenon skyrocketed, [99] which one critic called "technological supernaturalism." [100]

Other Writers after *Chariots of the Gods?*

Although New Age spirituality is not the focus of our book, aspects of the AAT syncretized with this movement – some writers as far as stating the Nazca Lines were deliberately made for religious rituals. Even if this was true, geometric notions, such as the Mayan and Egyptian pyramids, have been interpreted by some postmodern UFO believers as having hidden messages. From our *socio-skeptical* approach, to put forward the explanation that aliens from the ancient past deliberately encoded messages does not reflect the ancient past. This postmodern projection, hence, coincides with the present disenchantment toward institutions, namely government and institutional science. Consider how some ancient astronaut theorists have boldly argued there is a spiritual void to fill in this postmodern era. Out of sympathy, such feelings are pervasive and the desire to fill in spiritual emptiness is understandable.

---

[98] Anthony F. Aveni. *Between the Lines: The Mystery of the Giant Ground Drawings of Ancient Nazca*, Peru. University of Texas Press, Austin .
[99] Ibid., p. 107-15.
[100] Colavito, *The Cult of Alien Gods*, p. 177.

Confusing times, let alone confused persons, could bring about feelings of grandeur. Some may change their identities, believing they were given special gifts. Messianic fervor can result. One of these elected episodes happened to Claude Vorilhon. This Frenchman gave up being editor for race a driving magazine and also gave up his beloved passion, race car driving. Vorilhon told his story of the extraterrestrial experience that changed his life forever. Vorilhon's contactee experience was on December 13, 1973 while hiking in rural France. He was greeted by a short alien (1-2 meters tall), with long black hair, his eyes shaped like almonds. Taken on board a space vehicle, Vorilhon was flown to another planet. Vorilhon was told how ancient scientists from a distant planet created animals in test tubes. This was controversial among the ancient scientists, so ancient Israel was chosen as the place to conduct these scientific tests. Thus, the alien scientists watched their creations from their UFOs, which explain UFO sightings at the time. Vorilhon's name was changed to Raël. As "Light of God," the alien told him he was the Earthly representative of cosmic divinity. Raël met with spiritual leaders and learned that Jesus, Buddha, and Moses were cloned, as all religious leaders were cloned to save their wisdom. This sense of salvation is different than the traditional definition of Christian salvation. Since Raël was told science is the new religion, a materialistic form of worship, the soul did not exist, in this manner explaining the necessity of cloning. [101] Raël eventually moved from France and settled in Quebec, Canada where he started Raëlianism - a religion that worships cosmic beings.

---

[101] Claude "Raël" Vorilhon, *The Message Given to me by Extraterrestrials: They Took Me to their Planet*, AOM Corp., Tokyo, (1986) 1988.

Raël's radical materialism coincides with the search for radical spirituality in the 1970s. Many in the West embraced Buddhism, for example, the hippies during the 1960s. The Buddha himself, according to Rael, was cloned. There is reason to believe that Raël's radicalism was an offshoot of his times. Hippies and others accepted Buddhism as part of their nostalgia. Rather than the deluded present, the belief in reincarnation can remind one of the glorious days of old that are no more. From this perspective history is seen as a cycle, rather than linear. Future life could be much improved, given that higher awareness was searched for, an internal state of cosmic wisdom and spiritual transcendence. European contributions to the AAT during the 1960s with the publication of *The Morning of the Magicians* and *Chariots of the Gods?*, were influential works that may have influenced Raël. [102]

In the meantime, Robert Temple came onto the scene in 1976. In *The Sirius Mystery,* Temple asserts amphibian creatures arrived 5,000 years ago, welcomed by a sub-Saharan African tribe, the Dogon. Sirius is identified as the brightest star. Sirius B encircles its much larger neighbor, and mysteriously, the Dogon saw this star pair with their naked eyes, long before being discovered by the telescope in 1968. [103] It turns out that Sirius B had been known since the nineteenth century, French anthropologists discovering this in the 1930s after studying this tribe. [104]

These French anthropologists, taking advantage of their mother country's colonization on what is now called Mali, were Marcel Griaule and Germaine Dieterlen. Documenting Dogon's beliefs in an article

---

[102] Colavito, *The Cult of Alien Gods*, p. 314-5.

[103] Robert K.G. Temple, *The Sirius Mystery*, St. Martin's Press, Inc. New York, 1976.

[104] Liam Mcdaid, *Skeptic Magazine*, "Legends of the Dogon", 2004, Vol. II Issue 1; p.40.

in 1950, the Sirius Star was home to the half-human, half-fish gods. The Dogon called them the Nommos. Also, there was a savior god; his name was O Nommo. Crucified in a tree, his sacrifice allowed for the Dogon's sins to be redeemed. O Nommo's body was part of a redemptive meal, wiping the sins clean upon his resurrection. The Dogon's expressed hope by expecting the Nommos to return as promised. [105]

If this belief system does not ring bells that the Dogon's resembles the Christ story, then, perhaps, Temple is right in that the Dogon's story is much longer than Christ's. This implies that the real Jesus was descended of these aliens, like ourselves. Yet before Griaule and Dieterlan, French missionaries were busy proselytizing to Africans in the eighteenth and nineteenth centuries. [106] Upon further investigation, the religious beliefs of the Dogon do not resemble the Christian one. The Sirius Star, moreover, was not that important to the tribe – and nor was there a redeemer-savior. As early as 1967, other anthropologists began criticizing Griaule's methodology. In short, the Dogon's myth of the Nommos came from the mind of the French anthropologists. [107]

Temple published his book in 1976, when white Americans and Europeans had already been seeking and experimenting with religions outside of the Judeo-Christian tradition. While some looked to Mu, Lemuria, or Atlantis as the lost motherland, Zechariah Sitchin's was Sumer.

Like Temple, Sitchin published *The 12th Planet* in 1976. [108] He tells tales of space beings that can be

---

[105] Colavito, *The Cult of Alien Gods*, p. 187-91.
[106] Ibid, p. 196.
[107] Ibid, p. 200-03.
[108] Zecharia Sitchin, *The 12th Planet*, Stein and Publishers, New York, 1976.

found in ancient Sumerian texts, with these
sophisticated aliens giving birth to humanity. What
Sitchin did was cross-reference the Old Testament
with Sumerian tablets. As a linguist, he was born in
Russia, and then raised in Palestine. As the mother
of all future societies, Sumer – so states Sitchin
– would be a prototype for the ancient Hebrews and
the Greeks. If it were not for Sumer, there would not
be civilization. If it were not for the alien gods,
there would be no humanity.

For what it's worth, Sitchin was in direct
competition with von Däniken. It was Sitchin's turn
to make many sales of his books. After *The 12th
Planet*, many sequels were published, as though the
ancient alien narrative was a soap opera. 450,000
years ago aliens landed somewhere in Mesopotamia,
somewhere in the Near East during the last ice age.
The origin of the aliens is a distant planet in our
solar system. Rather than eight planets (originally
nine, once Pluto was demoted), Sitchin declared there
were twelve planets in our solar system. This planet
travels throughout space elliptically, like a comet
trekking across vast distances of outer space and
approaching Earth every 3,600 years. The gods return
in this time cycle.

Comparing other religious models of the 1960s
and the 1970s, Sitchin's cycle is comparable to
Buddhism's reincarnation, the anticipation of the
Age of Aquarius of the New Age movement, and the
Christian expectation of the Second Coming. What is
attractive about the AAT to believers is that the
once glorious days will come back when the aliens
return. Sitchin's translations of the ancient
tablets, led him to conclude the gods set up a
pecking order, the Anunnaki at the lowest, obliged to
work inside the gold minds. Exasperated of their
position, however, they rebelled millenniums later.
The story of humanity's origins actually began when

ape-like beings were enhanced into full humans through genetic manipulation. The first attempt was a failure. Once deformity was the outcome, the gods tried again – mixing their blood with clay – and out of this combination a human-like figure was created. Sitchin links the Sumerian story of creation with the Old Testament, where Adam and Eve were the first humans on Earth. Once the gods and humans intermarried, Sumer's population swelled. The god-leaders became so upset by their wicked ways that they decided to send a deluge to wipe out every single one of them. The Sumerian flood story is older than the biblical version. In the Sumerian tale, a god named Enki warns a human of what was to come, thereby sparing the human race. Once the Anunnaki return, a New Age will begin.

Richard Hoagland, supposedly a trained scientist, found a big hole in Sitchin's reasoning. This so-called 12th planet, a vast distance from the sun and further away than Pluto, would be too cold to support any life forms, let alone intelligent life. Despite this clever point by Hoagland, he believed Sitchin's methodology was superior to von Däniken's.

It is common for UFO believers to put a lot of weight whenever a scientist promotes the possibility of Earth-visiting aliens. It so happens this will occur from time to time, if not often. The bigger question is why the vast majority of scientists do not even want to bother with such endeavors, even for debunking purposes? For the most part, UFOs and alien abductions, let alone ancient aliens – are all nonsense and not worth the effort. There is a stigma attached to pseudoscience and any believing scientist crossing over would be branded a pseudoscientist. There are a few, dedicated skeptics with scientific backgrounds, namely Michael Shermer and Steve

Novella. In recent years, skeptics have gained respect, no doubt by laymen skeptics.

Continuing with Hoagland, one could assume that accepting Hoagland's rationale implies his aliens have superior technology to protect themselves from what would be yearly-round and very severe winters. Using Sitchin's assumption the aliens reached Earth 450,000 years ago, Hoagland speculates the aliens arrived 500,000 years ago, colonizing a Martian region called Cydonia. He bases this on the Martian Face, a face like structure that stares right up into outer space. Near the face are other pyramidal structures. In Hoagland's awestruck reaction, he saw a resemblance between the pyramids on Mars and the Pyramids of Egypt.

Since ancient astronaut theorists have been speculators on a science fiction level, Hoagland claimed an ancient alien race landed on Mars and may also be the founders of ancient Egypt. Once again, in the pivotal year of the AAT in 1976, the face was discovered when NASA sent a probe to Mars that year. It was explained as a trick of sunlight. Subsequently, a photo with a better angle revealed that particular edifice was a natural Martian mountain. [109] Hoagland has been hosting a radio show, telling his listeners the face is no trick of light and that NASA is engaging in a massive cover-up. [110] Only the most cynical of institutional authority would buy into Hoagland's accusation.

Looking at the Mars photo, one can see there is an eye, a pair of lips, but the right side of the face is shadowed, obscuring any mountain features. NASA explained that the sunlight hitting the Martian mountain creates the illusion of an intelligently

---

[109] http://skepdic.com/faceonmars.html
[110]

http://www.cnn.com/2004/TECh/space/03/17/alien.debunk/index.html

made face. Upon looking closer, the solar light does not envelope the entire mountain and the facial features are the result of the awkward angle of the light falling on this pyramid-looking object. In relation to the psycho-social hypothesis, some skeptics alluded to the inkblot effect – where anomalous objects are given meaning to randomness. Hoagland's Martian Face has a Nazcalian effect, a huge construct by advanced aliens leaving their calling card.

Graham Hancock and his colleagues championed Hoagland's theory. During the 1990s, Hancock and his crew argued there was a Martian civilization on Mars, currently a cold and barren red planet. [111] Hancock, Bauval, and Grigsby were also adamant that the Martian Face had a redress and is reminiscent of the pharaoh's of Egypt. They also argued that pyramids of Mars were purposely designed in Pythagorean style, which means there is a mathematical code waiting to be cracked, providing humanity a long lost message. This message was either suppressed or denied by NASA. The three co-authors of *The Mars Mystery* were intrigued by the Great Pyramid of Giza and asserted the pyramids of Mesoamerica, Stonehenge, and other ancient ruins are all connected to Mars. The biggest concern these three authors offer is that the ancient Martian civilization was destroyed by a meteor and that the Earth may be subjected to the same fate. They conclude our home is somewhere in the stars and we must reconnect with our spiritual roots and syncretize it with science. From the perspective of the AAT, this sums up the disenchantment of postmodern society.

---

[111] Graham Hancock, Robert Bauval and John Grisby. *The Mars Mystery: A Tale of the End of Two Worlds*, Michael Joseph, Ltd., London, 1998.

Part 2

Advanced Aliens and the Science of UFOs

Mythologizing Technological Beings

4

Science and Technology versus Pseudoscience and Science fiction

Concern arose that pseudoscience encourages anti-science,[112] but other findings say this is not the case at all.[113] In one critic' s opinion, "Many people believe in both pseudoscience and science because they can' t tell the difference."[114] This view seems like the best one. Science and pseudoscience are dualist concepts. While science is associated with material progress, pseudoscience appears to focus on the moral regression of society, using it as political philosophy against the status quo. Society scientifically and technologically advanced; modern and postmodern society, however, resulted in a spiritual void. These contrarian notions are more complementary than given credit.

The UFO myth was born in an era of unprecedented growth. Such ideology of advancement inspired the belief that aliens are more advanced than humans. As it was eons ago, angels were second to God, although they were superior to humans.

[112] Paul Kurtz. "The Growth of Antiscience." *Skeptical Inquirer*, Spring 1994 V. 18 no.3 p.255 (9).

[113] Kendrick Frazer. "Science Is Still Well Regarded In U.S., NSB Report says." Skeptical Inquirer, V.17 (Fall 1992) p. 8-11; Andrew Lawler. "Support for Science Stays Strong." *Science v.* 272 (May 31, 1996) p. 1256.

[114] Gerald Holton. "The Antiscience Problem." *Skeptical Inquirer*, Spring 1994 v. 18 n. 3 p.264.

Aliens, as the new angels or new demons, became updated supernatural beings.

The UFO myth emerged as an expression of the end-times. In post-Hiroshima, the ambivalence towards science and technology is apparent. In one sense, the new *technologized supernatural* saved society from malnutrition, control or cure of major diseases, to name a few examples. On the other hand, science and technology have shown a tremendous capacity of what many call evil. When the Cold War began, the UFO myth became an alternate approach to old-time religion to provide meaning in a hostile, volatile, apocalyptic world, destroyed by atomic bombs.

Redefining Paranormal

What we have in the UFO myth is its idealism. We saw this with the Ancient Astronaut Theory. This idealism of the UFO myth is positioned in a grey area between scientific theory and ideal religion. The UFO myth does have metaphysical qualities, but it is not exactly that either. The best we can describe it as superstition dressed up in scientific garb. The materialist view was down played by UFOlogists, especially when the position that science overemphasizes "physical evidence." [115] One way to counter this is to suggest the elusiveness of the aliens is due to their technological ability to hide themselves. [116] UFOs have religious dimensions, physical phenomena behaving in supernatural and magical terms,

---

[115] Jacques Valle. *Anatomy of Phenomenon: Unidentified Flying Objects: a scientific appraisal.* Henry Regnery, Chicago, 1965.
[116] Budd Hopkins and Carol Rainey. *Sight Unseen: Science, UFO Invisibility and Transgenic Beings.* Pocket Books, a division of Simon & Shuster, Inc. New York, 2003.

in what Christopher Partridge calls "UFOs as *physicalist* religion." [117]

Seeing a UFO is a mystical experience. It is quasi-spiritual; it is technologized spirituality. The West was once dominated by theology. Its dominance was dethroned by science and scientific theory. When the Space age began, UFOlogy came into being to tackle new modes of how existence was now perceived. Theosophy has had a major role in shaping thoughts and beliefs of UFOs and aliens.

Using theosophy, George Adamski (a contactee in the 1950s) claimed that intelligent beings from other planets, namely Mars and Venus, are made of etheric matter. [118] In order to sell his books, Adamski needed the right motifs. Describing aliens as supernatural would simply not work. Even attributing complete material properties would not be convincing. The best, as Adamski saw it, was to describe extraterrestrials as ethereal. Even such a term is not the best description. A glimpse of nineteenth-century theosophy should help us.

Although theosophy goes back further than the nineteenth century, ideas brought forth by the Theosophical Society would eventually influence the UFO and alien abduction movements of the twentieth and twenty-first century. As founders, Helena Blavatsky (1831-91) and Henry Olcott (1832-1907) stitched together a complex form of religion and philosophy. They meshed a doctrine of Eastern religions and sciences with the intent to unlock nature's secrets via psychic and spiritual powers. [119] It is an attempt to reconcile magic, materialism, and

---

[117] Christopher Partridge, "Understanding UFO Religions and Abduction Spiritualties", in Christopher Partridge, ed., *UFO Religions,* Ch. 1. Routledge, London & New York, 2003, p. 21-6.
[118] Ibid, p. 18-9.
[119] Ibid, p. 9-10.

religion, as the stereotype of the animosity between religion and science has been exaggerated.

When it comes to social change, sightings of all kinds can manifest. Sociologist Robert Bartholomew calls this "Symbolic Community Scares," writing, "These community scares endure in a waxing and waning fashion for years, encompassing countries and geographical regions. There is less of a concern for security and welfare, and more of general long-term threat... consisting of fear over the exaggerated erosion of traditional values." [120] Social-psychological uneasiness can be seen in objective reality. These were expressed in explosions of apparitions of the Virgin Mary, the physical movements of Catholic statues in Ireland, widespread fairy sightings in nineteenth-century England, and the hysteria of UFO sightings ever since 1947. [121] Bartholomew succinctly explains, "These sightings serve as projected Rorschach test of the collective psyche, underscoring the promise of intellectual advancement during a period of spiritual decline." [122] So much for Jung's Collective Unconscious.

Adamski furthers that any form of "operation of technology is spiritual work." Among contactees, the synthesis of the scientific and the spiritual are transcending components. [123] The way Jennifer Porter sees it, extraterrestrials are superior to humans because of their superior technology and because of their advanced scientific knowledge; space aliens are also spiritually superior. In short, there is no science without religion and there is no religion

---

[120] Robert Bartholomew. *Little Green Men, Meowing Nuns, and Head-Hunting Panics: a Study of Mass Psychogenic Illness and Social Delusion*. McFarland & Company, Inc. Jefferson, NC, 2001, p. 19.
[121] Ibid., p. 21.
[122] Ibid., p. 27.
[123] Ibid, p. 15.

without science. [124] The Raëlian religion, however, has completely severed the Western roots of the supernatural. This movement is atheistic and materialist. [125]

In fairness, UFO organizations of the 1950s and 1960s were not cultists like contactees were. Members of UFO groups believed they were involved in activities in the name of science. The most successful groups were the Aerial Phenomena Research Organization, the National Investigations Committee on Aerial Phenomena and the Mutual UFO Network. UFO groups tried to unlock the mysteries of UFOs, emphasizing the 10 percent of unsolved UFO sightings. Brenda Denzler's surveys reveal that while members of the UFO community rely on science to unravel the UFO mystery, those seeing one was described in religious language. To put it simply, UFO witnesses had higher confidence understanding mysterious aerial objects in religious terms, but lower confidence in understanding them in scientific terms. When it comes to alien abductees (largely from the 1980s onwards), confidence in understanding the UFO experience from a religious basis is even higher. Science is not entirely mistrusted, although many abductees are not confident science can understand the non-physical aspect of reality. Unlike the 1950s and 1960s when attitudes toward contactees was very negative, UFO researchers have been more willing to be open-minded towards the alien abduction experience. Besides sympathy from the UFO community and a few abduction researchers (social scientists, therapists, and such), even old-time institutionalized religion is not supportive since it declares aliens to be demons.

---

[124] Ibid, p. 15-6.
[125] Ibid, p. 45.

As far as skeptical scientists are concerned, the experience is nothing short of fantasy. [126]

In the 1990s, alien abduction researcher and Harvard University professor John Mack saw aliens as physical and spiritual. Mack explains that the alien abduction experience occurs in some other dimension. The experience is physical, but it is also spiritual and psychological. As an anomaly of its classification, Mack rejects the rigid dichotomous approach. [127] If one is a skeptic, the reaction is one of confusion. In a sense, Mack asserts, alien abduction claims are measurable, but not exactly in the traditional materialist sense. Thus, how reliable is science in explaining UFOs? Is science just 90 percent reliable? What about the ten percent that is not explained?

UFOlogists have for decades emphasized the *unknown* explanations of UFOs. It has really bothered UFOlogists that 10 percent must be explained; it is the missing link. Institutionalized science was closely intertwined with the American military, namely the Air Force. UFOlogists (starting with Donald Keyhoe) believed something was hidden from the public and possibly the government was lying to the taxpayers. UFOlogists, specifically Jenny Randles and Peter Warrington, understood the 1950s and 1960s were the beginning of the Cold War, thereby covert government operations were a must. Even public disclosure of UFOs seemed to be to cover covert military operations. Scientists who worked for the Air Force were under strict guidelines. Randles and Warrington's beef was similar to that of the Condon Committee, headed by Dr. Edward Condon to investigate

---

[126] Brenda Denzler, "Attitudes Toward Religion and Science in the UFO Movement in the United States." In Christopher Partridge, ed., *UFO Religions*, Routledge, New York & London, 2003, p. 301-13.
[127] Partridge, ed., *UFO Religions*, p. 35.

UFOs in 1968, but for a different reason. Not only was he biased and a skeptic, Condon would repeatedly make jokes about the whole project and insinuate that UFOs are products of crazed minds. In subsequent years, Dr. Hynek addressed this issue. Indeed, in 1981 Hynek – once a skeptic working for the Air Force – was the leading UFOlogist at that time. He blasted the fact that most UFOlogists tended to lean towards fringe speculation, while only a minority have been doing competent work. The superstitious and occultists are drawn to UFOs. These mysterious objects can trigger fantastic and embellished theorization, often an embarrassment to "nuts-and-bolts" UFOlogists. [128]

From a skeptical standpoint, UFOlogists have yet to prove Earth is being visited by space aliens or some kind of beings from another realm. From a social-psychological perspective, the anxious concern of the unexplained 10 percent says more about UFOlogists than the UFOs themselves. It is hard to ignore the need for mystery. Although it is only 10 percent, it feels like a large gaping hole.

Science & Technology Inspires Fantasies of ETs

There is a lot of room in the imagination. Some more than others, of course, can get carried away. Just because Western Civilization has scientifically advanced and eroded religion, does not mean magical thinking went by the waste side. Probably more than ever, science has inspired magical thinking. Just as science influenced the UFO myth, technology is probably more important in our discussion.

---

[128] Jenny Randles and Peter Warrington, *Science and UFOs*. Basil Blackwell, New York & Oxford, 1985.

We mentioned the airships of the late nineteenth century, in anticipation of the new invention that was rumored and soon-to-be invented, some suspecting it already was. Because of the novelty of new, revolutionary technology, the best way to relate to it was through magical terms. Magic, we reiterate, has been part of human culture for a very long time.

In 1947, therefore, new technologies were introduced that directly influenced human misperception. There were many who described UFOs that flew at incredible speeds. Considering that it was the Cold War, the military – as a covert operation – were experimenting with high-speed airplanes. Chuck Yeager broke the sound barrier, a feat that broke the flight record the very same year Kenneth Arnold saw his flying saucer. [129] Weather balloons, satellites, and Air Force jets were misconstrued as flying saucers. In fact, during the late 1940s and the early 1950s, many civilians believed flying saucers might be secret weapons, either of Soviet or American origin. What was flown was top-secret, but it was not a weapon per se. Whenever it was, the CIA provided the media a yarn because of the political nature at the time. [130] This was part of the Skyhook program that was strictly classified, in which weather balloons were launched and very often misidentified as UFOs. [131] This furthers our crusade against Jung. The only thing mysterious about UFOs is that they are misidentified.

---

[129] "Breaking the Sound Barrier," p. 44-46 in Neil Schlager's, ed., *Science and Its Times: Understanding The Social Significance of Scientific Discovery*, Vol. 6: 1900-1949, The Gale Group, Farmington Mills, MI, 2000.

[130] William J. Broad. "CIA Admits Government Lied About U.F.O. Sightings." New York Times (Late Edition)(East Coast)) New York.N.Y.: August 3, 1997, pg. 1.12.

[131] B.D. Gildenberg. "The Cold War's Classified Skyhook Program: a participant's revelations." www.csicop.org/si/2004-05/skyhook.html.

Stress has been known to contribute to sightings of apparitions. Indeed, contactees (as we saw earlier) were probably hallucinating or in some kind of dream state – as the beautiful, blond-haired, blue-eyed aliens magically appeared to save them from technological disaster. Considering that observing UFOs is accompanied with magical interpretations, flight descriptions and maneuverability are often exaggerated. When Kenneth Arnold described the nine objects flying at 1200 miles per hour, one must ask how he knew this. Otto Billig, author of *Flying Saucers-Magic in the Skies: a Psychohistory*, explains the socio-historical circumstances:

> The democratic West, feeling psychologically overpowered, attributed greater, almost magical powers to Russia. Some believed that the USSR had a secret weapon, the flying saucer, an aircraft that could move with remarkable speed and perform unbelievable maneuvers against the law of gravity.[132]

It goes without saying that the UFO myth borrowed from science and technology. In subsequent decades, during the 1980s and 1990s, the Greys were abducting people by the multitude. The stereotypical human scientist, described as highly intelligent, cold, rational, introverted, and workaholic [133] – spilled over to describe the grey aliens. They are emotionless, the alien leader wears a lab coat, are economical, impersonal, and business-like. [134] These similar characteristics are not coincidental. What the abductees were describing were their alienated lives; in the postmodern age, science and technology has brought more anxiety than happiness. Of course,

---

[132] Otto Billig, *Flying Saucers-Magic in the Skies: A Psychohistory*. Schenkman Publishing Company Inc., Cambridge, MA, 1982, direct quote on p. 72.
[133] David C. Beardslee and Donald D. O' Dowd, *Science*, "The College Student Image Of The Scientist." V. 133, March 31, 1961, p. 997-1001.
[134] David M. Jacobs, *Secret Life: First Hand Accounts of UFO Abductions*, 1992.

these sentiments are related to millennial fears, UFOs and aliens as motifs of religiosity and spirituality. Taking away the mechanics of magic and reducing them to deluded states of interpretation is akin to stripping away the mystique of the universe. Religiosity and spirituality have depended upon these from the faithful. Believing in the mundane is one thing, believing in the extraordinary is preferred.

In comprehending the science and technology of UFOs, it was around late 1947 that Project Sign was put together. A number of German scientists who crossed over to the American side were asked if flying saucers were confiscated, V-rockets being used by the Soviets. The German scientists responded that flying saucers could not be secret Soviet weapons. It was simply unwise to fly over enemy territory, but then again some of these scientists thought the technological sophistication was way beyond human limits, and as such, many of them believed these flying saucers were coming from Mars. [135] Those who believed outnumbered the skeptics. Eventually, these beliefs spilled into the public's hands. Writing an article for *True* magazine, retired Marine Donald Keyhoe shocked the world when he published, "Flying Saucers are Real." Even the brightest can be fooled. This was because of stress - turning to supernatural explanations was the result. We could see this crisis of belief brewing in the prior century.

From this time, despite the industrialization of the nineteenth century (perceived as progress), it acted more as displacing individuals from their jobs. Many farmers in the Midwest could not compete with the new technological monster. As far as the South, post-civil war recovery only got so far until the 1890s when the American economy hit a depression. This inspired the nativist movement. As such,

---

[135] Otto Billig, *Flying Saucers-Magic in the Skies.*

foreigners were hated and targeted with prejudicial and racial violence. Only the wealthy few did very well. Ignatius Donnelly addressed the wide disparity of wealth with his novel, *Caesar's Column* in 1891. The hero went up against the plutocrats in his airship. By 1896, sightings of airships were abundant, most especially in the Midwest and in the South where the agrarian economy plummeted. Sightings would come back to coincide with the Cold War. [136] Sociologist Robert Bartholomew and psychologist George Howard have shown how the tendency towards the fantastic is influenced by the trends of the time. [137]

Anticipation in science fiction sometimes leads to technological reality. Jules Verne's *Around the World in Eighty Days* (1872) hinted at traveling the globe through flight in a timely fashion. Journalist Nellie Bly broke Phileas Fogg's record by a little more than a week. Bly left New York on November 14, 1889 and returned on January 25, 1890. [138]

Anticipation of something novel can influence perception. Howard Menzel recognized the revolutionary change of the era where,

> By 1950, when space travel had at least become a theoretical possibility and scientists were discussing ways to reach the moon, uneasy persons fantastically overestimated the height and size of mysterious lights in the sky and sometimes saw birds as spaceships from another planet.[139]

---

[136] Ibid, Ch.6.

[137] Robert E. Bartholomew and George S. Howard. *UFO's & Alien Contact: Two Centuries of Mystery*. Prometheus Books, Amherst, New York, 1998.

[138] Jason Colavito, *The Cult of Alien Gods: H.P. Lovecraft and Extraterrestrial Pop Culture*. Prometheus Books, Amherst, NY, 2005, p.57.

[139] Donald H. Menzel & Lyle G. Boyd. *The World of Flying Saucers: A Scientific Examination of a Major Myth of the Space age*. Doubleday & Co., Inc. Garden City, NY, 1963, p. 122.

Contactees believed these aliens came from our own solar system – either from Mars, Venus, Jupiter, or the Moon. However, the home planets had to be pushed further away once science made it clear none of these planets' atmospheres are equipped to support life. The vast distance between solar systems is suggestive of disgruntled disconnection. Between mainstream scientists and UFOlogists there is only a narrow bridge. There are UFOlogists who remind us how ideas that were once rejected eventually are accepted. They fail to forget that theories and hypothesis are often adjusted or discarded because of thin evidence. When claims were posed in the 1950s that aliens came from planets in our solar system, they were immediately dismissed. A brave few UFO enthusiasts still felt compelled to continue their search for the truth.

Jacques Vallée, subsequently, brought the aliens much closer to Earth, instead of light-years away. Vallée's approach to the UFO problem was cautious, because of the capacity of the human imagination. In 1969, this French scientist left open the possibility that humans throughout history have been interacting with beings from other realms, [140] at the very least an abstract hypothesis that challenged the extraterrestrial one. Many years later, in a UFO conference, Vallée stated that, "I believe the UFO phenomenon represents evidence from other dimensions beyond space time, but from a multiverse which is all around us..." [141] Coinciding with the birth of his interdimensional hypothesis, the 1960s was a decade where the occult and interest in the supernatural rose. What was apparent was how folk beliefs were making a comeback from the glory days of the

---

[140] Jacques Vallée. *Passport To Magonia: On UFO's, Folklore, and Parallel Worlds*. Contemporary Books, Ins. Chicago, (1969) 1993.
[141] C.D.B Bryan, *Close Encounters of the Fourth Kind: Alien Abduction, UFO's and the Conference at M.I.T.*, Alfred A, Knopf, New York, 1995.

Victorian supernatural, although it must said that aliens depicted in films during the 1950s had magical characteristics. Vallée's interdimensional hypothesis, at first met with scorn, was very slowly accepted by some pro-UFOlogists. Among UFOlogical circles, it was subsequently wondered whether fairies and aliens were one in the same. [142] Fairies, according to popular culture of northern Europe, were known to abduct people prior to the twentieth century. In fact, by the new millennium, traditional, otherworldly encounters, to some investigators, may be extraterrestrials after all. [143] And by the 1990s, abduction researcher John E. Mack from Harvard University, championed the incorporeal paradigm. [144]

The most famous and most notorious alien abduction researcher was Budd Hopkins. To support his theory of the aliens' origins, he speculated there was a parallel universe. Hopkins argued that it is in conjunction with scientific theory. [145] Parallel Universe was a notion thought by two German

---

[142] Nick Pope. *The Uninvited: An Expose of the Alien Abduction Phenomenon.* The Overlook Press. Woostock & New York, 1997, p. 3-14; Jenny Randles, *Alien Abductions: The Mystery Solved: Over 200 Documented UFO Kidnappings Investigated.* Inner Light Publications, New Brunswick, NJ, 1988, p. 32.

[143] Lynn Schofield Clark, *From Angels to Aliens: Teenagers, the Media, and the Supernatural.* Oxford University Press, New York & London, 2003; Keith Thompson, *Angels and Aliens: UFOs and the Mythic Imagination.* Addison-Wesley, Reading, Mass., 1991.; Philip J. Imbrogno, *Ultraterrestrial Contact: A Paranormal Investigator's Explorations into the Hidden Experience.* Llewelyn Publications, Woodbury, MN, 2010.

[144] John E. Mack. *Abduction: Human Encounters with Aliens*, Macmillan Publishing Co. New York, NY, 1994; John E. Mack. *Passport to Cosmos: Human Transformation and Alien Encounters.* Crown Publishers, New York, NY, 1999.

[145] Budd Hopkins and Carol Rainey. *Sight Unseen: Science, UFO Invisibility and Transgenic Beings.* Pocket Books, a division of Simon & Shuster, Inc. New York, 2003.

theorists, Werner Heisenberg and Erwin Schrodinger. [146] The theory was used in science fiction, and the concept was traced to folklore. [147] Physicist Michio Kaku, an enthusiast of the "fourth dimension," admits that it is only theoretical. [148] From this sense, the supernatural – of which there is no proof – is *physicalized*. Like the influential H. P. Lovecraft who we discussed earlier, UFO theorists drew a lot from science fiction. The skeptics of alien abduction have said the evidence is elusive. Hopkins explains the reason aliens are unseen is due to their cloaking technology. [149] Nonsense. The Romulans, a race in the *Star Trek* series, used cloaking to hide from enemy humanoids. The science fiction genre borrowed cloaking from fairy folklore that gave them the capability to elude humans. [150] Fairies were rehashed into gray aliens who abduct people. Once they roamed the forests, now they returned as technological beings. [151]

Science may have chased away ghosts and goblins, but science also encouraged space aliens. There are various kinds of alien species/humanoids. [152] The most infamous are short, not even five feet, creatures with bluish-gray skin color. These are called the "Greys."

[146] Charles Seife. "Physics Enters the Twilight Universe." *Science*, July 23, 2004, Vol. 33, issue 5683.

[147] See "Parallel Worlds" in John Clute and Peter Nicholas, editors, *The Encyclopedia of Science Fiction*. Orbit, Inc. UK, 1993, p. 907.

[148] Michio Kaku. *Hyperspace: A Scientific Odyssey through Parallel Universes, Time Warps, and the Tenth Dimension*. Oxford University Press, Inc. New York, 1994.

[149] Budd Hopkins and Carol Rainy, 2003.

[150] See invisibility at Wikipedia.org.

[151] Thomas E. Bullard, "UFO Abduction Reports: The Supernatural Kidnap Narrative Returns in Technological Guise", *The Journal of American Folklore*, April 1989, Vol. 102, Issue 404, p. 147.

[152] Diana G. Tumminia, Ed., *Alien Worlds: Social and Religious Dimensions of Extraterrestrial Contact*. Syracuse University Press, Syracuse, 2007, see Exhibit B: *Some Types of Aliens*, p. 313.

5

Alien Abduction

Technological beings kidnap people, and as such, alien abduction is the most bizarre of all UFOlore. Only the Raëlians who publicly claimed they cloned a human baby can top alien abduction. But while the cloning scandal was a hoax, the alien abduction narrative is not. It is real. It is only real insofar as the imagination goes. Delusional is the hallmark of human behavior, most especially by mystics. Abductees, as well, describe their abduction experience as they are shamans. Although alien abduction can be a transcendent experience, we will discuss its religious significance later. For now, we want to focus on its pseudoscientific aspect and increasing relation to the science of psychology.

Overview

Whether in a car, a bedroom, or in a crowd of people - aliens abduct their victims and take them to a UFO (presumably a spaceship) - to conduct medical examinations. Because of the invasion of privacy, these tests are humiliating. Men have their sperm stolen while women have their eggs confiscated. Women are often injected with a hybrid fetus, only to have it taken away upon birth after a brief glimpse of the newly-born crossbreed. Strangely, the aliens tell their human captives they will not remember what happened; memory will be "blacked-out."

Of course, the abductees cannot remember what happened. When waking up from bed, they are unable to account for unusual marks on their skins. Not only lesions and scars are found, nasal and anal bleeding are reported. Tracking devices might explain the reasons for the unexpected bleeding. In addition, abductees lose track of time and have difficulty accounting for this. Returning from the supermarket is a mere 15-minute walk, but one does not reach home for another two hours. These are odd instances and the abductees are baffled and are at a loss as to what is going on. The tricky part is that the abductees do not know they are abductees yet because of the erasures of their memories. Some of the missing pieces come together through dreams, something seen on TV, and in some cases seeing a picture of an alien. Budd Hopkins calls the unrecalled phenomenon as "missing time," the very title of his book published in 1981. [153]

Like many clients who went to Hopkins, in their attempts to resolve their sense of time loss, were treated by hypnotherapists interested in alien abductions. Further probing during the altered state of consciousness, allowed objects, animals, and people to be remembered. There are blockages but upon digging deeper into the far reaches of the mind, aliens have set "screen memories." They are false memories to confuse the abductees about the real ones. After several hypnotic sessions, it becomes clear the abductees have been abducted since childhood. They were continually abducted and observed until reaching adulthood. After the aliens and their captives get to know each other, abducted humans are told (although such information is not clear) the aliens may come from the Sirius star system or possibly from some other dimension. These

[153] Budd Hopkins. *Missing Time: A Documented Study of UFO Abductions*. Prentice Hall, 1981.

aliens came to Earth because their planet was blocked-out from the sun, after being destroyed. Since the aliens are dying, the goal is to hybridize with the human race. However, as we noted above, alien abductions are real only in fantasies. Upon numerous sessions of hypnosis, clients are led to believe (in a sort of brainwashing way) they were abducted by aliens - when the actual occurrences were not authentic. These memories of alien encounters are *false memories*.

This is when psychology comes in. It has become sophisticated enough to let us know how false memories can easily be implanted. Further, hypnosis does not function like alien abduction researchers, especially like Hopkins, say it does. Psychology has taught us that humanity can, has, and will continue to delude itself with dream states.

Sleep paralysis is thought to be the cause of an alien abduction episode. As a rare, yet not so uncommon experience, it takes place at night during sleep. Just before waking the sleeper is unable to move, and unnerving as it is, shadowy figures are seen in the dim-lighted bedroom. Other types of hallucinations include lights, sounds, and floating. The actual memory of the experience may be unclear. Once alien abduction is mentioned in the popular media, aliens immediately become the culprits. [154] Through magazines and books, abductees read related stories and wonder if they were also kidnapped without knowing it. Some psychologists believe that

---

[154] Susan Blackmore. "Abduction by Aliens or Sleep Paralysis?", *Committee for the Scientific Investigation of Claims of the Paranormal,* www. Csicop.org/si/9805/abduction.html.; Dr. Peter Dodzik (managing editor) "Is Sleep Paralysis the Cause of Alien Abductions?" *Sleep & Health Newspaper,* www. Sleepandhealth.com/Newspaper/2003/April/14.htm.

abductees are escapists and masochists. [155] Others disagree, but do agree abductees are a suggestible population, [156] vulnerable to fantasies.

Hypnosis, skeptics say, can crystallize any fuzzy recollections. The evidence also suggests abductees have vivid imaginations. Neuroscientist Michael Persinger explains, "Fundamentally, except they have an unusual creativity. That also means suggestibility. [157] " One does not need to be imaginative to be abducted by aliens, but the imaginative, seemingly, are attracted to the unusual and the bizarre. Persinger continues, "We have looked at individuals who claimed abduction experiences. There's a tremendous spectrum of experiences that take place. What makes the experience often very rigid and formulated when they go to a particular therapist who has (a) particular idea of what the alien is. [158]"

Not all alien abduction hypnotists see the experience in the same way. The type of professions hypnotists have had has influenced particular themes of this fantasy role-playing. Budd Hopkins saw the alien encounter as a surreal story. His original

---

[155] Leonard S, Newman and Roy F. Baumeister, "Toward an Explanation of the UFO Abduction Phenomenon: Hypnotic Elaboration, Extraterrestrial Sadomasochism, and Spurious Memories." *Psychological Inquiry*, 1996, vol. 7, Issue 2, p.99, 28p.

[156] Jamie Arndt & Jeff Greenberg, "Fantastic Accounts Can Take Many Forms: False Memory Construction? Yes. Escape From Self? We Don't Think So." *Psychological Inquiry*, 1996, Vol. 7 Issue 2, p. 127, 6p; Kenneth S. Bowers and John D. Eastwood, "On The Edge Of Science: Coping with UFOlogy Scientifically." *Psychological Inquiry*, 1996, Vol. 7, Issue 2, p. 136, 5p; Steven E. Clark and Elizabeth F. Loftus, "The Construction of Space Alien Abduction Memories." Psychological Inquiry, 1996, Vol.7 Issue 2, P.140, 4p.

[157] Quote in Kidnapped By UFO's ?: the true story of alien abductions, NOVA: adventures in science, WGBH Education Foundation, 1996 (video).

[158] Ibid.

trade was art. As such, it more than seems Hopkins was also fantasy-prone. Most importantly, Hopkins was not a certified psychologist even if he was using hypnosis to regress his clients.

David Jacobs did his Ph.D. dissertation on the history of UFOs after completing The *UFO Controversy in America*. Like Hopkins, he was not a certified psychologist. As a history professor, Jacobs asserts that aliens were secretly invading Earth through their discreet alien abduction program in progressive stages. [159] His suspicions sound very much like the covert operations of the Cold War and also reminiscent of McCarthyism (Senator McCarthy was paranoid that communists were secretly moving about to take over the U.S.). The film *Invasion of the Body Snatchers* portrayed a similar theme in the 1950s. Jacobs' two books on alien abductions, were respectively published in 1992 and 1998. [160] The 1990s were filled with millennial fears, of which included the "illegal alien" under the radar, the stereotype being that these foreigners were "taking" jobs away from Americans. In the meantime, alien abduction enthusiasts and the general UFO community emphasized the credentials of these hypnotists. Besides Jacobs, a certified historian, John Mack was the most credentialed of all the alien abduction researchers. Once again, the UFO community has had the habit of holding high hopes of solving UFO matters whenever a real scientist, such as Dr. Allen Hynek, comes over to their side.

Harvard University professor, John Mack, did just that. He was a credentialed psychologist, professor, and researcher with tenure. However, Mack

---

[159] David M. Jacobs. *Secret Life: First Hand Accounts of UFO Abductions*, Simon & Shuster, New York, NY, 1992. *The Threat: Secret Agenda: What the Aliens Really Want and How They Plan to Get It*. Simon & Shuster. New York, NY, 1998.
[160] See footnote 159.

was unorthodox. He interpreted the alien abduction experience as not physically real. Rather, these otherworldly events take place in an altered state of consciousness. His actual definition of physicality, although leaning more towards metaphysics, is difficult to pin down. To be sure, Mack's approach was philosophical. He had a keen interest in non-Western perceptions of reality, calling Western materialism and its scientists as elitists. He, evidently, rejected the Western method of science. [161]

Carl Sagan came to the defense of the scientific method. He was a scientist who was very excited about the prospect of life in outer space. In reality, it is one thing to hope to find life outside of Earth, it is another to claim aliens are here, mastering time and space to perform hideous sexual, medical experiments. In an interview with Sagan on the TV program *Nova* aired on PBS, the conversation was about alien abduction reports and was asked to comment on John Mack:

> Many of the principal advocates of UFO abduction seem to want the validation of science without submitting to its rigorous standards of evidence. When John Mack talks about parallel universes or other dimensions, he is using scientific ideas. Those have long been in play in the physics and astronomy community. But there is no evidence for them. He also criticizes the current paradigm that is the scientific method. But, this isn't validated. We don't believe it just out of prejudice; we believe it because it works. [162]

Like we saw earlier, Jacques Vallée proposed there is a multiverse that envelopes all surroundings. Mack went a step further. The so-called parallel universe notion became popular. If Mack

---

[161] John E. Mack. *Abduction: Human Encounters with Aliens*, Macmillan Publishing Co. New York, NY, 1994; John E. Mack. *Passport to Cosmos: Human Transformation and Alien Encounters*. Crown Publishers, New York, NY, 1999.

[162] See, "I want you to comment on John Mack." www.pbs.org/wbgh/nova/space/sagan-alien-abduction.html. Accessed on October 3, 2014.

demonstrated that knowledge can be extracted by an alternate approach to science, the UFO community was ready to accept this notion. UFO buffs were already believing in this kind of reality. Mack just put a more, academic spin to it. This is, in fact, a game-changer. Because science relies on proof, pseudoscience now says their ideas cannot be disproved, remaining dogmatic and becoming deliberately deaf to any rebuttal from skeptics. We want to respect the dead, since Mack died in an automobile accident, but we must not avoid criticizing his methods. Mack embraced New Age spirituality. Like himself and his clients, he searched for new meaning. Keep in mind that the hypnotist and those hypnotized influence each other's fantasies. Scientific research strongly attests to this. Mack was a credentialed psychologist, but then again fell into the pseudoscientific trap. It is clear, as we have been arguing all along that even Mack's relationship with his colleagues at Harvard exemplifies the discontent of postmodern society. Mack is the hero who must slay the bureaucratic dragon. In this case, it is Harvard University.

Therapeutic Healing v. Hypnosis

Like Mack and others, whether one is a New Ager or not, what has been pervasive is the quest for meaning. That life, in itself, is inherently meaningful and has a purpose. In recent years, many have been attracted to psychological healing. Physical exercise has been promoted. Others use drugs and/or drown themselves in alcohol. The second half of the twentieth century has seen a resurgence in God. In the final analysis, science and technology can only go so far in fulfillment. Humans have been and will continue to search for some kind of transcendent meaning. The alien abduction narrative is simply a form of escape in what appears to be a meaningless world.

As psychotherapists, Richard and Lee Boylan view the alien experience as a healing mechanism. [163] Although Karla Turner is also a psychotherapist, her own abduction experience was deceptive and hostile. [164] Edith Fiore is another psychotherapist who used hypnosis on her clients. She suggests the abductees have paranoid tendencies, but trusts hypnosis as a reliable tool. Interpreting her own abduction experience, she realized the influence reading materials had on her. [165] Fiore, finally, was precise with this observation. Wherever the evidence leads, as honest researchers and theorists that is where we must go.

Expertise is not pretended here. Dr. Benjamin Simon was an expert and was the psychologist who treated Barney and Betty Hill with hypnosis. On the morning of September 20, 1961, the Hills spotted a UFO as Barney was driving through upstate New York on route to their home state of New Hampshire. Returning from vacation, it was 2:00 AM when the married couple noticed an unusual flying object. They arrived home two hours later than they should have. Shortly afterwards, Betty began having dreams, but more on the nightmarish side. She divulged this to her colleagues at work, where one of her co-workers recommended writing her dreams down. Other co-workers, and especially her supervisor, insisted her dreams were not fantasies but an actual event, an authentic UFO experience. A UFO investigator was

[163] Richard Boylan and Lee K. Boylan. *Close Extraterrestrial Encounters: Positive Experiences With Mysterious Visitors*, get rest of info
[164] Karla Turner Ph.D. *Taken: Inside the Alien-human Abduction Agenda*. Rose Printing Co., Inc. Tallahassee, Fl. 1994.
[165] Edith Fiore. *Encounters: A Psychologist Reveals Case Studies of Abductions by Extraterrestrials,* Double Day, 1989.

called to the Hill's home. He believed it was a good idea to consult with Dr. Simon, since the UFO investigator thought the spotted UFO might be the reason for the two unaccounted hours. This is three years later, in 1964. From late February throughout March, both Barney and Betty drove on Saturday mornings to meet with Dr. Simon to undergo hypnosis. After several hypnotic sessions, Dr. Simon ended therapy and came to his conclusion that Betty and Barney Hill were not abducted by aliens. What really happened was that they experienced a shared dream,[166] or better said a shared nightmare. The reason it was shared because it started with Betty Hill and as a close couple that they were, Barney wound up absorbing her dreams unconsciously. The author of *The Interrupted Journey*, John Fuller – biographer of the Hills – did not really accept Dr. Simon's conclusion, throwing subtle hints that there must be something more to the story. *The Interrupted Journey* was quite influential, considering how it captured people's attention and how many read the book. A few though wondered if they were also abducted, attributing missing time to UFOs right after spotting them. This became the newly transformed contacteeism that had petered out by the early 1960s.

Phillip Klass, the most admired and hated UFO debunker (and often plucked the nerves of Bud Hopkins), was busily writing during the period when Hopkins published *Missing Time* in 1981. Eight years later, Klass published *UFOs: a Dangerous Game,*[167] renouncing the claims of alien abduction reports. Klass was hostile towards the UFO community, calling them pro-UFOlogists. One can guess Klass was their demonic counterpart. Even though Klass was not an

[166] John G. Fuller. *The Interrupted Journey: Two Lost Hours "Aboard a Flying Saucer."* The Dial Press, New York, NY, 1966.
[167] Phillip Klass. *UFO Abductions: A Dangerous Game.* Prometheus Books, Buffalo, NY, 1989.

expert in hypnosis (neither am I), he knew something was amiss. He believed, like many skeptics since (including the great Carl Sagan), there must be verifiable evidence, something tangible to prove alien abduction claims. So Klass consulted an expert on such matters, Dr. Martin Orne. He told Klass one must be cautious when using hypnosis because it can lead to pseudo-memories.[168] Other experts echo these observations, adding active imaginations contribute to fantasies.[169] There is evidence of fantasies, not of otherworldly beings. Instead, memories can become distorted; for this reason legal courts do not trust hypnosis.[170]

Before Hopkins died, he declared on his website, IntrudersFoundation.com, that 70% of abductees recall their violent alien encounters without hypnosis. Only 30% need hypnosis to retrieve their hidden memories. Hopkins furthered that hypnosis is reliable as long as it is used carefully. Hopkins totally disagreed with Harvard's Susan Clancy, a skeptic of alien abductions and a specialist on memory, berating her research by calling it "faith-based science."[171] Clancy's argument is very simple. With a formula consisting of media-filled science fiction through teletechnology in combination with hypnosis, the alien abduction myth was created.[172] 70% of Hopkins' abductee population had total recall without hypnosis, because

---

[168] Klass cites Dr. Martin Orne, *UFO Abductions*, p. 57-63.

[169] Robert G. Kunzendorf, Nicolas P. Spanos, and Benjamin Wallace, editors. *Hypnosis and Imagination*. Baywood Publishing Company, Inc. Amittyville, NY, 1996.

[170] Kevin McConkey and Peter W. Sheehan. *Hypnosis, Memory, and Behavior in Criminal Investigation*. The Guilford Press, New York, 1995.

[171] Budd Hopkins. "Faith-Based Science" *Intruder Foundation.com*, October, 2005, www.intrudersfoundation.org/faith_based.html.

[172] Susan A. Clancy. *Abducted: How People Come to Believe They Were Kidnapped By Aliens*. Harvard University Press, Cambridge, MA & London, 2005.

they did not need it. This information was uploaded in 2005, in response to Clancy's work. Unlike in 1981 when *Missing Time* was published, by the 2000s, the alien abduction experience was much more known. It was no longer necessary to wonder if aliens did any kidnapping. Such "total recall" come from deluded individuals, imaginative and creative types, and even from a few hoaxers.

There is this misconception that non-clinical or non-pathological people are immune to hallucinations and suggestibility. For example, Dr. Elizabeth Slater evaluated five men and four women, individuals who were abducted, but Slater was not told this. She did note how these nine persons suffered from anxiety, low self-esteem, though not paranoid. When it was revealed to Slater the individuals were abducted, she was surprised. Psychopathology in the population she evaluated was absent. [173]

Not only is this assumption a leap of faith, those evaluated were disturbed as they had characteristics that may need clinical care. Even those that were evaluated did not show severe symptoms of psychopathology does not prove they were abducted by aliens. Alien abduction researchers and enthusiasts have failed miserably in not noticing how the imagination can mislead some of us:

> Consider the fact that thousands of sane and intelligent people with no evidence of psychopathology speak in terror-stricken voices about their experience aboard flying saucers. They *remember*, clearly and vividly, being abducted by aliens. [174]

Gregory van Dyk, *The Alien Files: The Secrets of Extraterrestrial Encounters and Abductions*. Element, Rockport, MA, 1997, p. 79.
Dr. Elizabeth Loftus and Katherine Ketchman, *The Myth of Repressed Memory: False Memories and Allegations of Sexual Abuse*. St. Martin's Press, New York, 1994, p. 66.

All that is needed is to be convinced of one's past experiences. Once suggestion is injected in a rigid environment – where the therapist calls the shots – one can start believing there was trauma of being sexually abused, either by one's own parents or members of a satanic cult. [175] Nicolas Spanos subjected adult subjects to hypnotic regressions to their previous past lives. Before meeting with Spanos, these individuals did not have past life identities. When suggested they were sexually abused as children, the number of child abuse reports went up. Spanos concluded that clients who exhibit some form of psychopathology sometimes confabulate memories which tend to correspond to their therapists' expectations. [176]

During sleep paralysis, the figures and shadows are mere fuzzy figments. *Fuzzy* is the key word here, because when one goes to a hypnotherapist who believes in aliens (even if he or she might be skeptical), the likely scenario is false memories of being abducted. After being subjected to vivid recollections of torture (although they are believed to be fantasies), the memories become imbedded into the abductees. As such, it is unfortunate how they developed characteristics of posttraumatic stress. Can fantasies really do this? The evidence points in that direction. The evidence also shows that these bedroom captures, as extracted under hypnosis, were influenced by movies and other forms of popular culture. Fantasy proneness of abductees' personalities is connected to confabulating fantasies. The creative types sometimes report having "higher awareness." Abductees, some more than others, as observed through the case studies, demonstrated some form of psychopathology – which includes a tendency for masochistic fantasies. In

---

[175] Loftus and Ketcham, *The Myth of Repressed Memory*, 1994.
[176] Ibid, p. 79.

short, sleep paralysis is a significant component of an alien abduction episode – although hypnosis is much more pivotal. [177]

Alien abduction panic has similarities to retrieving "repressed" memories of child sex abuse and satanic ritual abuse. The False Memory Syndrome Foundation was founded in 1992 to combat the misconception of repressed memory retrieval. False memory is a distraction to dealing with the real issues of a person's life. [178] There also is something to be said about fear, fear of personified evil living life under our very noses. [179] Children may be afraid of the boogeyman man; for some adults, their boogeyman might be the Greys.

---

[177] Stuart Appelle, Steven Jay Lynn, Leonard Newman, and Anne Malaktaris, "Alien Abduction Experiences." In
Eztel Cardeña, Steven Jay Lynn, and Stanley Krippner, eds., *Varieties of Anomalous Experience: Examining the Scientific Evidence*, second edition. American Psychological Association, Washington, D.C., 2012, Ch. 8.

[178] Bridget Brown, *They Know Us Better Than We Know Ourselves: The History and Politics of Alien Abduction*. New York University Press, New York & London, 2007, p. 66-7.

[179] Loftus and Ketchman, *The Myth of Repressed Memory*; Richard Ofshe and Ethan Watters, *Making Monsters: False Memories, Psychotherapy, and Sexual Behavior*. Charles Scribner Sons, New York & London, 1994; Lawrence Wright, *Remembering Satan*. Alfred A. Knopf, New York, 1994; Dale McCulley, "Satanic Ritual Abuse: A Question of Memory." *Journal of Psychology and Theology*, Fall 1994, Vol. 22, No. 3, p. 167-172; Robert Passantino and Gretchen Passantino, "Satanic Ritual Abuse in Popular Christian Literature: why Christians fall for a lie searching for the truth." *Journal of Psychology and Theology*, Fall 1992, No. 3, p. 299-305.

Part 3

Millennial and Apocalyptic Fears

6

Nuclear Fears

Growing in importance since the discovery of radioactivity in the late nineteenth and the early twentieth centuries, the future city was visualized as an ideal urban center that no longer depended on the pollution from using coal. Nuclear energy was deemed more reliable. By the 1930s, electricity not only illuminated darkness, it enlightened those to think the future is brighter than ever. On the other hand, critics began distrusting scientists as the twentieth century wore on, seeing military weapons imbued with radioactive energy. This was viewed in a negative light, drawing pessimists. Satirists began depicting the clumsy oddball, a kind of evil figure, the mad scientist, since this person could potentially bring chaos and destruction with his military weapons.[180]

In this section of our book, we will continue to discuss technology in relation to fear. More precisely, advancement of science and civilization may be beneficial in one sense, but more perilous in another. UFOs and alien abductions serve as expressions of technological decadence and discontent brought on by bureaucracy. In this matrix, many struggled to find themselves, a period filled with the anxiety of atomic energy. To the point, postmodernism brought nothing but coldness.

---

[180] Spencer R. Weart. *Nuclear Fear: A History of Images*, Harvard University Press, Cambridge, MA & London, UK, 1988, chapters 1 and 2.

Is Technology Evil?

Should we mess with the impermissible, like Adam and Eve did when they ate the Forbidden Fruit of Knowledge and were expelled from the Garden of Eden? This Old Testament story teaches the price to be paid by becoming self-aware. As the old cliché says, curiosity killed the cat. We can get into serious trouble for unlocking knowledge. According to ancient Greek myth, Zeus gives Pandora a jar (although the story is known as Pandora's Box). She is explicitly told not to open it, for doing so will unleash all the evils known to man. Pandora's curiosity got the best of her, figuring a slight opening, a peek, would do no harm. Even with a small crack came the rushing out of ghostly figures, all of the evils stored away now became permanent. However, there was one last item left in the Box; that one last thing happened to be hope.

In the early years of the twentieth century before World War II, the public came to realize the dangers of radiation. Clergy members saw the exotic glow emitted by radium as a mystic event. Even spiritualists were writing that radioactivity is a supernatural source, warning scientists to keep their hands off foreign territory. [181] UFO sightings tend to have strange lights, often glowing and turning off while other lights turn on. Modern culture borrowed from the ancients that light is a divine source, sunlight in particular is associated with the sexual prowess of procreation. Some saw electricity as a supernatural agent. [182] This new form of energy scared many, since they could not comprehend it. Given the

[181] Ibid., p. 37-8.
[182] Ibid., p. 40-1.

suspicion of its potential danger, technophobia arose.

Folklore is filled with the all-seeing eye penetrating into one's deepest secrets. The invention of the X-rays was received ambiguously. It is a device to examine the inner parts of the human being while emanating a small amount of radiation, although it gave the feeling of the invasive stare. [183] Abductees have reported the Greys' large eyes are able to communicate telepathically with them. Abductees are most impressed with the leader's gaze. This gives the impression authority is closely watching with intrusive technology.

On a cosmic level, it is alluring to explore the secrets of nature. Scientists probing into God's realm are pleasant for some, though the mastering of the atom by smashing it terrified some critics. Science fiction writers took advantage. In this genre, the world is a technological totalitarianism ruled by a mad scientist who uses science to politically oppress his victims. This includes the fear of being mutilated, a notion that falls in line with the scientist's child, his invention, a monster or a robot. [104] As a monstrous oppressor, it rings of a secular antichrist, a familiar religious motif for the end of the world.

As symbols of rebirth after Armageddon, the Greys have been described as fetuses. [185] It's no accident that alien abductions increased in the post-war era, an era perceived as the development of globalization, which owes gratitude to technology, a billion dollar industry devoted toward the massive

---

[183] Ibid., p. 44-5.
[184] Ibid., p. 55-69.
[185] Bridget Brown. *They Know us Better than we Know Ourselves: The History and Politics of Alien Abduction*, New York University Press, New York & London, 2007, p. 92.

buildup of militarization. Hence, it is correct to say that some were vehemently angry over military zealousness. The alleged intergalactic secretive breeding project - like any secretive government plot - symbolizes the amalgamation of the globe, but dictated by the superpower called the United States. The Counterculture movement, as we discussed previously, became disgusted with their own government and the overall state of affairs in its own society and the world.

The American government oversaw atomic bomb tests, irritating many despite the government's downplaying the dangers of radioactivity. There were concerns of possible birth defects, as well as the concern of acquiring cancer. Bureaucrats were accused of being "cancerous" themselves. The fear of radioactivity was projected onto the silver screen, where contamination caused mutations of giant ants in the movie *Them*. *Godzilla*, a giant-living dinosaur, was another movie mythologizing this fear. Hollywood beat the dead horse by making films about oversized insects running around terrorizing humans. It is clear that fears of radiation were expressed as guilt after the destruction of Hiroshima and Nagasaki. The movement of protesting against atomic tests was initiated. Moreover, there were films and novels conveying a chaotic world after the decimation of an atomic war. There were protagonists welcoming man-made destruction, surviving a dreadful society to begin with and fantasizing of running free after everyone has died.

Several novelists in the 1950s and a lesser amount in the 1960s, wrote stories about the end of the world. It is better to obliterate wickedness, these authors barked, so we could start anew.[186] Hence,

---

[186] Spencer R. Weart. *Nuclear Fear: A History of Images*, Harvard University Press, Cambridge & London, 1988, p. 199-230.

the fetus-looking Greys resonate with this mythology – where technology and humanity is the new synthesis – the metaphors of rebirth from death. Even those apathetic towards UFOs and alien abductions cannot deny the post-war epoch is so remarkable and unlike any in history. Skeptics say extraordinary claims require extraordinary evidence. Conversely, it is extraordinary historical circumstances that require an extraordinary myth.

The alien abduction myth serves as expressions of American decadence, globalization, and invasive technology. [187] Bridget Brown argues that the alien abduction narrative takes on a movement of victimization, similar to survivors of incest and the sexually abused. The abductee population, composed of both men and women, go to alien abduction hypnotists to learn of being raped by aliens. Ironically, they come to realize their lives make more sense in an age of discontent. Being submissive to authority figures, alien abduction regressions done by experts is akin to psychiatrists, dentists, and doctors – all of whom are traditionally associated with treating their clients laying down while standing over or near them. Though suffering and victimization, argues Brown, the submissive role of abductees becomes a form of empowerment through relinquishing control.

Brown calls the alien abduction scene *Techno-Sexual Violation*, noting stories of abductees detailing the violation of humans by inserting or removing gadgets and displaying phallic, technological devices. [188]

[187] Bridget Brown, *They Know Us Better Than We Know Ourselves: The History and Politics of Alien Abduction*. New York University Press, New York and London, 2007.
[188] Ibid, p. 54-5.

UFUs: Symbols of Death and Rebirth

Watching a ball of fire from the superb energy coming from an atomic blast is accompanied with awe or despair. Ancient civilization had great admiration and fear towards light; this natural source came from the gods. Nuclear energy could be both beneficial and destructive and both satanic and Godly. Preachers from the 1950s and the 1960s saw the unprecedented nuclear fireball as a sign of the Second Coming. Those in the 1980s, including Ronald Reagan, believed the same thing. The rapture was evoked in the same decade, [189] during the increase of alien abduction reports. The golden era of UFOs, from the 1950s through the 1970s, was referred as "atomic psychosis" by some. [190] Technology, according to some, was the new salvation, [191] although contactees of the 1970s warned of nuclear peril. [192]

UFOs are products of nuclear fear. Mysterious sightings represent the uncertainty of where progress was headed, as transformative symbols during the transformation of postmodern civilization, their inhuman speed indicating that society was changing too quickly. Are we headed towards self-destruction? The mushroom-cloud artistically became part of films, books, pamphlets, and other textual forms of popular culture. The media was always ready to photograph the mushroom-cloud during atomic bomb tests. Folklore studies reveal the symbolism of fungi, the process of rotting and the last destination referred as death. But the mushroom as a food source also represents life. They have been associated with witches and fairies related to the supernatural (while aliens are believed to be from outer space or another

---

[189] Weart, *Nuclear Fear*, p. 395-8.
[190] Ibid., p. 399.
[191] Ibid., p. 400.
[192] Ibid., p. 401.

dimension). The "magic mushroom" of the 1960s counterculture was self-administered to travel to the other side, copying the shaman's spiritual journey.

The mandala is believed to be a universal archetype that stands for spiritual transcendence. The same theme was taken by the ringed atom as the most popular iconography of postmodern science, "mandalizing" the incredible power of nuclear energy. [193] The first man of the world, Adam, is in a sense replaced by an atom, the basic element of the universe. The mandala can be expressed through the flying saucer as an archetype of death according to Carl Jung. [194] The problem with Jung's interpretation of this universal symbol, if universal at all, is not entirely clear. His analysis, though, of universality – not the objectivity of the archetype, but its interpretation – anticipates drastic social change.

Stories of Biblical visions are especially good examples. Preaching in the tumultuous period during the Jewish captivity in Babylon, Ezekiel describes his heavenly vision as a sign of God. Approaching from the northern skies was a giant cloud. From a great ball of fire, emerged four hideous creatures with four wings and four faces. Then, Ezekiel notes the appearance of four wheels. When the winged-creatures lifted up, the wheels ascended as well. [195] There are some who perceived Ezekiel's wheel as a UFO. These are the Ancient Astronaut Theorists. Actually, Ezekiel's vision expresses the crisis his Jews were going through, fallen victims of the mighty civilization of Babylon. Those interpreting this mystic event as a UFO are expressing their current

---

[193] Ibid., p. 399-407.
[194] Carl G. Jung. *Flying Saucers: A Modern Myth of Things Seen in the Skies*, Princeton University Press, Princeton, NJ, 1979.
[195] *Ezekiel* 1:1-21.

crisis of postmodernism, namely the anxiety the world
will end.

There are numerous websites, YouTube videos,
documentaries, and books – all positing UFOs are
nothing new and are signs of God at the end-times.
Christians, most particularly right-wing Christians,
engage in hybridization of their own. They combine
UFOlogy with Christian theology. Conservative
Christianity has been pushing its sales pitch on how
we are living in the days of the impending
Apocalypse. Signs and religious imagery on strange
clouds of medieval or Renaissance art work as UFOs,
when in fact they must be interpreted within their
own context. There is a very old painting done 1200
years ago of Jesus on the Crucifixion, where there is
an object on the upper left-hand corner that looks
like a piloted UFO. On the upper right-hand corner is
another object that looks like a UFO with what looks
to be a pilot inside, flying over the spectacle
below. We know what these objects are. Medieval art
works tend to feature the sun and moon as icons
during the Crucifixion of Christ. [196]

There are many medieval art works with Jesus at
the Crucifixion with the same two objects on each of
the upper-hand corners. These art works were done in
the Byzantine style. The sun and the moon witnessing
the death of Jesus were carried over from pagan Rome.
There are also many paintings with clouds, sometimes
a fireball within the clouds. Sometimes angels were
added inside the clouds, other times the artist may
only have luminous clouds. These clouds are symbols
of God. There are also paintings of clouds (some say
spaceships) that shine a ray of light right above
Mary. The light itself is the representation of the
Holy impregnation of Mary. Finally, Ancient Alien

[196] http://godless-skeptic.blogspot.com/2012/04/ancient-aliens-i-dont-think-so.html, retrieved on 10/11/2012.

Theorists say that the Soviet satellite Sputnik was deliberately painted. Jesus is on the left, God is on the right, both holding on to each antenna. The globe is a symbol of the creation of Earth, made possible by the Trinity.[197] Such postmodern interpretations of medieval Christian paintings reflect Cold War anxieties and nothing more. The reality is that a nuclear holocaust can have devastating consequences.

Due to the Bomb's awesome power, its omnipotence comes from the release of great energy. The tiny atoms that we all carry enable us to exist, as living, physical beings, yet these minute objects can destroy us. The primordial need of powerful release, it is argued, can be perceived through sexual orgasm, and we attribute this microcosm analogous to the release of nuclear energy. It is a mythological drama reenacting the Big Bang Theory. We now have a sense of timelessness, for it is not clear if there is a beginning or an ending.[198]

In the so-called amnesia of the alien sexual-medical examination, missing time cannot be accounted for. Missing time is associated with fairy folklore, directly linked to death. The forest was believed by pre-modern northern Europeans to be teeming with these little rascals ready to trap humans. After returning from Fairyland, humans realize that time has passed; two hours with the fairies is the equivalent of decades, a hundred years may pass unnoticed and those returning to human civilization wound up dying and turning to dust.[199] This mythology

---

[197] http://www.youtube.com/watch?v=-gqHOjCNMTk, retrieved on 10/11/2012.

[198] Ira Chernus. *Dr. Strangegod: on the Symbolic Meaning of Nuclear Weapons*, University of South Carolina Press, Columbia, SC, 1986, p. 12-31.

[199] Fairyland is a land of death. In one legend, two Scottish fiddlers played for a fairy gathering on a hill, the performance lasting a few hours. They both returned to their human homes, afterwards going to

implies the lack of power one has in the cosmic sense.

The nuclear age has intensified victimization, powerlessness, and fatalism. [200] This can be perceived in the alien abduction ritual, since when it comes to the powerful and the overpowered, such a ritual is a feature of hypnotic regressions. The hypnotist penetrates any wall of stubbornness on his client, the alleged abductee, a wall of separation analogous to the Iron Curtain.

The Bomb, it is suggested from a philosophical-psychiatric point of view, can instill a touch of psychosis. That a trip to fantasyland by those affected, whether Hiroshima survivors or by those thinking about the existence of the Bomb (in terms of its devastating potential), is denying its reality by "psychic numbing." The effects of nuclear war, paradoxically, are felt more profoundly in the illusions of fantasy. Irrational thoughts may be symbolisms of the Bomb. Fears are visualized in fantasies, a possible side effect of guilt.

Fear and guilt have been expressed through short, Asian-looking aliens stealing reproductive necessities for their regeneration in order to survive; these Asian-looking aliens are reminders of Hiroshima. Western abductees are reliving fantasies of nuclear oppression. They have reported aliens showing them scenes of explosions, chaos, and destruction on panoramic screens. Abductees of the 1980s and 1990s relive their abductions with these

---

their local church. When the priest began the sermon, however, the two individuals turned to dust. See Janet Bold, *Fairies: Real Encounters with Little People*, Carroll & Graf Publishers, Inc., New York, NY, 1997, p. 129.
[200] Chernus, *Dr. Strangegod*, p. 57-9; Also see Bridget Brown, *They Know us Better Than We Know Ourselves: The History of Politics and Alien Abduction*. New York University Press, New York & London, 2007.

apocalyptic scenes as environmental guilt.[201] The alien abduction narrative would develop into a form of antinuclear protest that was vocal during the late twentieth century.

The realization of a nuclear Apocalypse is played out in theatre, and the objective reality of drama, which coincides with the ever-rising of telecommunications, i.e., radio, television, cinema, newspapers, and the like. War is mimicked by games people play, with rules that separate life and fantasy.[202] When it is explained to abductees of the nature of their otherworldly experiences, they are not convinced. Alien abduction is a classic example of myth-making. Like the angel of death, the Greys come on a whim to forcibly grab people to reenact the symbol of death. The Greys who can float, go through walls and closed windows, behave like ghosts and as disembodied spirits, return to haunt the sons and daughters of those responsible for dropping two atomic bombs.

In the new secular divinity, it is argued, the Bomb is a divine object, and therefore, God is a machine invented by humans. He is perceived as an It, a thing with a powerful energy source of life and death, while the rest of us are mobilized like soldiers in times of war. As human agents of the Bomb, we behave like automatons.[203] The sex-freaks automatons, the Greys, with Asian-like eyes, reflect the guilt of dropping the Bomb on Hiroshima, the majority of abductees having been Western whites. White American abductees of the 1980s and 1990s were protesting nuclearism. The hybrid project of the alien abduction narrative is a metaphor for the merger between technology and humanity and conveyed

[201] Brown, *They Know Us Better Than We Know Ourselves*, p. 162-7.
[202] Chernus, *Dr. Strangegod*, p.73-84.
[203] Ibid., p. 136-7.

as an aggressive act of social change. The imposing
of "progress" through dangerous technology could
have catastrophic consequences, and by blowing
ourselves up we all become ghosts, wandering
aimlessly.

Conclusion

The year 1945 marked the beginning of a new era.[204] The
UFO myth, commencing two years later, is a very theme
in the overriding parent of the nuclear era. The
scientist's child, the atomic bomb, could rebel
against his master. As children of the atomic bomb,
it seems the Greys' mission is to avenge themselves,
the flip side to guilt. The UFO and alien abduction
myths represent projected anxieties onto objective
reality.

Flights of fancy are conducted to find
inspiration, whether for religious or secular
purposes. Scientists have been compared to shamans
(or more precisely alchemists have been compared to
shamans.) Metallurgy has rudiments of spiritual
transformation, where various elements are
manipulated to achieve the desired state, the perfect
metal called gold. In order to do this, fire is
needed. In the religious tradition, fire is both
destructive and purgatorial. A shaman works within
time and space to temporarily leave Earth to find
hidden wisdom, for his religious experience is golden
to him.

Nuclear scientists who have unlocked the
secrets of the atom have elevated themselves to great

---

[204] Ira Chernus. *Nuclear Madness: Religion and the Psychology of the Nuclear Age*, State University Press of New York Press, Albany, NY, 1991, p. 229.

status – as creators and destroyers of life, as God or the Devil, and as Dr. Jekyll and Mr. Hyde. As possessors of power of the sun, its secrets are locked away and closely guarded by the State.[31] As such, the likes of Hopkins, Mack, and Jacobs, and others, have been wizards to unlock what they believe are repressed memories of UFO kidnappings.

To be sure, the alien abduction narrative that exploded during the 1980s and 1990s was inspired by 1950s flying saucer films. During World War II and the post-war period, a plethora of movies with the theme of technologically savvy aliens bent on conquering Earth, were very popular. There was the movie version of *War of the Worlds*. *Killers from Space* and *Invasion USA* are two more examples. In *Invaders from Mars* (1953), citizens are implanted on the back of their necks to make them docile for a smooth takeover.[205] As Brown tells us, Aldous Huxley's novel published decades before, *Brave New World* (1932), resonates with evil threats of "Communism, Fascism, and industrial mass-production, all of which conspire in placing the needs of the state above the needs of individuals."[206]

We now turn to Chapter 7, where we will show how individualism is expressed through metaphors that describe modern bureaucracy as an incarcerator.

---

[31] Ibid., p. 229-41.
[205] Brown, *They Know Us Better Than We Know Ourselves*, p. 73.
[206] Ibid, p. 73.

7

The Cadaver and the Grey

As strange as the title is for this chapter, we address the fear of death by attempting to show how the UFO myth reflects such a fear. We do so by analyzing the motifs of alien abductions and the myth of Roswell. The fear of death, seemingly the main overriding theme, is related to the belief of *advanced civilization* by virtue of science and technology. Material progress is one thing, moral and spiritual matters are another. Further, bureaucracy may be highly efficient, vis-à-vis the military-industrial complex, but it is so at the expense of individual freedom and knowledge. We have been arguing that the UFO and alien abduction myths arose in the post-war era for various reasons. Undeniably, the future has been looked upon with ambivalence. Ever since Hiroshima and Auschwitz, the million-dollar question is: Can science and technology really save us – or have they been total failures?

The Abducted Body

During the sixteenth and seventeenth centuries, visual artists were painting dismembered bodies. Of particular interest, were the paintings of scientific anatomical demonstrations. These works of art, either of medical students or well-dressed men, involved an audience of onlookers. It could be argued it is as though the painters were depicting the line between life and death as being just inches away from each other, even though the viewers were in denial of death. [207]

Abductees have complained of not having control of their bodies during alien abduction ordeals. Corpses are just as helpless. During the early modern period they were stolen from their graves by body snatchers. Body parts, jewelry, and other valuable items were sold on the black market. Disturbingly, corpses were also subjected to sexual violation. [208] These types of illegal activities, in one form or another, still occur today. The difference between abductees and corpses is that the abductees are alive and conscious while being "sexually ravished" by aliens from another realm.

The dead body has been viewed with great awe and fear. The symbolism of the corpse as the representation of death was expressed through superstitions long ago. Among the beliefs were the careful preparations by the survivors to enact necessary rites so that the corpse was protected from evil spirits or to prevent the release of the body's spirit from becoming a haunting ghost. It was believed the cadaver could return as a pesky witch or a blood-sucking vampire if it was buried the wrong way. Therefore, meticulous funeral preparations were required so the body's soul acquires its new "life." [209]

The main theme of the alien abduction narrative is that these aliens are dying and are in dire need of human sperm and eggs. According to the alien

---

[207] Christine Quigley, *The Corpse: a History*. McFarland & Company, Jefferson, NC, 1996, p. 26; Phillip Ariès, *The Hour of Our Death*: *The Classic History of Western Attitudes Toward Death Over the Last One Thousand Years*. Vintage Books, 2008, p. 369-87.
[208] Ibid, p. 292-301.
[209] Quigley, *The Corpse*, p. 16-7.

abduction narrative, if the aliens do not steal
humans and their reproductive abilities, they will
surely die and go extinct. (Certainly, extinction has
been a bothersome concept throughout modern and
postmodernity.) Survival, therefore, is dependent on
stolen vital, bodily fluids. According to vampire
folklore, the nocturnal blood sucker must force his
or her way into the bedroom in order to keep on
living by feeding on the sleeping, involuntary host.
Vampire victims and alien abductees both assume in
their submissive positions. In fact, the alien
abduction theme is traceable to the succubus and the
incubus when these evil spirits of the late medieval
and early modern periods entered their victims'
bedrooms to have sex against their will.[210]

Such bedroom experiences, though, have been
hallucinations of one form or another. Although the
particular characteristics may be different to
coincide with time and culture (i.e. 19th century
British fairies, or 1990s alien abductions) the very
bare nocturnal experience with creatures from other
realms points to sleep paralysis,[211] a harrowing

---

[210] Walter Stephens, *Demon Lovers: Witchcraft, Sex, and the Crisis of Belief*. University of Chicago Press, Chicago, 2002.
[211] Susan Blackmore. "Abduction by Aliens or Sleep Paralysis?", *Committee for the Scientific Investigation of Claims of the Paranormal*, www. Csicop.org/si/9805/abduction.html.; Dr. Peter Dodzik (managing editor) "Is Sleep Paralysis the Cause of Alien Abductions?" *Sleep & Health Newspaper*, www. Sleepandhealth.com/Newspaper/2003/April/14.htm.
[211] Leonard S, Newman and Roy F. Baumeister, "Toward an Explanation of the UFO Abduction Phenomenon: Hypnotic Elaboration, Extraterrestrial Sadomasochism, and Spurious Memories." *Psychological Inquiry*, 1996, vol. 7, Issue 2, p.99, 28p.
[211] Jamie Arndt & Jeff Greenberg, "Fantastic Accounts Can Take Many Forms: False Memory Construction? Yes. Escape From Self? We Don't Think So." *Psychological Inquiry*, 1996, Vol. 7 Issue 2, p. 127, 6p; Kenneth S. Bowers and John D. Eastwood, "On The Edge Of Science: Coping with UFOlogy Scientifically." *Psychological Inquiry*, 1996, Vol. 7, Issue 2, p. 136, 5p; Steven E. Clark and Elizabeth F. Loftus, "The

experience where it is favorable for nightmares to occur; what is disturbing is that one is half-awake (but still in dream state) and a presence, like a shadow, can perpetrate victimization – giving the illusion of a supernatural experience.

The sense of helplessness can be overpowering when pondering the end of physical existence. [212] Even if we deny physical death, our bodies' major functions, such as eating and having sex, or the failure of these functions, remind us of death. A way to distance oneself from our bodies' failings is by dehumanizing it. The female body, in particular, becomes an object since it is the source of regeneration. [213] There are men and women who have claimed to have been abducted; both serve as objects of regeneration. The objectification of the abductees' bodies is the key since the aliens treat their kidnappings as objects; it is rape, it is impersonal.

Impersonal death tells a different story altogether. From the painting *The Triumph of Death*, we learn the following:

> Another theme that was contemporaneous with, if not older than, the *artes moriendi* and the *danse macabre*, and just as popular, was the Triumph of Death. The subject is different. It is no longer the personal confrontation between man and death, but the collective powers of death. Death, in the form of a mummy or a skeleton, stands with his symbolic weapon in his hand, driving a huge, slow chariot drawn by oxen. One recognizes this vehicle as the heavy cart used for holiday

Construction of Space Alien Abduction Memories." Psychological Inquiry, 1996, Vol.7 Issue 2, P.140, 4p.

[212] See Mikulincer and Shaver, Chapter 2, "Helplessness: A Hidden Liability Associated with Failed Defenses Against Awareness of Death." In Phillip R. Shaver and Mario Mikulincer, *Meaning, Mortality and, Choice: The Social Psychology of Existential Concerns*. American Psychological Association, Washington DC, 2012.

[213] Jamie L. Goldenberg, Chapter 5, "A Body of Terror: Denial of Death and the Creaturely Body." In Shaver and Mikulincer.

processions, inspired by mythology and intended for the grand entries of princes into their local towns. Here it is driven by a prince whose emblems are skulls and bones. It could also be the chariot from a royal funeral procession, and might carry the waxen or wooden "representation" of a body decked out for the obsequies, or the coffin covered with the pall. In the fantastic universe of Bruegel the elder it became the congruous little cart in which gravediggers piled the bones to transport them from one part of the church or cemetery or another.[214]

The skeleton has personified death, although it is the skull that has struck the most nerve. It reminds one that once the flesh decomposes the skull is exposed, albeit much more long-lasting, a gruesome reminder of the permanence of death. The depictions of skeletons are referred to as "vanities," many of which predate the twentieth century.[215]

The Dance of Death, however, is older than vanity paintings. First appearing in early fifteenth-century France then spreading throughout Western Europe, these images depict the coercion of dancing with skeletons or dead bodies in alternating fashion or in procession against the living's will. The skeleton, arriving uninvited, will crash a banquet to seize a living and breathing human being. Other painters portrayed the skeletons as seducers of women, although at times the female skeleton was the seducer of living men. Victims of either gender, though, were grabbed and kissed on the lips. To be sure, Dance of Death painters were creative and experimented with subthemes with the same overriding theme. At times skeletons were also depicted as kidnapping-killers by snatching the living through flight as they are winged creatures. The Grim Reaper, of course, is the most fearsome character of death. He appears with many weapons to aid him in the stealing of his victim. Although these objects are

---

[214] Ariès, *The Hour of Our Death*, p. 118.
[215] Quigley, *The Corpse*, p. 27-8.

razor sharp, the most infamous weapon is the scythe. During the Middle Ages and onwards, the skeleton became the dreadful symbol of the Apocalypse, yet it is collective death that resulted in the resurrection.[216]

There is no doubt that footage of the aftermath of Hiroshima, Nagasaki, and Auschwitz have left lasting, scarring impressions. The skeletal-looking large cranium Greys are symbols of our collective death - by processes of oppressive bureaucracy and deadly technology - better known as the end of the world. As we have been arguing the alien abduction narrative symbolizes the renewal from death, not physical, but spiritual rejuvenation. They swoop into people's bedrooms, escort them to their UFOs, and with sharp objects perform some of the nastiest medical examinations on their captives. The impersonal aliens and their impersonal medical procedures are similarly striking to the training medical students go through.

Medical school students are indoctrinated to detach themselves from their experiences of dissecting cadavers during their anatomy lab training. Future doctors are given vigorous psychological training to perceive the cadaver as an object. Thus, the detachment approach becomes the platform to learn about the human body by dehumanizing it from a scientist's standpoint in order to collect data.[217] Well-known sociologist Robert Nisbet, explains how individual freedom, resulting from the triumph of secularism, came with a price. Individual freedom did not emerge alone, since it is accompanied by disenchantment and alienation. Free

---

[216] Ibid, p. 28-30.
[217] David Wendell Moller, *Life's End: Technocratic Dying in an Age of Spiritual Yearning*. Baywood Publishing Company, Amityville, NY, 2000, p. 91-4.

from the moral restraints of history, the postmodern individual became alienated from his fellow man. [218] This makes sense in understanding alien abduction mythology. The detachment of the aliens and hospital staff are also eerily similar.

The hospital is compared to a hovering spaceship, where dying patients are assisted by machines in the process of dehumanizing them. Patients are described as human cyborgs, entities that are made of half human and half machine that are transported from "planet death." It was after World War II when hospital technology took off. Devices that can scope the insides of a patient's body, like the brain or the heart, made it possible to prolong life. However, the merger between humans and hospital machines excludes the soul as the basis of its life-given source. Of course, this is symbolic. Before the patient finally dies, oftentimes hospital staff treats him with great detachment, numbing their feelings as though he is already dead. [219] One should recall the hospital scene that aired on *The Outer Limits*, where the episode the "Bellero Shield" aired on February 10, 1964. Therein, a human patient is implanted with an object by an alien. The patient himself and the doctor attending him are far removed from personalization because of bureaucratization.

Roswell

Prehistoric man believed in life after death. Since death came early and sudden, normally by violent means (through intertribal warfare or during the

---

[218] Ibid, p. 107.
[219] Sandra M. Gilbert, *Death's Door: Modern Dying and the Ways we Grieve*, W.W. Norton & Company, New York & London, 2006, p. 164-203.

hunt), preparation for death would not have been as likely. When humanity became agricultural, our imagined ways of dealing with death changed as well. One could live longer, but could also suffer from terminal illness that could last for weeks or months before death relieves the pain. The continuation of life after death was still expected. Modernism, on the contrary, created urbanized structures of anonymity, where bureaucrats participate in the patient's slow, isolated, lonely death. As administrators, i.e. doctors and ministers, middle class urbanites began managing their deaths. It was their attempt to control an uncontrollable situation. By "managing" death, preparation for the next world is made. This is not so when it comes to the stigmatized who have died social deaths because of dementia and bodily deterioration. The elderly and those dying of AIDS are institutionally controlled.[220]

We cannot say for certain the AIDS epidemic contributed to the alien abduction narrative. It is known how dying from AIDS causes a significant loss of weight, making one to look slim and sickly like the Greys. Likewise, the bald head, the result of hair loss due to chemotherapy procedures, has become an iconic symbol of struggle while facing death itself. The image of a bald-headed child dying from cancer is even more hurtful. Indeed, the Greys have been described as looking like fetuses or like small children, who are sickly because they are dying.

The authenticity of alien abductions has been challenged by skeptics. Although both are entitled to their own beliefs, it could be argued postmodernism denied us truth. The fact that relativism gives free expression to everyone, has also contributed to the

---

[220] Allan Kellehear, *A Social History of Dying*. Cambridge University Press, Cambridge & New York, 2007.

loss of faith in progress. [221] The Roswell myth, which will be explained in detail, teaches lessons of the nefarious control of modern institutions.

In the twentieth century, bureaucracy entered life and death as well. Hiroshima and Auschwitz are two examples of systemic death. This is an expression of controlling collective death. When pulling the plug, it demonstrates the politician's power over the dying body. The individual, now a body, is stripped of any sign of humanity. Since his identity is taken away, this leaves him with as a mere mechanical object of biological existence. [222] The biggest bureaucracy, it seems, is the military. It has become a giant, and there are many who dislike it for hiding information from the public, accusing of a massive cover-up involving intergalactic beings that are visiting Earth. Moreover, one of the biggest accusations against the government is their denial of recovering a crashed UFO.

Referred to as the Roswell Incident, it was on June 14, 1947, when ranch owner William Brazel stumbled upon strange debris while riding on horseback. Ten days later, Kenneth Arnold spots his infamous flying saucer. It was July 4th when Brazen and family members went out to collect the debris. Brazen was not aware of flying saucers, but his brother-in-law was and urged him to make a report with the local sheriff's office in Roswell, New Mexico. After the sheriff notified the army station, representatives went to Brazel's ranch to collect the debris. This was when a public officer called the local radio station and announced the Air Force recovered a "flying disc." On July 8, the *Roswell Daily Record* placed the flying saucer occurrence on

[221] Steve Bruce, *God is Dead: Secularization in the West*, Blackwell Publishing, Malden, MA, 2002, p. 230.
[222] Benjamin Noys, *The Culture of Death*. Berg, New York, 2005.

the front page. Still, by the next day the Air Force cleared things up by saying what was recovered was a weather balloon.[223] This shut the door on Roswell and all was forgotten until the late 1970s. By the early 1980s, several books were published by purported experts accusing the government of covering up the existence of intergalactic beings.

TV-movie *Roswell* aired on July 31, 1987. Its premise was that the U. S. government recovered a crashed UFO and its four occupants. Only one, however, survived. The only survivor was able to communicate telepathically. Accordingly, the local funeral home director was phoned by a military official, who was asked about the availability of child-size caskets. Many eyewitnesses came forward claiming they did not see the dead aliens but knew someone who did. Additionally, it was alleged a team of Roswell staff studied the alien cadavers.[224]

This is a very strange twist that needs further analyzing. The Roswell Incident becomes the reverse of alien abduction. For the onlookers were now human scientists rather than alien scientists studying their abductees. The Fox television network took the Roswell Incident to another level. In the summer of 1995, *Alien Autopsy*: *Fact or Fiction?* aired. Experts who were interviewed for the film affirmed its falsity. One Hollywood special effects expert, several medical experts, even pro-UFOlogists, all vehemently declared the film was a hoax.[225] Such assessment is the easy part. The most difficult

---

[223] Kendred Frazer, "Introduction," in Kendred Frazer, Barry Karr, and Joe Nickell, *The UFO Invasion: The Roswell Incident, Alien Abductions, and Government Cover ups*. Prometheus Books, Amherst, NY, 1997, p. 9-10.

[224] C. Eugene, "Top-Secret Balloon Project Looms Over TV Movie on the Roswell Incident." In Frazer, Karr, and Nickel.

[225] Part Three: Roswell and "The Alien Autopsy." In Frazier, Karr, and Nickell, p. 135-57.

position is looking into the folklore and understanding its possible meaning. It is obvious the Roswell Incident points to aliens who died upon impact while taking the surviving alien captive. This is the reverse of the alien abduction narrative. Conversely, it is different from alien abductions insofar as the sexual component is not even mentioned. Recovering an advanced space ship flown by an advanced race suggests the power to control information even on the cosmic level. Air space is monopolized by the U. S. government and the richness of possible wisdom that can be acquired by space beings is completely cut off. In a sense, the bureaucracy of the government is worse than vampires by denying food of the mind, information.

What actually fueled the Roswell myth frenzy was when the Majestic-12 documents were introduced to UFOlogists anonymously, only to be shot down by them. These documents divulge information on twelve top government officials, with President Harry Truman as the biggest, who were responsible for overseeing an intergalactic project. [226] This strongly coincides with the Cold War theme, where actually it was a weather balloon that crashed in the summer of 1947, a spy device launched to measure radio activity due to Soviet atomic tests.

The Roswell Incident ballooned in the 1980s in perfect unison with Reaganomics. The Cold War intensified to the point of bringing down the Soviet Union. The apex of the Cold War also coincided with the rise of alien abduction reports, when the Greys became the appropriate symbol of nuclear Apocalypse. In *Alien Autopsy*, the alien being analyzed resembles the Greys to a significant degree even if the eyes

---

[226] Bridget Brown, *They Know us Better Than We Know Ourselves: The History of Politics and Alien Abduction*. New York University Press, New York & London, 2007, p. 112-4.

were smaller than the alien from the alien abduction narrative. But the Asian-like features are rather obvious. Hence, the Roswell Incident tells the story of a race of beings whose technology failed when presumably spying on a military-making facility. This alien race was the heroes while the U.S. government was the villain. This strongly corresponds to Western guilt (a very dark act) of when the Bomb was dropped.

The alien abduction story mentions time and again how the Greys came to Earth to spread the message of their own nuclear catastrophe that made them homeless wanderers. Even if not so subtle, there is more than a tinge that is reminiscent of Hiroshima. Attempting to be godlike with superior technology can lead to disastrous consequences. Indeed, man could fall. That is what the dead aliens suggest. That lone survivor also suggests the brink of extinction. When we combine this theme with the Ancient Astronaut Theory, what we have are lost civilizations who rose and fell. The mythical Atlantis, in particular, was an advanced civilization that fell when it sunk into the sea, taking its wisdom and technological know-how with it. We could visualize the dead aliens (even in mummified form) in a museum as a reminder of what was once a remarkable civilization that saw its end. Caveman was barely smart enough to populate the planet. On the other hand, future man was too smart for his own good.

To further the Roswell myth, in 1994, the U.S. Air Force took the opportunity to tell their side of the story. Simply, what was recovered was a weather balloon. This was not enough and so in 1997, the carting away of dead aliens was addressed. It was years later, after the weather-balloon incident, when the Air Force was dropping anthropomorphic dummies from high altitudes to determine if human pilots can withstand the force upon descending back to Earth. UFO investigators who interviewed the locals near

Roswell, how much older, if they could recollect what they saw. Air Force officials at the time were heavily guarding the secrets of these tests. After the dummies hit the ground, these officials would come to the land site to pick up their equipment. They would also tell civilian eyewitnesses to forget all that was seen, not because the equipment was from another world, but because it was the Cold War. Looking from a distance, some witnesses remembered telling UFO investigators seeing dead human-like beings, some of which lost their heads, fingers, legs, and such. Carted away in containers, they resembled small caskets. There were witnesses who did say they saw dummies on the ground, unlike UFOlogists who insist they were not dummies at all. To UFOlogists, they were dead aliens and their remains were taken by the U.S. government.[227] As the vampire is associated with sucking the blood of their victims, government agents steal dead aliens, while denying they did so. After trekking from far away distances, they crash in the desert of New Mexico.

Life itself has been perceived as a journey where the final destination is bodily death.[228] Life commences during the conception of birth, yet some belief systems add that once the soul attaches to the body is when life begins. The Western tradition though has taught how one can lose one's soul sleeping overnight. Children have been encouraged to say a prayer right before going to sleep. Notice it is children-like aliens who are entering bedrooms of adult abductees; the UFO abduction narrative may be an expression of the deathbed scene. It was believed if death occurs while sleeping, the soul may be taken by angels or devils. It is often the case how upon

---

[227] James McAndrew, *The Roswell Report: Case Closed*. U.S. Government Printing Office, Washington, D.C., 1997.
[228] Robert Kastenbaum, *On Our Way: The Final Passage Through Life and Death*. University of California Press, Los Angeles & Berkeley, 2004.

the very last moment before death the dying may go through a personal transformation, a psychological acceptance of death. In the postmodern era, the institutionalization of death and dying emerged to cater to death and dying, but not many fully trust agents (i.e. funeral homes) of death. What has become pervasive is the impersonalization of death — the body equating as a thing. One can blame the alienation from the dead on the technologizing of advanced societies.

8

The UFO Conspiracy Theory
1947 - c. 2000

The Roswell Incident is more relevant to the *UFO Conspiracy Theory*. Before the 9/11 conspiracy theory became popular, the UFO Conspiracy Theory was the most talked about. This theme speaks volumes about the relationship between the masses and the government. It should not be any surprise that this controversy was so heated up in the post-war era at the very dawn of the Cold War.

This belief subscribes to the idea that the world's governments have been covering up extraterrestrial visitations making it the largest conspiracy of all time. The UFO Conspiracy Theory was born during the Cold War era and was influenced by the Space age. It was a time of military buildup and bureaucratization of the government. Secret activity has long been part of the government's culture, which inspired distrusting it. This was a time when the political climate was one of paranoia. Ideas are influenced by their culture and times. The UFO Conspiracy Theory has been no exception.

Donald Keyhoe: 1949 - 1977

Recalling that Kenneth Arnold saw flying discs in the air in June of 1947, setting the stage for the flying saucer myth, later to be called UFOs. It was thought to be secret weapons of the Soviets or of domestic origins. Such a presumption reflected Cold War conditions. The Cold War did not cause Kenneth Arnold to see a flying saucer. Rather, it was the public reaction to his sighting which sparked media sensation. The political climate influenced others to perceive a possible secret weapon in the skies, especially a Soviet one. It is a given how the "top secret weapon theory" reflects the political climate.

Flying saucers would be associated with outer space visitors once the public was made aware of space travel. Retired Marine major and writer Donald Keyhoe influenced such a perception. Hired by *True*, a popular men's magazine of the day, Keyhoe asserted in his article "Flying Saucers Are Real," that the government was covering up the existence of extraterrestrial visitations and the flying saucers were being flown by beings from another planet. Before he expanded the article into a book, newspaper writer Frank Scully stepped in with wild claims. But it was Keyhoe who had already opened the door to this bombshell of an accusation.

After Keyhoe's long magazine article, Frank Scully published the first book on UFOs entitled *Behind the Flying Saucers* in 1950. Two men, Dr. Gee, a supposed scientist and Silas Newton, an oil baron, told Scully that a crashed flying saucer was recovered along with 34 dead aliens. Using magnetic devices from the saucer, these two men claimed they could locate oil underground, a ploy to lure investors. At the time, the U.S. Air Force was engaged in investigating flying saucers. However, Scully like Keyhoe, suspected the saucers to be interplanetary.[229] Unfortunately, Scully's credibility suffered a blow as it turned out that Dr. Gee and Silas Newton were con artists. The supposed technology they were using was nothing more than metal made from pots and pans.[230]

Before Scully's publication, Donald Keyhoe laid the intellectual groundwork for the UFO Conspiracy Theory. *Flying Saucers Are Real* went from a long article to a full-fledged book where he interviewed Air Force personnel. To his dismay, Keyhoe became frustrated with top officials, but also decided to interview pilots as well. They told him they have also seen UFOs and they believed the Air Force was not telling all there was. Keyhoe boldly stated that the Air Force is covering up the reality that Earth was being visited by interplanetary beings.[231] The most logical explanation as to why top Air Force officials were dancing around Keyhoe is that they could not divulge top secret information. As far as the pilots, who were of lower rank, would not know much information either. Keyhoe, for whatever was his motive, took a giant leap of faith. Although many among the public were skeptical, the genie was already out of the bottle. In such times of stress, some welcomed magical answers to aerial mysteries.

In *Flying Saucers From Outer Space (1953)*, the U. S. Air Force allowed him to see unclassified sightings. Some in the Air Force told Keyhoe they believed some kind of secret activity was going on. Keyhoe interviewed several individuals who speculated

---

[229] Frank Scully, *Behind the Flying Saucers*. Henry Holt and Company, New York, 1950.

[230] David E. Thomas, "The Aztec UFO Symposium: How This Story Started As A Con Game." *Skeptical Inquirer*, Sep/Oct. 1998.

[231] Donald E. Keyhoe, *Flying Saucers Are Real*. Fawcett Publications, New York, 1950.

on the origins of UFOs. In his second book, Keyhoe emphasized pilots as key and reliable witnesses. Keyhoe entertained the notion of flying saucers being Soviet secret weapons and was also concerned whether they were hostile. (This relates to the theme of the invasion of UFOs, to be discussed in the following chapter.) Also of significance, the Air Force press conferences did not provide all the answers Keyhoe was looking for, feeling the Air Force should have been honest from the beginning and should have admitted flying saucers were from outer space. Keyhoe wondered if they were from Mars or the Moon. He was basing this on astronomical speculation at the time. Keyhoe was sure of a cover-up, [232] then again he got carried away with romantic ideas.

One could say Keyhoe's era was ripe for idealism, since the "truth" was denied. The Cold War was a time of distrust and paranoia, not to mention theatre for con artists. Gray Barker wrote *They Knew Too Much About Flying Saucers* in which UFOlogists were threatened to stop UFO research by stern-faced men in black suites. These men were thought to be from the government or from another planet. [233] The folklore of the "Men in Black" was born. UFOlogists and other believers were duped. Barker was known to be a practical joker. Decades later, after his death, Barker's friend John Sherwood, confessed to helping Barker execute the Men in Black hoaxes. [234] The difference between Keyhoe and Barker is that Keyhoe wanted aliens to visit Earth,

---

[232] Donald E. Keyhoe, *Flying Saucer From Outer Space*. Henry and Holt Company, New York, 1953.

[233] Gray Barker, *They Knew Too Much About Flying Saucers*. University Books, New York, 1956.

[234] John C. Sherwood, "Gray Barker: My Friend, the Myth Maker." *The Skeptical Inquirer*, May /June 1998; "Gray Barker's Book of Bunk: Moth, Saucers, and MIB." *The Skeptical Inquirer*, May /June 2002.

while Barker (most likely an unbeliever) got a few laughs from behind the scenes, a play on those who have information versus those who do not.

Donald Keyhoe continued to be convinced of a cover-up. In his third book, *The Flying Saucer Conspiracy*, Keyhoe believed there was a "silence group" responsible for withholding information who were using legal documentation to hush up eyewitnesses. Keyhoe believed there was a mothership hovering over Earth as smaller crafts were dispatched to observe our planet. He believed they would land on a massive scale. Some astronomers of his day played with the idea that there were advanced civilizations on other planets. Keyhoe believed that there may have been intelligent life on Mars. He linked the increase of sightings due to Mars getting closer to Earth, which it does in the natural course of circling the sun. Also, Keyhoe talked about the rumors circulating that the government knew of a space station on the Moon. In addition, Keyhoe emphasized the "mysterious" sightings. This reinforced the logic that if a sighting is unexplained, then it must be of extraterrestrial origin since nothing else on Earth could fly with such capabilities at top speeds conducting inhuman maneuvers. [235]

Keyhoe outright dismissed the skeptics and placed a lot of weight on scientific theory. For example, a UFO speculator told him that the UFOs could fly with incredible speeds using "electromagnetic power" [236] and that "such technological capability can be found in science fiction." [237] Not only did Keyhoe entertain the idea of invisible saucers, he thought that perhaps saucers

---

[235] Donald E. Keyhoe, *The Flying Saucer Conspiracy*. Henry Holt and Company, New York, 1955.
[236] Ibid, p.95.
[237] Ibid, p. 95-96.

might have taken planes. This suggests alien abductions. In fact, stories, "…in which spaceships from another planet come to Earth and capture humans, appeared in the science fiction of the 1930s – years before the first flying saucer reports!" [238] Slowly, nuts and bolts began to gravitate to fringe theory.

In 1960, Donald Keyhoe published *Flying Saucers: Top Secret*. Keyhoe was the director of the National Investigations Committee on Aerial Phenomena (NICAP). NICAP was a civilian organization with amateur UFOlogists investigating mysterious aerial sightings. They often put pressure on the Air Force to admit to a cover-up of extraterrestrial visitations. Keyhoe explained that the renowned organization of UFO research was going through internal struggle. NICAP allowed new members from the military and believed those UFO eyewitnesses testimonies' and those of other pilots as reliable. At first glance, this seemed impressive. However, the content of the conversations between them and Keyhoe were theoretical only, such as the idea that the Earth was an ancient space colony. [239]

This notion strongly coincides with the Ancient Astronaut Theory, where as we noted earlier, is a theme that emerged parallel to the decline of the West. Western whites have long assumed their superiority over others not of Western European stock. When the space-alien myth is added, the Third World is represented by the entire planet. The role is reversed where it is Earth colonized by a civilization from another world. This makes sense in the Space age, a myth now purports to make humans inferior to space aliens. They are angelic and are

---

[238] "Alien Abduction: Part one of Two; The Invasion Begins" *Skeptical Inquirer*, Nov/Dec., 2006, see quote in cartoon drawn as a book.
[239] Donald E. Keyhoe. *The Flying Saucers: Top Secret*. G.P. Putnams' and Sons. New York, 1960.

purer than mortal men. Unfortunately, their wisdom
(let alone their presence) is denied by government
bureaucracy. Yet Keyhoe, as the hero, is going up
against top evil officials. And one must take note
how decolonization and secularization are two themes
relevant to the post-war era.

Keyhoe was careful when believing claims of
alien contact, "…meeting a space crew wasn't
impossible; we knew there had been brief landings.
But all of the contact claims we examined – tales of
long talks, with spacemen, being flown to the Moon,
Mars, Venus or Saturn – appeared to be dreams,
delusions, or frauds." [240] Keyhoe desired the contact
claims to be true, "…it was the lure of the UFO
mystery, the hope of finding a link with other
worlds…" [241] Keyhoe's aliens are part racial and part
angelic. Because the latter had declined, this was a
clever way for Keyhoe (and others like him) to grab
onto some form of hope during moral backwardness.

Continuing with the theme of moral regression,
Keyhoe published *Aliens From Space: The Real Story of
Unidentified Flying Objects* in 1973. Unluckily for
Keyhoe, he was no longer a NICAP member since he had
been ousted by that time. This last book was a look
back at the UFOlogical contributions throughout the
years. Keyhoe considered pilots to be reliable
witnesses since they were trained observers. He did
not consider UFOs to be aggressive, but they did take
defense measures, such as permeating heat and
inflicting psychological effects, like headaches,
dizziness, and nausea. Keyhoe believed that the
aliens possibly came from a dying planet and perhaps
were here to colonize Earth. He suggested a way for

---

[240] Donald E. Keyhoe, 1960, p. 130.
[241] Ibid, p. 139.

the aliens to land in peace in "Project Lure." [242] This idea strongly sounds like the Hippie movement and its message of "peace and love." Keyhoe admitted, "But even with all detailed UFO evidence, the aliens' purpose has not been discovered." [243] In the moral regression of history, one must ask what the purpose of life is. In such a disenchanted world, Keyhoe believed aliens could save humanity from its own suicide.

Keyhoe, however, was not scientific unlike renowned astronomer Dr. J. Allen Hynek. The *Hynek UFO Report* released in 1977, was more critical of the government's UFO investigative body, Project Blue Book's, methodology rather than the silence of information. [244] As far as the Air Force, he felt they were rigid in their views on UFOs and he also criticized the Condon Committee, the body of scientists the government hired to investigate UFOs. He did give credit to the Air Force for admitting that there were unexplained flying objects. The letter "U" did stand for "unidentified" after all, Hynek explained. He refrained from using the word cover-up in his analysis Hynek also keenly observed, "Why flaps occur just may be more of a problem for the psychologist than for the physical scientist; perhaps they are triggered by awakening public interest that follows one or two well-publicized spectacular sightings." [245] Here he recognized the media playing a role. Hynek also said, "…it is likely that during the summer months there

[242] Donald E. Keyhoe, *Aliens From Space: The Real Story of Unidentified Flying Objects*. Doubleday & Co. Inc., Garden City & New York, 1973.
[243] Ibid, p. 164.
[244] Dr. J. Allen Hynek, *The Hynek UFO Report*. Souvenir Press, New York, (1977) 1998.
[245] Ibid, p. 244-5.

are more conventional objects around to misinterpret!" [246]

Like Keyhoe, Dr. Hynek did emphasize the unexplained sightings, but was not as speculative about explaining them. As a trained scientist, he was prudent and very hesitant to speculate. Dr. Hynek was a skeptic and a trained scientist before finally announcing he was a believer. Perhaps the government's bias in their investigations of UFOs left Dr. Hynek with a bad taste.

Going back to Donald Keyhoe, let us look at his writing career before the UFO craze, which was science fiction. Keyhoe wrote for several pulp fiction magazines during the 1920s and 1930s. *Dr. Yen Sin* was a pulp magazine of 1936 whose main character was Dr. Yen Sin. His intention was world domination using advanced science. [247] *Weird Tales* was perhaps the best known magazine that Keyhoe wrote for. In a 1926 story "Through the Vortex," a pilot gets caught in a vortex and ends up in a floating island with dinosaurs and hostile sub-humans. In a 1927 story, "The Master of Doom," a Navy pilot and passengers fly to an island thought to be deserted. The masters' loyal followers who intend to rule the world capture them. Blond-haired giants save the day by invading and overthrowing the master. [248] Imperialism should be clear, since Keyhoe's stories were filled with superior technology, airplanes, and exotic places with strange humanoids and were replaced by technologically advanced beings originating from a dying planet.

---

[246] Ibid, p. 245.
[247] John Clute and Peter Nicholis, editors. *The Encyclopedia Of Science Fiction*, Orbit, Inc. A Division of Little Brown and Company Limited, London, 1993.
[248] Everett F. Bleir, ed. *Science Fiction: The Early Years.* The Kent State University Press. Kent, OH and London, 1990, p.405.

Leaving Keyhoe behind, we are now in the late 1970s. This was when the Ancient Astronaut Theory was making waves. Like von Däniken who, inspired others to ponder ancient aliens, Keyhoe opened the speculative door wide open. Speculation on the UFO Conspiracy Theory would take on exotic themes, to the point of ridiculousness.

The Fringe of UFO Conspiracy Theory

Not since the 1950' s did UFO research spark such a great interest as it did in the 1980s and 1990s. It attracted many who firmly believed in a cover-up. Not all will be mentioned here, only the prominent figures. As we will see, they provided their own individual twist to the UFO Conspiracy Theory. This theory took on a bizarre turn. The Air Force, after years of silence, published additional books telling their side of the story. The UFO Conspiracy Theory thrived in this atmosphere. What was being addressed in the latter part of the twentieth century was the Roswell Incident.

On July 7, 1947, it was announced that a flying saucer had been recovered after crashing in a New Mexico ranch, near the town of Roswell. The military changed their story, saying that it had recovered a downed weather balloon. UFOlogists Charles Berlitz and William Moore set out to investigate this incident around 1978. They gathered eyewitnesses who could provide firsthand accounts of what they saw that day in 1947. They included Major Jesse Marcel and the individuals who were children at the time. By 1980, Berlitz and Moore concluded the government covered up the story. A fierce lightning storm brought down the believed interplanetary craft. The interviews of the eyewitnesses revealed that the debris did not resemble a weather balloon. Some even claimed to have seen humanoids as part of the recovery. To Berlitz and Moore, The Roswell Incident pointed to a possible recovery of a crashed UFO.[249]

At first glance, this part of the UFO Conspiracy Theory seemed plausible and certainly not as sensational as Donald Keyhoe's. There were first-hand witnesses, who never said that the downed weather balloon (whom they believe it wasn't) was a flying saucer. That was Berlitz and Moore's contention, although they were not absolutely certain. Considering the debris was scattered for more than a mile after the storm, it was likely that the lightning hit the weather balloon causing it to scatter within a wide area. Berlitz and Moore's eyewitnesses say that the foil was flimsy. To Berlitz and Moore, this was proof of a possible spacecraft. Of course, this does not explain the supposed dead aliens that were allegedly carted away by the military. There seemed to be something to the story. From a skeptical point of view better evidence is needed. If Berlitz and Moore's eyewitnesses could not figure out this strange foil, it does not mean it is evidence of extraterrestrial origin. The fact that the witnesses were not familiar with that substance simply explains that they were not familiar with such an item. The *extraterrestrial hypothesis* is not needed.

It would seem safe to conclude that an urban legend has been in the making since 1947. Even if the extraterrestrials were technologically advanced, they would have to travel a long way from a planet from a nearby galaxy which could take multiple lifetimes. It seemed more likely that a weather balloon was the craft that crashed in the New Mexico desert. This is

---

[249] Charles Berlitz and William L. Moore, *The Roswell Incident: The Classic Study of UFO Contact*. Berkerley Books, New York, NY (1980) 1988.

the most likely scenario given that weather balloons were so often used for atmospheric experimenting, a device the public were already acquainted with. To the most ardent UFO conspiracy theorists, space aliens were given magical abilities. Besides, granting these beings immense powers to break the laws of nature sounds more like a fairy tale. Yet, in its irony, with their godlike qualities, the aliens crash. What a waste of a trip.

The UFO Conspiracy Theory gained momentum in UFO circles during the 1980s. A momentous time arrived, when purported proof of the alien cover-up made itself available with the introduction of supposed government documents known as Majestic-12, or MJ-12. This was believed to be a memo prepared for then President-elect Eisenhower in November of 1952. Co-author of the *Roswell Incident* William Moore and author Jaime Shandera anonymously received a 35 – mm film. Upon analysis, a conclusion was made of the authenticity of these documents. There are UFOlogists, however, that deemed them a hoax. [250] The MJ-12 documents have been a controversial piece of evidence within the UFO community ever since.

The 1980s and 1990s welcomed millennialism and it stands to reason the UFO Conspiracy Theory became more bizarre than ever. Alleged scientist Bob Lazar came forward to claim that he worked in alien technology and was engaged in reverse engineering of a downed spacecraft. Lazar said he had worked at Area S-4 of the Nevada Test Site (near Area 54). [251] Some supported his claims while others did not. UFOlogist Stanton Friedman vehemently opposed Lazar's claims, saying he had not provided any proof, including

---

[250] Kevin D., Randle and Donald R. Schmitt, *The Truth About the UFO Crash at Roswell*. M. Evans and Company, New York, 1994, Appendix A p.187-191.
[251] www.wikipedia.org., see Bob Lazar, December, 2006.

proper documentation. A background check showed that Lazar did not have the scientific training he said he claimed to have. [252] Bob Lazar made Area 51 famous by stating he worked there. Area 51 is known in UFO circles as a secret military base where it is believed aliens were captured and held and where their technology is studied by scientists. There is ample evidence the base does exist. Whether or not there are aliens there is a matter of faith, for what we have here is an urban legend.

The times, according to some, were terrible and elitists hiding behind secret circles were to blame. Milton William Cooper was the most controversial figure within the UFO conspiracy myth community. He has made accusations about the U.S. government, aliens, and world events. He traveled making speeches and drew crowds. Cooper served in the military, first the Air Force, then the Navy. As a high-ranking officer, he understood that the military engaged in secret activities. During the early 1970s, he claimed he had secret documents regarding an alien cover-up. According to Cooper, the government had knowledge of alien visitations since 1936. Cooper added that even Germany possessed a downed spacecraft that the Nazis were trying to duplicate but were unsuccessful.

Alien technology was believed to be militarily advanced. Cooper asserted in 1947 that the U.S. had their hands on a downed UFO. Many more crafts were recovered and used as military tests, such as those in Area 51. Accordingly, he claimed that the government acquired their extraterrestrial technology, superior to our own. In exchange, the U.S. government allowed alien abduction and animal sampling to take place. Cooper's further proof was that he had seen photos of aliens both dead and alive. Eisenhower also knew of the secret activities

---

[252] www.stantonfriedman.com, see Bob Lazar Fraud. December, 2006.

of the aliens, documented by twelve men within the government in the MJ-12 documents.

All of this information was kept from the public. A way to finance the secret activities with the aliens was to sell drugs to the populace. George H. W. Bush was allegedly part of this trade when he was president. Many in the military tried to expose this information to the public and were killed as a result. It is believed this is why John F. Kennedy was killed since he had ordered the release of alien information. According to Cooper, it was the limousine driver that killed the former president during his visit to Dallas, not Lee Harvey Oswald. The questions become, Who is in charge? Who is responsible for making the all-important decisions?

According to the imaginative Cooper, secret societies and the secret government, such as very wealthy bankers were believed to have been in control of the government and withholding information from the public. Since the end of World War II, the U.S. and the Soviet Union had been allies and have been participating in a secret space program. A base on planet Mars and the Moon were built. Cooper believed that NASA had been lying to the public about those celestial bodies not being habitable. Since the alien intent is to take over the planet, immigration out from Earth is necessary. Not everyone is welcome in the new outer space home. Only elitists (and those who are of Darwinian fitness) are. This plan is referred as "Alternative 3." [253]

"Alternative 3" was actually a television program broadcast in the United Kingdom in 1977. It was a final episode of a weekly science series, *Science Report*. The episode started off claiming there were missing scientists. They were part of an

---

[253] www.sacred-texts.com/ufo/cooper1.htm., December 2006.

American Ouvlet space program, which was to take the smartest and most educated individuals from Earth in case of planetary catastrophe. Overpopulation led to climate change which would make the planet unable to support life any longer. There were three alternatives: Alternative 1 was to explode nuclear weapons in the atmosphere to allow pollution to escape, Alternative 2 was to build underground cities, and Alternative 3 was to choose the most brilliant and transfer them to the Moon and Mars. The television series aired on April 1st (*April Fool's Day*), clearly a hoax, yet to some conspiracy theorists this was valid information.[254]

Although the 1970s saw conspiracy theories, in the 1990s, they blossomed like never before. Different types of conspiracy theories fused with one another. As was typical of alternate spiritualties to fuse with each other (Eastern and Western religion), the 1990s ushered in fusions of various types of conspiracy theories. "Cafeteria demonology" blamed the government for being evil and turning its back on its own citizens. This fused form of ideology was militant. What was accompanied with the militia movement and its right-wing rhetoric was utter rage. The extreme left was just as radical. In essence, the tone that dominated conspiracy theories during the 1990s was led by extreme beliefs, with radical individuals who wanted to take down the status quo.[255] This certainly sounds very much like William Cooper.

Others, though, jumped on the UFO Conspiracy Theory bandwagon. Retired military officer "Commander X" made claims of a government/alien deception. According to him, aliens were captured and frozen for research. The capture of a downed

---

[254] www.wikipedia.org., see alternative 3, December 2006.
[255] Jesse Walker, *The United States of Paranoia: A Conspiracy Theory*. HarperCollins, New York, 2013, see Ch. 11.

spacecraft took place in Hawaii in 1944. The Nazis even captured one. Sinister in cooperation, the cover-up was international. Commander X also contended that our technology came from the aliens. According to an interview with John Lear, there was a secret deal with aliens and the government. In exchange for technology (no doubt after they were thawed), the aliens would abduct humans and engage in cattle mutilation, just as Cooper had claimed. The aliens had abducted more people than was agreed upon. That explained the missing children by the late 1970s and early 1980s. Also, the aliens had underground bases which the government tried to get back, but lost because the aliens had advanced weapons. There are different types of aliens. The ones underground are Extraterrestrial Biological Entities (EBE' s), while the benevolent ones are blond. Commander X, pathetic as it sounds, partly acquired this information through telepathic means. The claim was that blonds provided spiritual guidance to the founding fathers of the United States by way of telepathy. Earthlings are caught in the middle of this war between the blonds and EBEs. [256]

This is reminiscent of the war between heaven and hell, where humans are stuck in the middle of this apocalyptic mess. The late twentieth century is replete with paranoia, fear, conspiracy, and the end of the world beliefs. One must bear in mind, the exotic features (some would call it fringe) of the UFO Conspiracy Theory was added after Berlitz and Moore are independent claims. Other believers may or may not accept these added claims. If one does so, there are apparent contradictions to consider.

---

[256] Commander X. *The Ultimate Deception: A Shocking Disclosure! The Most Sensational Government Conspiracy of Our Time Is Finally Revealed To The World By A Military Officer*. Abellard Productions, Inc. City not available, 1990

The UFO conspiracy took on millennial fervor. Milton Cooper's *Behold A Pale Horse* (the title extracted from the Book of Revelations), made an impact with fans. Reading Cooper's controversial book, one gets the sense of his political idealism and patriotism. He does not believe in random events, rather that the elite are ever-controlling. His anger towards the government may stem from anger toward his father. Cooper was a militarist and a vindictive character. During his Navy days, he was alleged to have observed a saucer-shaped metal object enter the water then re-emerge as it soared into the clouds, then enter the water again. During his time in Vietnam there were plenty of UFO reports, as he recalled in his book. Cooper described the UFOs as aggressive, even abducting soldiers. There are also secret societies hoaxing humanity into believing that aliens are taking over Earth. The real takeover is believed to be when the secret societies create a one-world government referred to as the New World Order. The secret documents that Cooper said he saw during his tenure in the military effectively declared war on the citizens of the U.S. The economy is controlled by these secret societies as they manipulate economic institutions and the flow of information. This makes people believe they are secure while the weak are exploited. Only the chosen can understand the wisdom and the malice of the secret societies. [257] As such, Cooper – like other similar UFO and alien abduction gurus – are self-proclaimed leaders. Cooper, therefore, emboldened himself as messianic.

Cooper was also outspoken against the government on his radio talk show, including bashing the IRS. He was clearly anti-authority. He was accused of bank fraud and tax evasion, and was killed

---

[257] Milton William Cooper, *Behold A Pale Horse*. Light technology Publishing, Flagstaff, AZ, 1991.

during a shootout with authorities.[258] Cooper was gone, but others – in the UFO conspiracy, in this fly-by-night adventure – stepped in to provide their own imagination. If one cannot fly in a UFO, taking a ride in the imagination is the next best thing. The ride itself evoked speculation of evil beings.

Jim Keith intertwined the UFO Conspiracy Theory with demonology. The Men in Black (MIB) were considered sinister by Keith. They usually wore black suits and are described as dark-tanned complexion, with almond-shaped (e.g. Asian) eyes, and a hypnotic facial expression. They also have ghostlike behavior. Some reported poltergeist activity after MIB visitations. Keith believed that MIB might originate from the supernatural realm. Therefore, awareness goes beyond the material. If they are not paranormal, then MIB are from the government Keith believed. He also believed the MIB may be from occult lodges. Keith also speculated that MIB may be hoaxers.[259] Keith, and others like him, were definitely hoaxed by Gray Barker.

In *Saucers of the Illuminati*, Jim Keith admitted experiencing a sleep paralysis episode where he hallucinated a grey alien. He asked, "Was the experience a hallucination at the edge between dreaming and wakefulness?"[260] This is a good question to ask; yet Keith would rather believe the government is partaking in mind control and aliens are invading Earth. Keith believes the government is administering the drug LSD or using microwave frequencies to control the mind. The government is also infiltrating UFO investigation groups and trying to trick

---

[258] www.wikipedia.org., see Miton William Cooper, December, 2006.

[259] Jim Keith, *Casebook On The Men In Black*. Illuminet Press. Lilburn, GA, 1997.

[260] Jim Keith, *Saucers of the Illuminati*, Illuminet Press, Lilburn, GA., 1999, p. 12.

UFOlogists. To Keith, this explains the MIB. Behind the scenes in all of this are the Illuminati, a secret society that is believed to have social-historical influence from the government to private individuals. There is a New World Order to take place where the abolition of money and religion will be part of a one-world government led by this group. The Illuminati may have contacted otherworldly beings during the Middle Ages, possibly demons. They may be the ones who invented UFOs. Also, occultists channeling aliens might be spies for the Illuminati. They summon UFOs through ritual, as they are possibly demonic entities. [261]

Among some abductees, there is a movement that believes the military, not space aliens, have been abducting people to perform their own sinister medical and psychological tests. This is *the Dark Side Hypothesis* and it purports that either the government is working on its own to control the masses or that the government and the aliens are working together to administer their instruments of mind control. Such tests take place in underground bases, many of which are located in the southwestern United States. [262] These underground chambers are a sort of modern-day hell, where mind torture takes place against people' s wills.

Evil plays a role in UFO conspiracy theories. British conspiracy theorist David Icke is no exception. After consulting with a psychic to heal his arthritis, he was told that he was here to heal the Earth. (Yes, Icke is another self-proclaimed messiah.) Inspired, he went to Peru on a spiritual quest. He went to find himself and tap into his

---

[261] Ibid.

[262] Bridget Brown, *They Know Us Better Than We Know Ourselves: The History and Politics of Alien Abduction*. New York University Press, New York and London, 2007.

gifted powers. For all we know, Icke might be schizophrenic, for he believes energy flows from his hands. He also believes that secret societies are manipulating life by controlling people's minds. The very sources of this manipulation are the extraterrestrials which Icke believes have already enslaved humans. These are reptilian aliens, whom reside in underground tunnels and operate in fourth- and fifth-dimensional reality. The aliens have crossbred with humans as the plan is to take over Earth. [263] It cannot be stressed enough that the UFO myth has been influenced by science fiction. Icke got the idea of the reptilian aliens from the 1980's television miniseries, *V.* The aliens in the program masqueraded with human faces. They also were deceptive in their supposed peaceful intentions. Their true faces and plans were revealed as the reptilians were bent on invading Earth. Millennial hysteria has seen a secular version of the end of times. In addition, the UFO conspiracy theme overlaps with the invasion theme, because behind the scenes secret society officials are plotting to control people. Not only is the government covering up knowledge of alien reality, the aliens themselves are believed to be malevolent. This is a far cry from the angelic form that contactees and abductees claimed them to be. But for all we know, Icke may be pretending he believes in such nonsense. Be that as it may, his beliefs are still nonsense.

However, from a sociological perspective, Icke updated Wells' novel, *War of the Worlds*. In effect, an advanced evil civilization has come to Earth to provide Western Civilization its own medicine. Icke's theory, albeit fantastic, demonstrates his own alienation.

---

[263] Michael Barkun. *A Culture of Conspiracy: Apocalyptic Vision in Contemporary America*. University of California Press. Berkeley CA, 2003, p. 103-107.

Even so, Stanton Friedman has been in the UFO
scene for more than twenty years. Although his
presence was undermined by the likes of controversial
and sensational figures during the 1980s and 1990s,
Friedman showed a consistency so that when the smoke
cleared, he stood as the leading UFOlogist. After
interviewing several witnesses and viewing secret
documents, Friedman and co-author Don Berliner
authored *Crash At Corona*. They conclude there were
not one, but two UFO crashes in the New Mexico
desert. [264] These events (and other possible UFO
recoveries) are claimed to be recorded by authentic
government documentation, in which Friedman gives
credence to the Majestic-12 documents. [265] These
government documents are the smoking guns and proof
alien space crafts crashed and its debris, along with
the aliens (dead or alive), was recovered by the
government then hushed.

Friedman has been known in UFO circles to give
talks to large audience members across the country,
even outside the U.S. He has been a constant presence
and has never backed down and continues to believe
and promote that the government is covering up
visitations by space aliens. What it boils down to is
that postmodern government institutions are disliked
by many.

It is they, like Hollywood, who have led us
astray, according to UFO conspiracy theorists.
Hollywood has played such a major role in shaping the
UFO myth. Author Bruce Rux of *Hollywood v. the Aliens*
believes this. He believes in a cover-up that
involves the government and the film industry in

---

[264] Stanton T. Friedman & Don Berliner. *Crash At Corona: The U.S.
Military Retrieval And Cover-up Of A UFO. Paragon House.* New York,
1992.
[265] Stanton T. Friedman. *Top Secret/Majic.* Manlowe & Company. New
York, 1996.

misinforming the public. Supposed life on Mars, for example, has been covered up. The structures of ancient Egypt and the Martian pyramidal mountains Rux believes to be artificial. The lost city of Atlantis he also believes to have been on Mars. Rux believes there are Martian underworlds the government knows about. These extraterrestrials may be a lost Aryan race. The Moon also has an interior city that is also being covered up according to Rux. Films have laid the groundwork for the furtherance of disinformation. Rux believes the aliens from the Roswell crash to be robots. He knows this as he accepted the abductees' accounts of what seemed to be robotic aliens. Rux is a firm believer that the government is engaging in mind control, reaching this conclusion by watching UFO-themed films. This gave the government the chance to openly portray their secret UFO activities by showing films as fiction, but in actuality are actual true events taking place. Secret societies, such as the CIA, may have been involved in this misleading of the truth about UFOs. [266]

Is Rux that naïve to believe what he describes as a UFO cover-up is being filmed for the entire world to see? Even the most hardcore nuts and bolts types do not buy into such terrible logic, let alone without any evidence whatsoever. Rux's work was published in 1997, two years after the Air Force came forward to explain the Roswell Incident.

With the buzz surrounding UFOs in the 1990s, the Air Force was compelled to put together an investigation. They reacted partly because of the request of Congressman Steven Shiff to investigate unusual aerial sightings, including UFOs. The investigative team found no evidence of a recovered spacecraft. Instead, what was found were documents

---

[266] Bruce Rux. *Hollywood v. the Aliens: The Motion Picture Industry's participation in UFO Disinformation*. Berkeley, CA., 1997.

related to Project Mogul, a top-secret government sponsored mission to detect Soviet nuclear bombs. Balloons were sent to the atmosphere to measure any radiation that had been detonated by a nuclear bomb. It was common for those balloons to be mistaken for UFOs. More importantly, Project Mogul's documents have long been declassified. [267] Therefore, it was a balloon that crashed on that June day after all, right? It still does not explain the humanoids that were carted away.

Two years later, in 1997, the Air Force published another report regarding the Roswell Incident. The alien bodies recovered at the UFO crash site were actually bald-headed anthropomorphic dummies used during high diving experiments. Upon landing, the dummies became damaged, where they lost fingers and legs. This influenced what aliens looked like since they were described as being four feet tall with only four fingers. These kinds of tests were done for safety reasons to determine whether pilots or astronauts could re-enter Earth's atmosphere with a parachute to escape desperate conditions. Space probes were also used that resembled flying saucers. These tests started during the 1950s. The government contended that UFOlogists had simply mistaken the dates of the Roswell Incident in June of 1947. The evidence that the Air Force provided is certainly convincing. There is no doubt that the UFO conspiracy theorists still cried cover-up, but the burden of proof is still on them. The conspiracy theorists made the claim of a cover-up; they must prove it. They do need to be given credit though. The Air Force wound up admitting to a cover-up. Cover stories were used for spy planes when misidentified for a UFO. The U2 and SR-71 had special

---

[267] Headquarters of the United States Air Force. *The Roswell Report: Fact Vs. Fiction in the New Mexico Dessert*. Washington, D.C., 1995.

flying capabilities that commercial airliners did not have. [268]

A participant tells of a classified Skyhook program that revealed secret activity by the Air Force during the Cold War days. He described different operations that were then classified. It was to keep their eyes on Soviet nuclear activity. It was typical of large weather balloons to be launched and confused for a UFO. The balloons changed colors in the atmosphere and were spotted as mysterious aerial objects. Reports tended to be covered up by the military since they were Cold War operations. It is only now that such information is coming out in the open. [269] There is more evidence that the government covered up its secret doings as part of Cold War strategy rather than withholding information of benevolent, or for that matter, evil conquering space beings.

Some UFO conspiracy theorists like Stanton Friedman insist the Air Force's revelations do not fly. They point out the dropping of anthropomorphic dummies were events of the 1950s, not the summer of 1947. This much is true. Again, the most likely explanation is that witnesses (of which were very old or were secondhand and even third-hand witnesses) misconstrued the dates. This evaluation is similar to the story, the Roswell Incident, which was not accepted as being a weather balloon. As an objective evaluator, when weighing the evidence presented by both parties - the UFO conspiracy theorists and the Air Force - the second is more convincing.

With all the terrestrial conditions taking place back then, the outer space explanation emerged

---

[268] William J. Broad. "C.I.A. Admits Government Lies About U.F.O. Sightings." *New York Times*, August, 1997.
[269] B.D. Gildenberg. "The Cold War's Classified Skyhook Program: a participant's revelations." www.csicop.org/si/2004-05/skyhook.html.

from imaginative Earthlings who felt rage against the government. It cannot be denied that the government does lie, but when it came to covering up UFOs they did so because they themselves were paranoid top-secret information might fall into the wrong hands. Unfortunately, they did so at the expense to the public. The UFO Conspiracy Theory teaches as folklore the bureaucratic monster achieving unprecedented powers equal to God. It is no wonder why Christian conservatives demonize the government, assuming the aliens are its agents and are demons abducting humans. The MIB, no doubt also products of the imagination, are evil henchmen working for the government.

In one of the most controversial UFO sightings ever where the military was involved, was a series of lights that were seen over the southwest on the night of March 13, 1997, known as the "Phoenix Lights". Arizona, Nevada, and the Mexican border state of Sonora saw these lights glide through the night sky around 7:30 PM MST through 10:30 PM MST. There were two events that evening. The first was as a triangular-shaped UFO. The second was a series of lights that were identified as flares. There were thousands of eyewitnesses. Many of those filmed the event as it was one of the most documented UFO sightings ever. One of the eyewitnesses was then-Arizona governor Fife Symington III. He was impressed with the lights and did not agree with the Air Force that they were dropped flares from military planes during an exercise. These lights gave the impression that they disappeared, but they fell behind the Sierra Estrella mountain range instead. UFOlogists and local residents did not buy the flares explanation. Many believe these UFO sightings were authentic extraterrestrial visitations (see http://en.wikipedia.org/wiki/Phoenix_Lights, June, 2008).

The U.S. government is given premier standing as all-knowing, but also all-secretive. They have documentations that hold keys to mysterious cover-ups. That suspicion led John Greenwald, Jr. to open up a website called www.theblackvault.com. He has collected thousands of government documents about secret activities including UFOs. These were released by the Freedom of Information Act. Greenwald showed that the government had extensive knowledge of UFOs, which included Area 51, cattle mutilation, and even the MJ-12 documents, which were considered totally "bogus." Greenwald has learned that the government has indeed engaged in cover-ups although he did admit he does not have "smoking gun" evidence of extraterrestrial visitations (see yahoo.com interview). As many UFO conspiracy theorists would have it, the evidence is buried or even destroyed. This is as though to say the government's intention is to mess with the minds of the public.

Conclusion

It is understandable the government would cover up military activity. This does not mean they are covering up extraterrestrial evidence. With all of the government documents recovered, nothing shows up as evidence that there is knowledge of extraterrestrial beings. Knowledge of extraterrestrial visitations the government is believed to be denying the public's thirst of cosmic wisdom. The government, along with the industrial-military complex, has become very powerful and can shut the door on top secret information.

For example, after the U.S. government was compelled to release classified information through the Release of the Information Act, it admitted to administering American soldiers LSD back in the 1960s to determine if they are susceptible to talking if captured by the enemy. Secondly, African-American men from the South were administered syphilis without any intentions of treating them. This warped study started in the 1930s and ended in the early 1970s. [270] Of course, Watergate was an embarrassment. Because of these actual nefarious government conspiracies, the government has opened the door to critics and haters of authority.

But the UFO Conspiracy Theory does not hold up. This conclusion is very simple; space travel from a theoretically inhabitable planet to ours is way too vast. As far as interdimensional traveling, there is no proof of that either. Thus, the UFO Conspiracy Theory delivers a mythic message. This message is saying that humankind has been alienated by those in power; they should stop pretending they are gods and let the people share in the democratic process.

---

[270] Bridget Brown, *They Know Us Better Than We Know Ourselves: The History and Politics of Alien Abduction*. New York University Press, New York and London, 2007, Ch. 6.

9

Invasion of Aliens

When UFOs (initially known as flying saucers) came on the scene, concern arose whether the extraterrestrials flying them were friends or foes. The invasion theme, the belief that extraterrestrials are bent on invading Earth, actually began before Kenneth Arnold's sighting in 1947. The idea of advanced hostile aliens coming to Earth started in science fiction. Since the Cold War helped to fuel the UFO myth, the invasion theme became a major part of it. It was believed that the Soviets would invade the United States. Cold War anxieties did not just reflect the invasion theme.

The invasion theme especially became a major concern as the new millennium drew nearer, when hysteria emerged as the year 2000 approached that aliens intended on conquering Earth. Conspiracy theorists speculated that a major plot was unfolding where the aliens were to be in charge of a new era, others speculating that alien abductions were a sign of invasive intentions. This notion started before Kenneth Arnold's sighting, decades before 1947. In the 1950s, during the beginning of the Cold War, the film industry took advantage of this anxiety. Guilt was projected onto the silver screen as fears of a reverse invasion by a malicious foreign power, a parody that was a continuation of the *War of the Worlds* novel by the British author H. G. Wells.

Collective feelings of guilt would be more prominent right before the new millennium.

Before 1947

Whether or not UFOs are Earth-threatening is an idea that began with science fiction; the British writer H. G. Wells was responsible for this. In 1898, Wells wrote *War of the Worlds*. It is a science fiction story about ugly Martians invading England. They wreak havoc with their aggressions and ray guns only to succumb to the bacterial Earth diseases they were not immune to. [271] Many critics have said Wells was satirizing Western imperialism. He certainly borrowed a page out of actual history; Native Americans became infected with diseases brought by Europeans. Those diseases debilitated the Natives into submission to the technologically sophisticated Western white man. Wells' novella is a reversal. Instead of the native English succumbing to the germs and bacteria, it is the Martians.

Wells' Martians were monstrous-looking beings with vampire attributes, since they have specially designed tentacles to suck their human victims dry, motifs that can be traced back hundreds of years before Wells' time. The invading Martians were hideous. We can trace this to devil folklore of the Middle Ages, which describes him as a horrific being, deformed in every way because of his fall. [272] According to the Judeo-Christian tradition, the air is filled with demons ready to swoop down to inflict pain and torment, [273] vis-à-vis alien abductions. This too is

---

[271] H.G. Wells, *War of the Worlds*, 1898.
[272] Jeffrey Burton Russell, *Lucifer: The Devil in the Middle Ages*. Cornell University Press, Ithaca and London, 1984, p. 68.
[273] Ibid, p. 71.

traceable to folklore, most specifically to beliefs in fairies. The traditional "little people" were converted to low-statured demons upon the arrival of Christianity to northern Europe. Trolls spent their time under bridges standing by to pounce on any travelers passing through. *Mares,* though, attack sleeping victims, thereby the word "nightmare." These demons enjoyed frightening people, but also enjoyed harming and killing.[274]

These traditions were not necessarily erased from objective consciousness just because of modern-day secularization. Such sightings of apparitions and supernatural encounters may reflect (although not always) guilt or fear. Incorporeal, secular expressions can be projections of collective death. And we credit Jung for pointing this out in his famous essay on flying saucers.[275] These feelings are harrowing, unnerving in that the globe led by the Western white race met its challenge by a more technologically advanced civilization from another planet.

A man with a similar surname, Orson Welles, made the *War of the Worlds* infamous when he performed it as a drama over the radio on the eve of Halloween on October 30, 1938. Many listeners tuned in late and missed the introduction indicating it was a fictional story. It was thought the play was an actual news story interrupting the regularly scheduled program. It described Martians invading New Jersey. It led to a small-size panic: some thought they smelled the aliens' gas raids, while others said they saw flashes from the rays from a distance. The police were swamped with phone calls and some shot at a farmer's water tower that was believed to be a

---

[274] Ibid, p. 78.

[275] Carl Gustav Jung, *Flying Saucers: A Modern Myth of Things Seen in the Skies.* Princeton University Press, (1958) 1978.

spaceship. The confused sought an explanation as they wandered into the streets. The public was not pleased when it was announced the drama was only fictional. Since World War II was an impending reality, some thought that the Germans were invading. Santiago, Chile also went into a panic when it heard the *War of the Worlds* broadcast. Many marched into the radio station and about twenty people were killed. In the minds of many, aliens were to be feared. [276]

UFO conspiracy theorists would argue some years later that the reason the government is covering up knowledge of extraterrestrial visitations is the fear a panic might result similar to the *War of the Worlds* broadcast. It was made into a movie in 1953. Even before Arnold's sighting of 1947, Americans showed signs of a nervous breakdown.

Feelings of insecurity resurfaced when an object was spotted in the night sky on the night and the early morning of February 24-25, 1942 in Los Angeles. Believed to be an aerial raid, the military opened fire on the object. Anti-aircraft missiles wound up damaging a few homes. The shooting eventually stopped. Newspaper accounts described the object as approaching airplanes. Since the Pearl Harbor attack was in the consciousness of America, the military speculated that it may have been a Japanese balloon, but that was ruled out. The official report from the Navy was that the incident was a false alarm. It was explained that "war nerves" influenced this incident. [277]

Impending war and great stress in general seems to contribute to aerial misidentifications. For

[276] "The War of the Worlds (radio)", www.wikipedia.org/wiki/The_War_of_the_Worlds(radio), September, 2007.
[277] "Battle of Los Angeles", www.wikipedia.org/wiki/West_coast_air_raid, September, 2007

example, one year before Arnold's sighting, the Swedes saw many strange aerial sightings, thinking they might be confiscated V-2 German rockets launched by the Russians. The Condon Committee reported, "There were 997 UFO reports that reached the Swedish government from private citizens in that country during 1946." [278] The actual origins of the phenomenon are unknown. Certainly, though, the Swedes were seeing things in the sky as it is not uncommon during times of stress.

It is common to view UFOs as a religious event. This is no exception to the Fátima miracle in Portugal. There were a series of sightings of the Virgin Mary from 1916–1917 by three Portuguese children, and on October 13, 1917, a crowd hoping to catch a sighting of the Virgin witnessed a "dancing sun" after a rainstorm. It appeared to drop from the heavens and back and forth from its original position as it changed colors. Back then the event was interpreted as a sign from God. [279] After 1947, some believed it to be a UFO. Social scientists would associate UFOs with unstable and insecure conditions. When the cultural and historical background is bound to a particular religion – namely Catholicism – the expression of apparitions is a familiar one. Thus, the Virgin Mary is witnessed as a plea for supernatural aid. [280]

---

[278] Daniel S. Gilmor, ed. *Final Report of the Scientific Study of Unidentified Flying Objects: Conducted By the University of Colorado Under Contract to the United States Air Force*. E.P. Dutton & Co., Inc. New York, NY, 1969

[279] Jerome Clark. *The UFO Encyclopedia: The Phenomenon From the Beginning, Volume I: A-K*, Omnigraphics, Detroit, 1998, see Fátima Miracle, pg. 405-406.

[280] John Whelan, "What's Mary trying to Tell Us?", *U.S. Catholic*, August 1991, p.30-36.

Instead of anthropomorphic apparitions, flying discs and cigar-shaped UFOs made their presence known. Of course, UFO sightings, especially in the 1950s, had everything to do with a potential showdown between two superpowers.

Are UFOs a Threat?

Five years and four months after the Battle of Los Angeles, Kenneth Arnold would see his flying saucer, sparking others to do the same. It was a nervous time because of the Cold War and UFO sightings took place all over the world, not just in the U. S. The national government became involved in UFOs to determine if they were a national threat. Officials also believed the Soviets would use UFO reports as propaganda. The U. S. government wanted to calm the public's apprehension. Therefore, they debunked UFO reports. Yet, pilots found themselves chasing flying saucers. A famous example was the Mantel Incident. Air Force pilot Thomas Mantel chased what he thought was a giant UFO. He climbed so high into the atmosphere that he lost oxygen and passed out. He met his death when his plane hit the ground. The public was alarmed and thought that there was more to the story. [281]

Cold War conditions inspired the military to keep its eyes out for any suspicious aerial object. One of the ways to do so was by radar. On the night of July 19, 1952, several objects were spotted on the radar screen. No objects were known to be flying at the time. These objects were seen over the capital in Washington D. C. Planes were dispatched to get a closer look. After searching the skies, they could not find anything. After the objects disappeared from

---

[281] See "The Mantel Incident" in Jerome Clark's *The UFO Encyclopedia: The Phenomenon From the Beginning: Vol. 2:L – Z,* Omnigraphics, Detroit, 1998, p. 603-607.

the screens, they would reappear. It was thought that an intelligent being was playing a trick. After further investigation, it was explained that temperature inversions created the blips on radar. This explanation did not sit well with civilians. [282]

1952 was a year where the extraterrestrial hypothesis was both popular and simultaneously disliked. The concern that UFO invasions from outer space gained paltry adherents, because most people who believed in flying saucers also believed the aliens offered something positive to humanity. Contactees were reporting beautiful, alien-saviors who came to Earth to prevent Earthlings from blowing themselves up. NICAP and APRO, though, put pressure on the Air Force to spill the beans.

Science Fiction Films, TV, & Books

As we saw, the invasion theme began before 1947. Here we will consider Paul Meehan's work, *Saucer Movies: A UFOlogical History of the Cinema* (1998). It is a fascinating scholarly analysis of UFO movies since the very first one until the 1990s. Meehan shows how Hollywood has influenced the perception of the UFO myth. [283]

There had been movies before 1947 that dealt with outer space themes. *Heavenship* (1917) was a film that recounted a voyage to Mars. Since it was made during World War I, it expressed European yearning for international peace. Other early movies included *A Trip to Mars* (1910), *A Message from Mars* (1913), and *The First Men on the Moon* (1919). This early

---

[282] See Washington National Radar/Visual Case in *Jerome Clark's The UFO Encyclopedia*, 1998, p.998 – 1003.

[283] Paul Meehan, *Saucer Movies: A UFOlogical History of the Cinema*, Scarecrow Press, Inc. Langhorn, MD, 1998.

period in film history was influenced by speculation that other planets, namely Mars, were inhabited by advanced civilizations.

The most influential UFO subgenre is the alien invasion theme. *A Thing to Come (1936)* was based on a H. G. Wells novel. A black aircraft flies over a town and lands on the town's square. The pilot emerges wearing a large-size helmet; he is the evil leader. Advanced-looking planes drop sleeping gas on the unsuspecting townspeople. They go into a deep sleep. When they wake up, they find themselves in a new era. *The Phantom Empire* (1935) and *The Undersea Kingdom* (1936) convey futuristic underground empires invading Earth. Later as the UFO era began flourishing, it was thought by some that UFOs were not from other planets, but rather underground cities. Even before the radio play by Orson Welles in 1938, science - fiction was already depicting advanced civilizations invading Earth. It was World War II, and thus, the appropriation of these kinds of movies. One must bear in mind that before 1947, referring to Arnold's flying saucer sighting, there were pre-conditions building up, eventually leading to the Cold War between the United States and the Soviet Union.

It was not just the militarization of new technology that brought on the pseudoscience of UFOs. What also surfaced was the belief in psychological techniques, reminiscent of mesmerism in the nineteenth century. Edward Hunter is the originator of the term "brainwashing," a journalist claimed Communist China was using methods of mind control on its citizens, and applying this on American prisoners of war during the Korean conflict between the Communist North and the Capitalist South. Brainwashing took off as a perceived reality that

Communist countries were using this type of stealth technology to conquer the U. S. [284]

As we discussed earlier, alien abductees often do not remember the actual event. Was this idea extracted from films? In the movie *Killers from Space* (1954), an atomic scientist disappears from an aircraft after having sighted a UFO. He is found in the dessert wandering alone with no memory of what happened despite a large surgical scar in his chest. A hypnotic drug was used to regain his memory and he remembers waking up on an operating table surrounded by aliens with huge hypnotic eyes. The first American abduction was not reported until 1961 when Barney and Betty Hill expressed that they experienced the same exotic and frightening experience under hypnosis.

UFOlore has a rich source of details extracted from science fiction films, especially the flying saucer movies. In *Superman and the Mole Men* (1951), the moles are played by midgets with large craniums and bald heads. In *the Man from Planet X*, the alien is a small humanoid with a large head enclosed a bulbous space helmet. The masklike face had horizontal slits for mouth, eyes, and a prominent nose. He is an abducting alien that hypnotizes folks to enslave them.

The actual first alien abduction took place in Brazil with Villa Boas. He described his aliens as small in stature with large heads and space helmets. The 1950s featured several films that dealt with abduction, amnesia, medical operations, hypnotic eyes, and vision screens all of which became part of UFOlore later on. Another example was *Not of this Earth* (1956), which entailed dark-suited individuals

---

[284] David Seed. *Brainwashing: The Fictions of Mind Control: A Study of Novels and Films*, The Kent State University Press, Kent, OH, 2004, see chapter 2.

with sunglasses. This paved the way for the Men in Black folklore.

There is also a tendency for abductees to relive the abduction experience with deceptive scenes of screen memories, memories planted by aliens to masquerade the real ones. Such an idea is found in the film *The Manchurian Candidate* (1962). It is set in the Korean War where a U.S. army patrol is captured by North Korean soldiers. They are taken to a research facility and brainwashed by Communist Chinese and Soviet Scientists. Their intent is to take over the U.S. government with the aid of American soldiers. They are sent back to fight, although some soldiers had nightmares. They dream they are attending a gardening lecture at a hotel in New Jersey given by middle-aged ladies. This is a screen memory, for the U.S. soldiers are actually in the Soviet institute under the authority of their Communist abductors. At the podium is a bald-headed Asian man of great intelligence who is infiltrating the minds of these young soldiers. During the abduction craze, it was typical for abductees to witness a taller alien who is wise.

Meehan mentions the psychological concept "cryptomnesia," a process in which the true source of the memory is forgotten. The theory is that the abduction scenario may be partially remembered from TV or a film and found their way into the abduction reports. There is plenty of culturally rich material in culture that would influence one's perception. The alien abduction scenario is just one example of how the media influences human behavior. Flying saucer films also portray environmental concerns.

Frank Scully's book, *Behind the Flying Saucers*, describes downed saucers in the southwestern U.S. desert along with small-statured humanoids that were carted away. He was hoaxed, but such an idea remained in the public's mind. It would appear in UFO films throughout the 1950s, with aliens portrayed as aggressive and bent on conquering Earth. They came from a dying planet worn by ecological disaster and warfare. They needed to interbreed with humans to survive. Such themes carried over well into the abduction myth. These advanced beings needed to genetically experiment and take human sperm and eggs to create a new hybrid race.

There were other films throughout the 1950s. For example, *It Conquered the World* (1956), is about Venusian bat creatures that leave needle implants in their victim's neck. This allows for the bats to control humans, in much the same manner aliens are believed to surgically implant tracking devices on humans. In *Invasion of the Saucer Men* (1957), little aliens have big, bug eyes similar to the Greys in the abduction reports. *Enemy From Space* (1957) is a film that depicts the idea of an alien conspiracy to overthrow the government and establish a dictatorship. *Attack of the 50-Foot Woman* (1958) conveys the abduction of a motorist by a UFO on a deserted highway. *I Married a Monster From Outer Space* (1958), dealt with reproduction and hybridization. Many of these themes made their way into the UFO myth.

Meehan cites Susan Sontag, saying that the flying saucer movies of the 1950s reflect the collective guilt of Americans of conquering the Native Americans. The aliens in the films were depicted as aggressive and technologically advanced, parallel to the Europeans conquering the Natives. Even though such a theme is significant to Sontag, UFO movies of the 1950s have to be looked at in their own context. Moviemakers were exploiting the widespread fear of the invasion of Soviet Communism. All of these films can thank H.G. Wells for writing *War of the Worlds* in 1898. As satire, it influenced the idea of conquering aliens where humans are the natives and the aliens are an imposing, advanced, foreign civilization. From this perspective, Sontag is not necessarily wrong either.

Meehan went further, asserting that flying saucer movies not only influenced the alien abduction narrative, but also UFO sightings themselves. It was common to report the flying disc throughout the years. The triangular-shaped UFO became part of the myth as well as a result of the silver screen. The movies *Star Wars* (1977), *The Empire Strikes Back* (1980), and *Return of the Jedi* (1983) all feature triangular-shaped space crafts. Waves of triangular shaped UFOs followed in New York's Hudson Valley and New Jersey during the 1980s, while Europe had waves in Belgium and Britain during the 1990s. The American southwest had sightings in 1997. While the timing of the waves may be questionable in terms of direct linkage, the reports seemed very plausible. UFOs were reported having all kinds of shapes. Objects in the skies are not what they seem to be. What is reported are shapes and sizes familiar to the culture, coinciding with *Cultural Optics*.

Reptilian aliens were considered evil as opposed to other types, also influenced by movies. Reptilian reports have a close parallel with movies such as *V* (1983), *The Last Starfighter* (1984), and *Enemy Mine* (1985), Meehan asserts. What is familiar in Western culture is the association with evil and the reptilian animal, the snake. It was the snake that deceived humanity in the biblical creation story of Adam and Eve. It might be expected that the film industry would use these pre-conceived notions in their movies. One must be reminded that movies are just to entertain. Some took material from UFO films and ran with the idea that aliens are evil and conquering beings; it is difficult to ignore the role reversal of actual history.

Meehan's work has been corroborated by Harvard University's Susan Clancy. Studying the fallibility of memory, she interviewed people who believed they might be alien abductees. Their suspicions were "confirmed" after going to a hypnotist. The source of the false memories is material traced back to the entertainment media where movies, books, and TV play a direct role in providing a "script" for the abductees and hypnotists alike. In Clancy's cases, her abductees saw the abduction experience as a religious one.[285]

In the last two decades of the twentieth century, there were many accounts of people taken against their will by small grey-skinned aliens with big wrap-around eyes. Many describe the alien that looks like the one drawn on the front cover of Whitney Strieber's book *Communion*, published in 1987. While some saw alien abduction as a spiritual experience, others were abducting humans in order to conquer our planet.[286] This theme strongly resembles racial fear. If this is the case, alien encounters should be nothing more than the representation of anxiety toward interracial mixing.

The Hill's Abduction in Context

Betty and Barney Hill was an interracial couple; Betty was white, Barney was black. We are told that they could not account for two lost hours driving back from Canada. Coming back from vacation they made their way through Upstate New York on their journey

---

[285] Susan A. Clancy, *Abducted: How People Come to Believe They Were Kidnapped By Aliens*, Harvard University Press, Cambridge, MA, 2005.
[286] David M. Jacobs. *Secret Life: First Hand Accounts of UFO Abductions*, Simon & Shuster, New York, 1992; Also by Jacobs, *The Threat: Secret Agenda: What the Aliens Really Want and How They Plan to Get It*. Simon & Shuster, New York, 1998.

to their home state of New Hampshire. They both
spotted a UFO as they headed home. This was a couple
that was in good-standing with their community and
fellow employees. In addition, both husband and wife
were involved in the Civil Rights Movement. The UFO
incident took place in the wee hours of the morning.
It was about 2:00 AM on September 20, 1961. [287]

Betty, in the passenger side of the car,
notices a strange aerial object. She tells Barney to
take a look, but has to stop the car on Betty's
urgent request. He grabs the binoculars, and then
takes them off to tell his wife that it is an
airplane heading towards Canada. As they continued
driving, Betty says the plane started behaving out of
the norm. The object was seemed to have flown right
behind them. Then, there were weird beeping sounds
coming from the trunk. They found themselves in an
inexplicable haze. They get home at dawn, although
they should've arrived two hours earlier. Betty
began to have recurring dreams, but more on the
nightmarish side. A friend tells Betty to write about
her dreams and she started doing so.

Both husband and wife would be referred to Dr.
Benjamin Simon, a psychiatrist and certified
hypnotist. The reason for the recommendation of
hypnosis is that a UFO investigator suggested that
there was something in the Hills' UFO story,
positing that the UFO may have been the cause of the
two lost hours. Because of the discrepancy of the
Hills' house clock when they finally arrived home
and their expected arrival, the UFO investigator
believed the couple's memories can be tapped into
through hypnosis. Betty began describing her dreams
to her friends and co-workers, when her supervisor
tells her such dreams are real events, an actual UFO

[287] John G. Fuller, *The Interrupted Journey: Two Lost Hours "Aboard a Flying Saucer."* The Dial Press, New York, 1966.

experience, not fantasies. Although Betty continued to persuade Barney that her dreams stem from an experience with alien visitors, Barney keeps his stance, vehemently brushing the dreams off as nothing more than that.

It's significant to mention the two individuals who opened up a can of worms for Betty. They were the UFO investigator, suspecting the Hills' late arrival, and Betty's supervisor, planting in her mind the physical reality of her otherworldly experience. The so-called UFO abduction that was recalled under hypnosis, wound up being Betty and Barney's false memories. The Hills stopping along the way while on their way home was not considered the real cause of their late arrival. The Hills did mention they stopped to walk their dog who was on the back seat. They mentioned they were in a town looking for an open diner and also stopped into a motel.

Before the Hills sought therapy with Dr. Simon, Barney was under Dr. Duncan Stephen's care, who saw his interracial marriage with Betty as a "a sociological condition that could not be ignored." [288] It was pages earlier when John Fuller, the Hills' biographer, wrote, "...what was to happen to them this night of September 19, 1961, had nothing whatever to do with their successful mixed marriage or their dedication to social progress." [289] Fuller is completely wrong about this. It was precisely because of the Hills' interracial marriage that brought them stress and anxiety in relation to their alien abduction experience. Let us see how this unveiled as Barney went under hypnosis.

Finally meeting with Dr. Simon, the therapy sessions began the first of which took place on

---

[288] Ibid, p. 53.
[289] Ibid, p. 3.

February 24, 1964, on a Saturday morning. Betty and Barney are separated. Dr. Simon has Barney undergo hypnosis first while Betty anxiously waits in an unoccupied room on the other side of the clinic. Barney is under hypnosis, in a sleep-like state; his memories regressed to the time when Betty asks him to stop the car. As Betty is walking the dog, Barney's curiosity got the better of him, leaving the road and going into an open field. He describes to Dr. Simon a strange craft with windows. Behind them were strange-looking humanoids. They stepped back as Barney noticed the leader gazing at him, as though he could see right through Barney. Petrified, Barney hurried back to where the car was parked in the middle of the road.[290] The reader may remember how we established how hypnosis can confabulate memories, false memories that seem vivid and picturesque and therefore very believable, no matter how subjective they are.

On the subsequent Saturday, Dr. Simon probed further into Barney's "hidden memories." Barney described the leader of the pack as a red-headed Irishman.[291] And added, "...the evil face on... he looks like a German Nazi. He's a Nazi.[292]" Dr. Simon asked for further clarification, prompting Barney to say, "His eyes were slanted...But not like Chinese...."[293] Barney then describes that after he gets into the car to drive away, he and Betty encounter men on the road wearing "dark jackets."[294] Barney says these men were using telepathy and their eyes to communicate with him.[295] We ought to mention a subtle tinge of evil, behaving in supernatural-like manner, when controlling Betty and Barney with their

[290] Ibid, p. 16-17.
[291] Ibid, p. 87.
[292] Ibid, p. 87.
[293] Ibid, p. 88.
[294] Ibid, p. 88-9.
[295] Ibid, p. 94-5.

minds. Indeed, these men on the road are similar to Men in Black.

When it was Betty's turn to be hypnotized, she describes Barney's intense fear when hurrying back to the car. Under hypnosis, she quotes Barney, "They've seen us, and they're coming this way." "And I laughed and asked him if he had watched *Twilight Zone* recently on TV. And he didn't say anything," explained Betty. Dr. Simon inquires, "Why did you mention *Twilight Zone?*" Betty responds, "Because the idea was fantastic." "Had there been anything like this on *Twilight Zone?*" inquires Dr. Simon. Putting the matter to rest, Betty's answer is, "I don't know. I never see *Twilight Zone*. But I had heard people talk about this program, and I always was under the impression that it was a way-out type of thing. And so when he [Barney] said that they had seen us, and that they were swinging around and coming in our direction, I thought his imagination was overactive." If only Betty knew how important her last six words are, extremely vital.

Back in 1961, Barney had no recollection of these so-called aliens, neither the craft's windows nor the men in the middle of the road. A major suspect was the television, but it wasn't *The Twilight Zone;* it was another show. UFOlogists have argued that Barney hardly watched TV since he had a very busy schedule. However, the key evidence is when Betty says that she hears people talking about TV shows like *The Twilight Zone*. It wound up being another show, *The Outer Limits*. Skeptics have pointed this out, but Jason Colavito's explanation is the best one.

In his website, jasoncolavito.com, [296] Jason Colavito makes it clear that there were several episodes just prior to Barney's very first hypnotic session with Dr. Simon, which took place on February 24, 1964. On February 10, an episode entitled "The Bellero Shield," there was a slanted-eyed alien. A week before that, February 3, "The Invisibles" featured the implantation of an object on a human subject. The aliens' intent was to take over Earth by possessing bodies. Although this particular human (played by Neil Hamilton) is face down on the operating table, Colavito asserts that the suggesting of sexual probing had to be implicit – since it was the 1960s – unlike Barney's alien procedures done face up, where it was "the manipulation of his genitals." [297] Finally, the episode just days before Barney's first therapy session, "The Children of the Spider Country," aired on February 17. There was an alien whose eyes lit up like very bright light bulbs. Barney did describe how the leader's eyes illuminated darkness, only eyes with no face. More importantly, says Colavito, the bright-eyed alien came from the planet Eros to get his hybrid, half-human half-alien son, the result of the alien's intergalactic relationship (where in the Hills' abduction account, the intergalactic union reflect Betty's and Barney's racial background being two worlds apart.) When the alien changes to human form, Colavito ties this with Barney's "German Nazi," where the alien has a serious and deranged facial expression. The alien's son, however, runs away with a white woman, reflecting Barney's estranged relationship with his former black wife and his children. Therefore, Barney's alien experience during regression is the manifestation of his guilt.

---

[296] http://www.jasoncolavito.com/alien-abduction-at-the-outer-limits.html, 09/07/2012.

[297] See quote in jasoncolavito.com. Search for the Hills' abduction account. Retrieval information is not available.

Bear in mind that during the Hills' era, interracial marriage was taboo. In addition, *The Interrupted Journey* did make it clear how Betty, a UFO believer (along with as her sister, also a believer) constantly discussed this relevant subject while Barney was present.

Communicating with Jason Colavito through e-mail, he suggests the producers of *The Outer Limits* may have been influenced by *The Manchurian Candidate*, which hit the movie theatres in 1962, a little more than a year prior to the three episodes of *The Outer Limits* that presumably influenced Barney in February of 1964. Colavito does caution that it "is a guess."[298]

However, Paul Meehan does not see a connection with the *Outer Limits* and the Hills' abduction. He did suggest the 1973 UFO wave prompted the Coyne helicopter and the Puscagoula abduction. There were other abduction claims, says Meehan, between 1973 and 1976. Meehen, via e-mail, writes, "The argument of the skeptics that *The Outer Limits* influenced the Hills, portrayed in the TV movie, *The UFO Incident* (in 1975), also assumes that Travis Walton watched the Hills' movie." Meehen does make the point such analysis does not do justice to the other pre-1975 alien abduction reports. In addition, "just because *The Outer Limits*' episodes preceded the Hills' hypnotic therapy sessions do not mean there is a causal relationship."[299]

On the contrary, Martin Kottmeyer did make the case that science fiction contributed to the alien abduction motif including what believers would view

[298] Jason Colavito, personal communication via e-mail, received on 08/21/2012.
[299] Paul Meehen, personal communication via e-mail, received on 09/14/2012.

as "the stunning coincidence" of an alien with wrap-around eyes in the "Bellero Shield" episode of *The Outer Limits*, the very episode that aired just days before Barney's very first session with Dr. Simon.[300] To say the least, the timing and the potential TV influence on the alien abduction narrative is indeed stunning. The evidence presented by Colavito and Kottmeyer is convincing. As well-intentioned as Meehan was, he did not provide an alternative explanation to how the Hills' aliens and the one from *The Outer Limits* were so similar. For that matter, Travis Walton's abduction occurred about a week after *The UFO Incident* aired, the very story regarding the Hills' alien experience it is hard to ignore the connection.

In Brown's estimation, images of reality or simulated reality appeared to have an effect on the popular mind during the 1960s and 1970s. Photography, film, and most especially television portrayed a thin line between reality and simulated reality.[301] She makes the point, as postmodernity took off, how individual identity and subjectivity were stressed. The accommodation of the new importance of multicultural perspectives also had an impact.[302] As such, Brown continues that hypnosis helps in the reconstruction of personal identity. In considering the decline of religion, hypnotists stepped in to provide quasi-magical answers to fill in the void.[303]

Perhaps technologically produced images are the new shamanist experience. According to Carl Jung, such experiences are rooted in the social psyche. However, Don McGowan shows how Jungian psychology is

---

[300] [22] Martin Kottmeyer, "Entirely Unpredisposed: the Cultural Background of UFO Abduction Reports, www.debunker.com/texts/unpredis.html., retrieved on 09/15/2012.
[301] Brown, *They Know Us Better Than We Know Ourselves*, p. 29.
[302] Ibid, p. 29-30.
[303] Ibid, p. 30.

flawed. [304] Visions and images are completely social constructs. In *What is Wrong with Jung*, we learn that Jung viewed religious visions – Buddhism for example – as projections of an innate mechanism he called the Collective Unconscious. According to Jung, it contains repressed memories, myths, and legends. They are projected as dreams, fantasies, or through symbols. The Collective Unconscious is innate; with Jung declaring some symbols projected by a culture may not have the same meaning for others. The differences in symbolic projection lie in the innate differences of what is projected. [305] If we understand Jung correctly, movies are projections of the collective psyche.

McGowan, however, convincingly argues that Jung is totally wrong. Suspension of disbelief is necessary when watching a film, viewers knowing full well of its fictitious content and characters. When suspension of belief takes place, movie watchers are taken in, in a quasi-magical manner and temporarily partake in it as though they are in the movie. If the suspension of disbelief does not occur, the film's plausibility can have interesting consequences. [306] Interpreting a movie about aliens as non-fiction, as opposed to science fiction, can cause subjective experience to take on a "reality" of its own. [307]

Thus, when we hear how supernatural entities of years past may be beings from outer space, what must be understood is how modern aliens replaced angels and demons in rehashed form. Aliens stepped in to coincide with the pervasive paradigm that supplanted the supernatural. Once demons lost their influence in swooping down to possess people, non-white races, by

---

[304] Don McGowan, *What Is Wrong with Jung*. Prometheus Books, Buffalo, 1994.
[305] Ibid, p. 27.
[306] Ibid, p. 39-41.
[307] Ibid, p. 43-5.

the start of the modern period (eighteenth and nineteenth centuries), replaced evil spirits. Racism became the justification to dominate societies that were not white.

Alien Abductions as Metaphors of Racial Fear

Essayist Annalee Newitz sees the alien abduction narrative as an old story where the advanced Europeans arrive on shore with their ships and change native culture by implementing an oppressive system. The West's conquering of the New World included the idea that civilization must be introduced even at the expense of non-white peoples; the natives were conquered and Africans were enslaved, all in the name of progress. The abduction story reveals a technologically advanced alien race taking humans against their will and creating a new racially-mixed society as a result. [308]

Most who have experienced the alien abduction scenario have been white people. Newitz saw this connection very clearly. Unfortunately, there has not been a writer or a scholar that has addressed this theme, a subject matter that is so obvious in what alien abductions are conveying, especially when these aliens are technologically advanced humanoids and sometimes referred as an "alien race." Susan Clancy noted the majority of the abductees are disproportionately Caucasian, but did not address the reasons why.

Bridget Brown also noted the majority of the abductees were, although not exclusively, white. [309] In

---

[308] "Alien Abductions and the End of White People", www.bad.eserver.org/issues/1993/06/newitz.html, September, 2007
[309] Brown, *They Know US Better Than We Know Ourselves*, p. 12, 25, 60.

chapter 8 of her work, "Look and See What You Have Done: Abductees and the Burden of Global Consciousness", Brown addresses the damage done by Western Civilization through the expression of alien abductions. Environmentalism is expressed through the alien abduction narrative, while the beautiful aliens of the contactees of the 1950s functioned like Christian missionaries. Rather than saving souls, Earth must be saved from nuclear catastrophe. After the 1960s, more so in the 1970s - as alien abduction reports began to soar - alien abductions merged with environmental concerns. Besides nuclear peril, other forms of environmental concerns, such as over-dependency on oil or even the exhaustion of natural resources and overpopulation, became part of the political agenda.[310]

Instead of conquering "nonwhite" civilization as history has shown, white abductees are imagining that they are the ones being conquered. This suggests the collective guilt of white dominance. Interestingly, this coincides with non-European migration into the U.S. and Europe at the time.

British UFOlogist Jenny Randles is skeptical of the idea that science fiction played a role in hypnotic regressions. To her credit, though, she does not duck the differences of alien encounters coinciding with their respective regions, namely hairy dwarfs of South America and blond-haired blue-eyed humanoids from Britain. She also went on to say that African and Asian abduction accounts are few. Therefore, alien abduction, like the rest of the UFO phenomenon, is a Western construct. This is our assertion, but Randles speculated, "Perhaps, a real alien race interested in breeding experiments does

---

[310] Ibid, Ch. 8.

not want non-Caucasian stock." [311] Nonsense. Randles, like other alien abduction researchers, are too literal. She goes on further, "…either the abduction is a product of the mind of Western white people or some intelligence behind the abduction prefers to contact such people." [312] Randles referred to the state of consciousness in the UFO experience as the "Oz factor," referring to the character Dorothy from the movie *The Wizard of Oz* who found herself in the Land of Oz after being knocked in the head by debris during a tornado. Randles writes, "…creates the impression of temporarily having left our material world and entered another dreamlike place with magical rules." [313] Randles recognized that the Oz factor might have played a role in sightings of fairies and apparitions, even tribal states of consciousness. Randles, as a pro-UFOlogist, must go where the evidence leads. We have shown how hypnotic regressions take on dream states, where *natural laws* are suspended. Besides that, alien abductions are dream states, and we will continue to argue that its political and social messages are manifestations of white guilt.

This expression is clear when examining the aliens' Asian-like features, a suspicion that is so apparent. There had been anti-Japanese sentiment late in the twentieth century. Throughout the 1980s and 1990s, there was also the perception that the Japanese were a technologically advanced society. There was fear that the Japanese would conquer the U.S. right after the Pearl Harbor attacks. American abductees have been imagining being conquered by

---

[311] Jenny Randles. *Alien Abductions: The Mystery Solved: Over 200 Documented UFO Kidnappings Investigated*. Inner Light Publications. New Brunswick, N.J., 1998, p. 158.
[312] Ibid, p. 158.
[313] Ibid, p. 22.

Japanese-looking aliens, parallel to the fear of a Japanese invasion.

Admittedly, however, the hypothesis of short-statured grey aliens (with wrap-around almond-shaped eyes resembling those of an Asian person) reflect fear or guilt towards the racial other, needs further clarification. It is true that alien abductions skyrocketed during the same period of "colored" non-white peoples immigrating to the U.S. and Europe. In order to support this hypothesis, socio-historical tracing has to be done. Paul Meehan has done some groundwork for us with his analysis of 1950s flying saucer films that influenced alien abductions. Actual historical circumstances strongly parallel alien pop culture. Decolonization, speeding up since 1945, is noted. [314] The idea of racial fear expressed in the alien abduction motif has not been explored thoroughly by any writer, Annalee Newitz as the exception. We think it is appropriate with the abduction experience of Betty and Barney Hill that took place in September 1961. Their experience received such sensationalism and gossip through media hype. This married couple started it all, the first Americans who alleged were kidnapped by extraterrestrials.

The most striking characteristic of alien abduction reports is that the abductee population has been overwhelmingly Caucasian. Kevin Randle discusses this in his blog. [315] Further, the kidnapping of humans by aliens resembles the Native American captivity narrative. In Colonial New England such narratives became very popular, although these types of stories were haunting. Whites who came back to their

---

[314] John Springhall, *Decolonization since 1945*. Palgrave, New York, 2001.

[315] Kevin Randle. "A Different Perspective: The Abduction Enigma," http://kevinrandle.blogspot.com/2007/08/abduction-enigma.html, retrieved on 09/14/2012.

communities were "Indianized," with some marrying their male captors. Puritan captives had a dualistic outlook, believing that Indians were the devil's agents since their residence was in the wild. The Puritans were well aware of the conversion process, giving oneself to God. Being taken away from white civilization is the very opposite. This is God's test, although many who returned experienced trauma and were also suspected of being impure since they became tainted from the devil's abode, the forest itself. [316]

During the nineteenth century, whites kidnapped by Indians were mentioned in newspaper articles and books. They enraged the white communities with disinformation; Indians were described as rude hosts. There were some men who were captured, but it was mostly women, many of them writing about their experiences in the form of diaries. These women described their experiences as benign, showing sympathy toward their Native American captors. The idea that the women were raped is false, lies that were deliberately told by the media of the day. [317]

When Barney Hill described the aliens who abducted him during consciousness, rather than under hypnosis, he told Dr. Simon these "men" had large heads and their eyes continued towards their sides of their faces. When he and Betty went to an anthropology conference, their reactions resonated strongly. A slide was shown of Indians living in the Magellan Straits who had, as Barney put it, "Oriental sort of eyes." These Indians living in the high mountains reminded him of the aliens who

[316] Richard Slotkin. *Regeneration Through Violence: The Mythology of the American Frontier, 1600 – 1800*, Wesleyan University Press, Middletown, CT., 1973, see chapters 4 and 5.

[317] Glenda Riley. *Confronting Race: Women and Indians on the Frontier*, University of Albuquerque, Albuquerque, NM, 2004, p. 38-40, 203-07, p. 209-11

abducted him.[318] Being in the same office at the same time with Barney and Dr. Simon, Betty went on to say, "...they look like mongoloids...comparing them with a case (as a social worker) I had been working, a specific mongoloid child. The surface of their skin seemed to be a bluish-gray, but probably whiter than that."[319]

Western men, in particular, have had racial fears of their white women having sexual liaisons with men of another race. Referred to as the *yellow peril*, Gina Marchetti explores Western films depicting Asian-Caucasian sexual relationships, female Asians as the sexual object of desire, while the antagonistic Asian male's role is one of asexuality with Caucasian women. Arguing from the feminist perspective, Marchetti maintains many films prior to the 1960s convey a white male romancing a submissive Asian woman as a metaphor of Western dominance over Asia. When it comes to an Asian male romancing a white woman, Hollywood has him play a submissive role to the Caucasian protagonist.[320]

Barney played a submissive role as a black man when he was married to his white wife. The manipulation of Barney's genitals by the aliens (whom he described as men) seem to suggest his *demasculinization*. Barney's aliens represent the system as his foe, a racist system he was fighting against since the start of the Civil Rights Movement. In the symbolic sense, Barney went through a humiliating racial, homosexual rape, albeit the aliens are asexual. We are only saying the homosexual rape in the spaceship is simply a metaphor that

[318] Fuller, *The Interrupted Journey*, p. 260.
[319] Ibid., p. 264.
[320] Gina Marchetti. *Romance and the "Yellow Peril:" Race, Sex, and Discursive Strategies in Hollywood Fiction*. University of California Press, Los Angeles and London, 1993.

represents institutionalized racism as expressed through Barney's forced submissiveness.

In Randle's abductee population, out of a 316, 23% said they are bisexual, 29% said they are homosexual – although the latter have not had sex in at least five years. (Though, notice the population of 52% when both categories are combined.) Besides being asked if they are gay, the women abductees said their abductors were male, while the leaders tended to be female. [321] Either way, the dominance of the racial other is demonstrated in the alien abduction scenario. The aliens, as foreigners of Earth (symbolizing foreigners of the West), are sexual colonizers of Earth (symbolized as white abductees). In other words, the role-playing abductees reversed the forced colonization of Western colonialism.

In fairness to those who may ask what about those abducted who are not white, consider the following. As we saw above, Barney's abduction reflected his fears and anxiety regarding his mixed race marriage. Abduction of non-whites may reflect anxiety of racism towards minorities. Yet, there is evidence of assimilation of minorities into Western Civilization. In order to really decipher this problem, abduction accounts of brown and black peoples must be reviewed. Analyzing the motifs and the type of conversations taking place with the aliens during recall (whether through hypnosis or fully conscious) are the best methods. Simply stated, one must hold evaluation until further information is gathered.

The yellow peril is tied together with the physical and intellectual inferiority of "colored" peoples. The mass media ingrained this belief in the late nineteenth and early twentieth century. White

---

[321] Kevin Randle.

Anglo-Saxon Protestants became familiar with the evil fictional character Dr. Fu Manchu. In Hearst newspapers, editorials were anti-Asian. In Homer Lea' s *The Valor of Innocence*, his 1909 text depicted Japan as an evil military monster. [322] *The Manchurian Candidate* (1962), says Paul Meehan through e-mail, is a film not about aliens but, "It anticipates many features that later become fixtures of abduction reports, including Asian-looking aliens, screen memories, induced amnesia, and brainwashing." [323]

Japanese-looking Aliens

One must ask the most obvious question; if alien encounters are nothing more than terrestrial happenings, why do they appear Asian? The fact that the aliens are described to have the type of eyes common to those of Asian heritage, should spell out the very idea that alien abductions are, indeed, nothing more than terrestrial happenings. Interaction with the supernatural has always actually been natural occurrences – via dream states, misidentifications, or hallucinations. Aliens, therefore, became *technologized* supernatural agents to fit into the begrudgingly accepted paradigm of materialism.

H. G. Wells' novel was so influential that the dramatic fictional radio account of 1938 resulted in a panic. This hysteria, appropriately, found its way into Hollywood – the theme reflecting the Cold War with brutally advanced, technological invaders. When Wells wrote his novella, materialism was challenging the supernatural. Instead of demons rearing their ugly heads, it was monstrous Martians. Draining their

---

[322] Gina Marchetti, *Romance and the "Yellow Peril:"*,
[323] Paul Meehan, personal communication via e-mail. Retrieved 08/21/2012.

Earthling victims of their life-sustaining fluids, Martian vampirism turned into hideous looking Greys, thieves of male sperm and female eggs. Such theft serves as a metaphor for the stealing of land of lesser technological natives.[324]

The message conveys that it was not the indigenous who were the savages. In the heightened sense of globalism, the depiction of white colonialism of the past is depicted in satanic terms. Although monsters and demons were often separate entities (according to medieval folklore), monsters were supposed to have been deformed humans without souls. Monsters and demons are thought of as moving away from God; monstrous entities not only are physically deprived, they are also morally deprived. Monsters were not exactly synonymous with demons. Demons and vampires, however, were strictly evil creatures bent on imposing disorder.[325]

The appearance of Greys in people's bedrooms came on the heels of supernatural belief. Like ghosts who come back to haunt the living, aliens make themselves "appear" to people. This is especially vital during the bedroom visitations of the Greys; that these entities have Asian eyes is no accident. The Greys received their motifs from planet Earth, not from outer space.

Writing through e-mail once again, is Paul Meehan's expertise answer on flying saucer films:

The first Asian-looking alien in screen history was probably Ming the Merciless in the three Flash Gordon Serials of the 1930s – early 40s. Ming, who was played by the Caucasian actor, Charles Middleton, was kind of an extraterrestrial version of the Oriental villain, Dr. Fu Manchu.

[324] Timothy A. Mitchell. *It Came from Outer Space: Faith, Science, Conquest, and the War of the Worlds.* www8.georgetown.edu/cct/thesis/TimothyMitchell.pdf, retrieved 09.20.2012.
[325] Russell, *Lucifer*, 1984, p. 78-9.

Hope this been helpful, keep watching the skies,

Paul.[326]

Dr. Fu Manchu, mentioned in the previous section, is a fictional character based on the yellow peril. As far as Ming, he is an evil emperor from the planet Mongo (obviously, a take on Mongolia). He falls in love with Gordon's sidekick, the beautiful Dale Arden. But Ming has to go through Flash since he is Arden's protector, which falls in line with Marchetti's filmography, just mentioned a moment ago. Ming wears a vampire-like cape, with deranged slanted eyes and a bald head.

Why a bald head? What is the symbolism behind this? It is reminiscent of the sinister Men in Black. Albert Bender claimed he was visited by three men wearing black suits, black shoes, and white shirts. This was Bender's selling his practical joke to UFO believers. [327] We do think there was government involvement in the harassment of UFO investigators, but it has nothing to do with space aliens. It was the Cold War, and the government was protecting its secret activities. Indeed, there have been many reports of MIB. Their behavior has been described as very odd, smirks on their faces, low monotone voices, and awkwardly walking in a wobbling fashion, their actions not resembling human-like qualities at all. They are always bald, have slanted eyes, and usually a pale grayish skin. According to one folklorist, the

---

[326] Personal communication with Paul Meehan. E-mail retrieved on 08/23/2012.
[327] http://www.theironskeptic.com/articles/bender//bender.htm, retrieved 07/06/2012;
http://www.csicop.org/si/show/gray_barker_my_friend-the-myth-maker/, retrieved 09/06/2012.

MIB phenomenon is strikingly similar to sightings of the devil. [328]

Whether it has been the Virgin Mary, angels, the devil, and especially aliens – these apparitions conform to *psycho-cultural* drama. The type of sightings reported has been bound by time, belonging to their historical backdrop. Equally, sightings of Mary have almost exclusively have taken place in predominated Catholic areas. Likewise, fairies have always been associated with northern Europe. [329]

The morally deprived have usually been depicted as physically unattractive. Expressed in movies and literature, the male bald head, like the mad scientist, has been associated with evil. This archetype is also related with aging and death. The bald head is a skin away from the skull. The Old Testament story of Samson' s hair, on the other hand, gave him vitality and strength. [330] Death is also not a pretty sight. With the fear of radiation in the 1950s, photos from Hiroshima' s disaster stunned Americans. Japanese survivors lost their hair and their gums bled. Some recovered from radiation

[328] Rojcewicz, Peter M. "The Men in Black Experience and Tradition: Analogues with Traditional Devil Hypothesis," *Journal of America American Folklore* 100 (April/June 1987): 148-60.

[329] Diane Purkiss, *At the Bottom of the Garden: A Dark History of Fairyland, Hobglobins, and other Troublesome Things*. New York University Press, New York, (2000) 2001; W.Y. Evans-Wentz, *The Fairy in Celtic Countries*. Citadel Press, New York, (1966) 1994; Carolyn White, *A History of Irish Fairies*. Carroll & Graf publishers, New York, (1976) 2005; Katherine Briggs, *The Vanishing People: Study of Traditional Fairy Beliefs*. Routledge, London and New York, (1978) 2003; Janet Bold, *Fairies: Real Encounters with Little People*. Carroll & Graf Publishers, New York, 1997.

[330] tvtropes.org/pmwiki/pmwiki.php/Main/BaldofEvil., retrieved 09/06/2012.

infections, but others died. The disfigured Japanese was a monstrosity and the face of unattractiveness. [331]

Henriksen's essay refers to the Berlin Crisis and the bomb shelter hysteria that gave rise to TV shows with bizarre characters. President Kennedy threatened thermonuclear war if Berlin was broken in half, (the eastern part of the city belonging to the Soviets, while the western portion belonging to the Western forces and the U.S.). Americans began to panic. This fervor led to the urgency to build bomb shelters. The survivalist mode was that of selfishness, everybody out for themselves. Some individuals did say they would stockpile food as well as weapons, and were more than willing to gun down anyone who threatened his small circle of friends and family members. This futuristic scenario was considered bleak. Dozens of magazine articles expressed the revulsion of Americans to such barbaric behavior if there was an outbreak of nuclear war. The response, says Henriksen, was an atomic age counterculture, a movement that was expressed through television. *The Munsters* and *The Addams Family* (both from 1964–66) were successful shows depicting families as oddballs. Herman Munster, the father of his family, is a Frankenstein and his son, Eddie Munster, is a vampire. In the other show, the name of the housewife – Morticia Addams – is a derivative of the word "mortician." She always wears black clothing, is a pale-skinned housewife, a walking corpse. We don't need to describe the rest of the family members to give the reader the sense of ghoulishness these shows were trying to convey. In addition, *The Twilight Zone*, emphasizes Henriksen, speaks of being in another space and time. When one crosses over, the rules of reality change. These

---

[331] Spencer R. Weart, *Nuclear Fear: A History of Images*. The President and Fellows of Harvard College, Boston, 1988, p. 106-11.

types of shows from the 1960s embodied the rebellion of their time. The protagonist breaks free from his villainous role. [332]

Derry calls "The Horror of Armageddon" films that have animal-beast mutants due to radiation. [333] Alfred Hitchcock's *The Birds* (1962), portrays humankind vulnerable to nasty and aggressive winged creatures. In *Them!* (1954), human society has to contend with giant ants, and in *The Beginning of the End* (1957), giant grasshoppers rule the planet. *The Deadly Bees* (1967) and *Eye of the Cat* (1969) have vicious bees and cats, respectively. *Night of the Living Dead* (1968) is a 1960s classic. Japan has *Godzilla* (1954) ruining Tokyo as a symbol of atomic destruction. *Planet of the Apes* (1968), some have argued, depicts the rebellion of an oppressed race. These movies portray the vengeance of nature and the racially oppressed. For example, *Invasion of the Saucer Men* (1957) is the first film "to depict aliens as bug-eyed dwarfs, similar to the Greys." [334]

White Guilt

Barrett's study of hypnosis in popular media reveals the nefarious male controlling his victim, invariably an adult female. [335] She schools us on "horror and science fiction." Hypnosis is utilized by villain Fu

---

Margot A. Henriksen, "The Berlin Crisis, the Bomb Shelter Craze and Bizarre Television: Expressions of an Atomic Bomb Age Counterculture," in Alison M. Scott and Christopher D. Geist, eds., *The Writing on the Cloud: American Confronts the Atomic Bomb*, University Press of America, New York & London, 1997, p. 151-173.

Charles Derry. *Dark Dreams: A Psychological History of the Modern Horror Film*. A.S. Barnes & Company, South Brunswick & New York, 1977, p. 49-84.

Meehan, *Saucer Movies*.

Deirdre Barrett, *Hypnosis and Popular Media*. ABC-CLIO, Inc., Santa Barbara, 2010, chapter 5.

Manchu in several films. In multiple Flash Gordon films, Flash's love, Dale, is hypnotized by the villain. With typical '50s restraint, marriage is always the nefarious goal. Flash inevitably shows up just in time... the white man comes to the rescue.

Racial mixing has been a great fear and hatred. The stereotype of the sex-crazed Negro was portrayed in a very popular film of its day, *The Birth of a Nation* (1915). African Americans were portrayed as arrogant and constantly on the look out to attack white women. In this film, blacks and mulattoes invariably attempt to rape their victims. [336] The lynching of black men in the South was justified to protect white women from black rapists, or more appropriately, alleged black rapists. Southern racists saw black progress (the Reconstruction era) with the hidden intent of interracial mixing. Racist white men saw this as losing their power, the basis of which was symbolized in the bedroom. The notion of owning the black man's body, even in death as he lifelessly hung from the noose and after being charred, was sending the message that despite the abolition of slavery, the black man's body was still owned. [337] This was brutal, indeed. It took a few decades before many youths and young adults expressed their white guilt in the form of outrage.

Alien abduction, of which we argued has no basis in objective reality, is a subjective experience and downright mythological. To the nuts-and-bolts type of people, this argument is not convincing. To skeptics – but more so, students of folklore, mythology, sociology, and the like – should consider that the alien abduction narrative expresses

---

[336] Frank H. Tucker, *The White Conscience*. Frederick Unger Publishing, New York, 1968, p. 56.

[337] Cynthia Carr. *Our Town: A Heartland of Lynching, a Haunted Town, and the Hidden History White America*. Crown Publishers, New York, NY, 2006, p. 51-2.

ownership of the human body by advanced otherworldly, bureaucratic beings. Bureaucracy is monstrous since everyday people are cut off.

The Holocaust was tied with nuclear fears in the early 1960s, together with the element of racism. The American public projected their current fears with the immensity of the scale of the Jews being slaughtered. The Cold War forced white Americans to consider their own evil political system. The oppressive racial segregation policies were an extreme motif during 1950s conformist America. What began was a hunger to expand consciousness, since Americans felt spiritually uprooted by technology and dehumanized by the government's obsession of its anticommunism. [338]

The Cold War, therefore, compelled Americans to look at themselves in relation to their historical enemies. It was not just rival Communist regimes, it was the racial otherness – films and television programs of the 1950s conveying the defeat of that otherness, while American Indians and the Japanese were shown hiding in the shadows, ambushing their enemies through sneak attacks. The war narrative though hardly paid any attention to blacks, although they were making public demands. The movies of the 1950s, which portrayed frontier battles against Native American Indians, parallel the obsession against Communism abroad, not to mention possible Communists from within, as shadowy and ghostly figures under the radar. White Americans were forced to look at their own arrogance, namely that it was they who were the evil other. There is an interesting correlation between the evil alien films and the abuse against African Americans. As the cinema showed evil aliens attacking and battering humans, many

[338] Margot A. Henriksen, *Dr. Strangelove's America: Society and Culture in the Atomic Age,* University of California Press, Berkeley, CA, 1997.

Americans were able to view blacks attacked in diners or mauled by police-rioting dogs, as shown on televisions throughout the country. This collective anxiety also included the hidden underworld – a realm filled with spies, traitors, and Communists.[339]

Elements of supernatural evil were hiding and were ready to pounce on innocent victims. The Men in Black, as was noted, filled the role of sinister evil men. Although these agents are all corporeal, there is an element of their perceived magical abilities. In this respect, sneaky natives and demon-like Japanese are given supernatural-like powers.

The injustices of bigotry from the past are preferred to be forgotten and buried. Steele's concept of "White Blindness" is defined as dissociating the target of racial oppression by identifying a substitute target that symbolizes racism. Steele gives the example of blackface. White men who paint their faces black during staged performances soften the emotional impact of white guilt since the white audience depersonalizes black individualism.[340] What is suggested is that such sentiments take place unconsciously. Unfortunately, Steele did not give us additional examples of White Blindness. We already belabored the fact how the majority of alien abductees have been Caucasian. Are they also practicing White Blindness? We just do not know. Alien abductees, however, were born into a civilization at a particular time period, where they witnessed unprecedented *progress* during a period of religious uncertainty. Not exactly trusting old-time religion, abductees wound up reconciling with an

---

[339] Tom Englehardt, second ed. *The End of Victory Culture: Cold War America and the Disillusioning of a Generation*, University of Massachusetts Press, Amherst, MA, 2007, p. 4-130.
[340] Shelby Steele. *White Guilt: How Blacks and Whites Together Destroyed the Promise of the Civil Rights Era*, HarperCollins Publishers, New York, NY, 2006, p. 128-9.

alien race (or races) in symbolic fashion. In the context of postmodern regression, this symbolic position of submissive rape speaks very loudly, as though saying that the Third World will rise up to take revenge. We could certainly argue that there is something to the notion of White Blindness when abductees substituted an alien race for non-white peoples behaving as the colonizers of the human race.

The depiction of aliens, whether through abduction or on film, arose right after the war. Entering the twentieth century, the white man had reached his apex. The last frontier became outer space. This upward mobility, however, was bound to lose momentum. By the end of World War II, when Japan suffered the destruction of two atomic bombs, began the downhill slide of the white man' s hegemony. [341]

The messianic Aryan aliens - with their blond, blue-eyed, and other attractive attributes - were the contactees' favorite aliens during the 1950s. Only they could save Earth from its own peril. These representations are expressions of youth, beauty, and vitality, qualities embodying love. It is a vibrancy that is the opposite of the ghastly and grotesque destruction of the atomic bomb. This anti-nuclear war movement was the springboard of the counterculture movement of the 1960s.

The Civil Rights Movement began as a pacifist struggle in the early 1960s, but in the latter decade it became radical and militant, a period when other minorities took advantage. Native Americans, Hispanic Americans, and Asian-Americans saw themselves as disenfranchised. By the 1970s, some minorities began to receive dividends in all fronts. Most particularly TV audiences began to see minorities portrayed in a favorable light for the first time. African Americans

---

[341] Frank H. Tucker, *The White Conscience*. Chapter 7.

and others were previously playing roles inferior to whites, [342] thereby white alien abductees are inferior to aliens. It should be clear how abductees have been role-playing a fantasy drama of submissiveness, with their captors being not from Earth.

The exotic and the extraordinary, including racial otherness from outer space, were now here to stay. Five years before the TV movie, *The UFO Incident*, concerning the Hills' alien kidnapping, the ABC TV network started airing movies with alien themes. NBC took their turn by airing *The UFO Incident* in October of 1975. [343] This sense of the exotic and strangeness of aliens began with flying saucer movies of the 1950s. The TV show, *The Outer Limits*, added this motif into their episodes, including the ones that aired right before the Hill's hypnotic therapy sessions. The image of the alien sketched by Barney under hypnosis, which he borrowed from *The Outer Limits*, would influence others. Fuller's novel begot *The UFO Incident* and in 1977, Steven Spielberg used Barney's sketch for his Greyish, glowing small-statured aliens in the blockbuster film, *Close Encounters of the Third Kind*. Hence, it is vital to point out alien abduction reports skyrocketed right after the movie premiered. Finally, this served as inspiration for Whitney Strieber and his bestselling book, *Communion* in 1987, Strieber's alien in the front cover of his novel serving as the prototype of the Greys. [344] The Greys,

---

[342] Thomas Adams Upchurch. *Race Relations in the United States, 1960 – 1980*. Greenwood Press, Wesport, CT & London, 2008.

[343] For examples, Meehan cites *The Love War* (1970), *Night Slaves* (1970), *The People* (1971), *The Disappearance of Flight 412* (1974), *The Stranger Within* (1974), and *The Night that Panicked America* (1975). See Meehan, p. 148.

[344] See Susan A. Clancy. *Abducted: How People Come to Believe They Were Kidnapped By Aliens*, Harvard University Press, Cambridge & London, 2005, p. 94-9.

partly stemming from white guilt and nuclear annihilation, were iconic throughout the late 1980s and 1990s as ghostly invaders.

The Spiritual Side of the Counterculture

We are still discussing the subject of white guilt, the kind of which is expressed through alternative spirituality. Spiritual awakening was a movement of the 1960s. It was established to break free from what was perceived as science's limited laws, to protect the weak, as well as turning away from the traditional religious bureaucracy. There was great interest in Eastern religions. This was the response against the rise of secularism. Moreover, some viewed Christianity as the white man's tool of oppression. As black leaders were busy fighting for equal rights, the leftist youth mobilized against the Vietnam War. By the middle of the 1960s, this type of activism began to have mystical qualities; there was a fusion of philosophy, political ideology, and the search for something spiritually new. Although racism was perceived by many whites as tyrannical and military intervention as evil, the counterculture movement wanted to move away from Manichaeistic dualism – encompassing all religions as a single whole of different existences. These developments, some have claimed, became the key to defining a new era, from modernism to postmodernism. [345]

In understanding the invasion theme of UFOlogy, the alien abduction narrative became more pervasive as more and more Anglo-Americans began to sympathize with non-Western type of religions. Many whites flocked to Third World countries for a variety of

---

[345] Robert S. Ellwood. *The Sixties Spiritual Awakening: American Religion Moving from Modern to Postmodern*, Rutgers University Press, New Brunswick, NJ, 1994.

reasons. Some realized they needed an answer to fill their spiritual emptiness, despite economic success.

Western tourists have had the tendency to romanticize poverty-stricken, non-Western countries. Even if such poor people do not have material wealth, Western tourists perceive them as innocent individuals, who have strong family ties and living in a tension-free reality. However, Westerners have also expressed guilt. It bothered them to see how poor men, women, and children can live in such impoverished conditions. Young people walking about without shoes and the ghastly sight of the deformed have all contributed to white guilt. [346] New Ager and alien abduction researcher John Mack blamed Western material science for the problems of spiritual emptiness and environmental pollutions. Mack makes it clear that Westerners (we could also add assimilated minorities) cut themselves off from their spiritual roots. [347]

Young men from Europe's middle classes of the 1960s and 1970s, known as backpackers, packed their belongings to trek the world in search of adventure. In the late 60s, hippies joined them. Many went to the Far East looking for spiritual experiences, most often through promiscuous sex and drug use. [348] Von Däniken and his version of the Ancient Astronaut Theory rose around this time. The 1970s was when many saw Western Civilization as spiritually bankrupt. The paradox with fusing Christianity with non-Western religions and adding ancient aliens as responsible

---

[346] Ton Van Egmond. *Understanding Western Tourists in Developing Countries*, NHTV Breda University of Applied Sciences, The Netherlands, 2007, p. 83-8.

[347] see Bridget Brown, *They Know us Better Than We Know Ourselves: The History of Politics and Alien Abduction*. New York University Press, New York & London, 2007, 161.

[348] Egmond, *Understanding Western Tourists in Developing Countries*, p. 89-93.

for the birth of humanity, shows the unwillingness to accept that Buddhism or Native American religions were created by human beings who did not need any help from intergalactic outsiders. From this angle, the notion of ancient aliens wreak of arrogance. According to the alien abduction storyline, however, ancient aliens appealed to many believers since it suggests that morality and spirituality are superior to the capitalistic ways of the West.

Therefore, white man's religion nor his materialism is the answer. The need to escape into an alternate reality in this context reflects the search for happiness. As such, Native American spirituality was symbolized by radical leftists as a staunch movement fighting the status quo. [349] Inspired by the Civil Rights Movement, white guilt was a manifestation of white hippies trying emulating the Indians by living off the land. Whites were also particularly fond of vision quests. The hippies were intrigued by peyote and other drugs and the appeal of that inner voyage by the early 1970s. Such aggressive insularism is, the alien abduction narrative suggests, is connected with globalization. [350] As the speeds of planetary wholeness come into full view, one reaction is to recoil and hide within the depths of one's mind, in whatever capacity suits one's individual needs.

If alien abduction reports are submissive acts, then what is needed is the very opposite of submission. This is when the hypnotist comes into play, an authority figure whose subjects' altered states of consciousness are easy pickings. These are also insular actions. The imagination of both,

[349] Phillip Jenkins. *Dream Catchers: How Mainstream America Discovered Native Spirituality.* Oxford University Press, Oxford & New York, 2004, p. 154-174.
[350] Brown, *They Know Us Better Than We Know Ourselves*, p. 172.

abductee and hypnotist, serve as a platform, and a dream state matrix to engage in actions where rules are different, in lieu of the real world. This sounds familiar to the rules of the silver screen and television. The abductee is the invaded, the hypnotist is the invader. As such, the tube viewer acts similar to an abductee. He or she watches TV while sitting or lying down. It is certainly common that televised imagery can infiltrate our dreams and nightmares. We saw this with the Hills' abduction case, let alone how visual and print culture influenced the rise of alien abduction accounts.

For example, some, namely David Icke, fervently argue how alien encounters have been deliberately portrayed through telecommunications. Thus, the series *V,* televised from 1984 through 1985, is premised on friendly, human-looking aliens. As a setup, the plot of the aliens is revealed; the human faces they wore were masks, underneath were reptilian and sinister-looking, evil aliens bent, as vampires, on sucking the resources of Earth dry. In Icke's demonology, the type of aliens abducting humans belong to reptilian species. [351] Even this movie, let alone Icke's demonology, coincide strongly with the counterculture movement's discontent, a disenchantment already expressed through H. G. Wells' *War of the Worlds* in 1898. Even if implicitly, Hopkins was also influenced by Wells' invasive aliens, and no doubt, Hollywood would also be influenced during the 1950s, a few years before Hopkins' life-altering experience.

Bud Hopkins grew up during the counterculture movement and would become the most influential alien abduction researcher. Hopkins was originally a

---

[351] Christopher Partridge, *Understanding the Dark Side: Western Demonology, Satanic Panics and Alien Abduction*. Chester Academic Press, Chester, UK, 2006, p. 46-7.

credentialed artist. What changed his life was when he saw a daylight disc in 1964. Originally uninterested in UFOs, Hopkins became a voracious reader about the subject after his UFO sighting. Hopkins became inspired to investigate alien encounters in 1975 when he spoke to his local liquor store owner, George O'Barski, who told him he saw a grounded otherworldly craft and its occupants digging into the soil, placing the samples into a bag while driving one evening. Hopkins wrote about this sighting in *The Village Voice* and the article was republished in *Cosmopolitan Magazine*. He started receiving phone calls from curious readers, wondering if they also were forcibly taken by advanced aliens. Hopkins went on to investigate on alien abductions from here on. He would allow certified hypnotists to digress possible victims, until he started doing so on his own. [352]

What is suspect is Hopkins' timing to start investigating UFOs, during the same year *The UFO Incident* was aired on NBC. Hopkins would eventually meet Whitney Strieber. Their corroboration led to the writing and publication of *Communion (1987)*, the catalyst for the explosion of alien abduction claims.

Japan-Phobia

We think it's not improper to link the increase of alien abduction reports to the rise of Japan bashing during the late 1970s. This has a lot to do with political and economic conditions when Japan's economy began to out produce the American economy. By 1982, the national collective became aware of this

---

[352] Sean Casteel. "A Journalist Remembers Budd Hopkins," Budd Hopkins Memorial Piece, www.seancasteel.com/A-Journalist-Remembers-Budd-Hopkins.htm, retrieved on 09/13/2012.

(five years before Strieber's *Communion*). Japan and America cleaved further apart in 1985, the year when the Japanese yen increased dramatically, while the American dollar dropped in value (two years before *Communion*). A multinational Japanese company was as a foreign power, a Cold War impersonal force with the purpose of technological conquest. Already occurring in the 1970s, the American economy hopped out of this decade only for its relations with Japan to fall further away. [353] We should make it clear that the Greys were not yet the dominant alien type until after Strieber's *Communion*. We will see how that novel was influenced by Japan-phobia.

Because of being so different, at least in the eyes of Westerners, Japan's economic might was suspect. The yellow peril further increased with high-intensity in 1941, after the Pearl Harbor sneak attack. By the 1950s, after Japan's World War II surrender, the Communist Chinese and the Communist North Koreans replaced the Japanese as the new yellow peril. Japan bashing blossomed in the 1980s until the mid-1990s (the time of Japan's unprecedented economic growth). What emerged were irrational fears of a Japanese economic invasion of the U.S. [354] The outspoken American criticism against Japan wasn't monopolized by economists and politicians, popular culture also jumping into the band wagon. From novels, plays, TV movies, and Hollywood films Japan was conveyed as an economic giant, a technological machine whose products were superior to America's. [355]

Japan bashing became noticeable by the late 1970s. In 1975, James Clavell published *Shōgun*, which was made into a TV miniseries in 1980. The

---

[353] Bill Emmott. *Japanphobia: The Myth of the Invincible Japanese*, Time Books, New York, 1992, see chapters one through 3.
[354] Narelle Morris. *Japan-Bashing: Anti-Japanese Since the 1980s*, Routledge, New York, NY, 2011, see chapters one through three.
[355] Ibid., see chapter six.

journalists of the 1980s were writing about the threat Japanese posed to America. Within its consciousness was the anticipation of the 50th anniversary of the Pearl Harbor attack in 1991. *Rising Sun*, both the novel (1992) and the movie version (1993), employed the Japanese as invaders of the U.S. by means of business conquest. In Michael Crichton's novel, the Japanese are technologically savvy, behave in stealth fashion, and are sexual savages who crave to have violent sex with white women. Additional criticism that followed made the Japanese soulless, sexually repressed monsters. Indeed, American novelists were expressing their fears of Japanese revenge for losing World War II. To understand the alien abduction myth, one must recognize the social developments of the latter part of the twentieth century.

The Greys were developed by the popular media, right here on our own planet. As it turns out, the alien from the episode, "The Bellero Shield," and the alien from in *Evil Brain from Outer Space*, a Japanese film imported in 1964 was designed by the very same person. The talented designer was sculptor and artist Wah Ming Chang, a Chinese American born in Hawaii, who was hired for his cinematic creativity.[356] Chang, no doubt, hit a nerve, and there is also no doubt the Asian facial features would work. The racial other merged with demons of old.

The Grey Bedroom Visitor

An Updated Ghost Story

Supernatural beings became secularized. In the mood of the new era, the paranormal had to be repackaged

---

[356] Martin Kottmeyer. "The Eyes that Spoke," www.CSiCop.org/sb/show/eyes_that_spoke/, retrieved on 09/15/2012.

to fit into the new mode of thinking. What used to be the incubi, the succubi, vampires, fairies, and such developed into aliens in the twentieth century. Whitney Strieber's impact with his novel *Communion* (1987) was enormous in American society, Western Europe, and other parts of the world.

The living are inventors of the supernatural and the type of beings encountered depend on the current cultural setting and the historical circumstances. The kind of societies human beings have influence motifs of the ghost story. As culture changes, so does the texture of the paranormal. [357]

Whitney Strieber admits to reading literature about nocturnal bedroom visitors, including Betty and Barney's story, [358] borrowing the motif of the Japanese-looking alien from Fuller's book. Strieber's aliens have a lot to do with his millennial fears:

> I may want powerful visitors to appear, to save a world that I'm pretty sure is in serious trouble. I'd spent the past three years working on books about war and environmental collapse...Maybe the idea of visitors coming along and saving our necks was more appealing to me.... [359]

Strieber compares the dominance of the aliens to human dominance over nature. The idea of a slaughterhouse or the study of monkeys by scientists, killing them so that their brains can be studied are two examples of reverse human colonization. According

---

[357] Ronald C. Finucane, *Appearances of the Dead: A Cultural History of Ghosts*, Junction Books, London, UK, 1982; Ronald C. Finucane, *Ghosts: Appearances of the Dead and Cultural Transformation*, Prometheus Books, Amherst, NY, 1996; P.G. Maxwell-Stuart, *Ghosts: A History of Phantoms*, Ghouls and Other Spirits of the Dead, Tempus Publishing Ltd., Gloucester-Shire, UK, 2006.

[358] Whitley Strieber, *Communion: A True Story*, HarperCollins Publishers, New York, 1987, p. 42.

[359] Ibid., p. 49.

to Strieber the aliens look like insects.[360] We already discussed some of the 1950s films concerning the attack of these giant creatures, monstrosities poisoned by radiation and whose only goal was to destroy human society.

Not only is Strieber's imagination very vivid, it is also off-color. He became a movie buff at a young age and as well as a voracious reader. He became a writer, using his imagination in horror-fantasy genre. Strieber is an ideal hypnotic subject. He was already practicing meditation, combining his alien abduction experiences with Hinduism, Taoism, Zen, and the like. The intensity of nuclear arms buildup and the response of the anti-nuclear movement against such escalation of weapons of mass destruction[361] had an intense bearing on Strieber's imagination.

There are three books by Strieber that paint the end of the world scenario. In *Nature's End: The Consequences of the Twentieth Century* (1986), Strieber and his co-author present a dismal picture of future history. In the twenty-first century, Earth has way too many people.[362] Extraordinarily resembling the intergalactic interbreeding program, the novel

---

[360] Ibid., p. 102-04.

[361] Christian Peterson, *Ronald Reagan and Antinuclear Movements in the United States and Western Europe, 1981-1987*, The Edwin Mellen Press, Lewiston, NY and Queens, Ontario, 2003; Ronald E. Pavaski, *Return to Armageddon: The United States and the Nuclear Arms Race, 1981-1999*, Oxford University Press, New York, p. 14-44; Andrew Rojecki, *Silencing the Opposition: Antinuclear Movements and the Media in the Cold War*, University of Illinois Press, Chicago, 1999, p. 107-158; Robert D. Holsworth, *Let Your Life Speak: A Study of Politics, Religion, and Antinuclear Weapons Activism*, The University of Wisconsin Press, Madison, 1989; Milton S. Katz, *Ban the Bomb: A History of SANE, the Committee for a Sane Nuclear Policy, 1957-1985*, Greenwood Press, New York & London, 1986, Chs. 6 and 7.

[362] Whitley Strieber and James W. Kunetka, *Nature's End: The Consequences of the Twentieth Century*, Warner Books, New York, 1986.

describes genetically enhanced intelligent children as the result of their parents providing fertilized eggs for illegal genetic manipulations, creating super-intelligent freaks incapable of joining normal human society. [363] *Nature' s End* was published one year before *Communion* (1987). For some reason, Strieber identifies with a lonely soul. In *Wolf of Shadows* (1985), an alienated wolf overcomes his strangeness by overpowering the leader of the pack right after nuclear war. Nuclear winter sets in as Wolf of Shadows guides his fellow wolves, a lady scientist (his human friend), and her daughter across the Minnesota wilderness in search of food to survive. Strieber' s message is that we have taken the Native American respect for the land for granted. To Strieber the wolves are not the savages. Rather, humans are the savages. [364]

But of all the novels, it is *Warday* (1984) that has a lot to do with environmental catastrophe and alien abductions. [365] The date the novel is set in the future. On October 27, 1988, the Soviets launch a nuclear sneak attack, devastating the borough of Queens and Brooklyn. As for Washington D.C., the nation' s capital was totally destroyed. With the death of the President, the Federal government was beheaded. Whitley Strieber and his friend, James W. Kunetka, the main characters, set out to trek the country to gather information on post-war America. The initial destruction of the bombs caused tens of millions to perish, with tens of thousands to follow in the coming weeks because of mortal radiation exposure and additional hundreds of thousands in coming years due to delayed cancer developments.

---

[363] Ibid., p. 277.

[364] Whitley Strieber, *Wolf of Shadows*, Alfred A. Knopf Inc., New York, 1985.

[365] Whitley Strieber and James W. Kunetka, *Warday and the Journey Onward*. Holt, Rienehart and Winston, New York, 1984.

Lastly, The Cincinnati Flu wiped out tens of millions across the globe.

With the American infrastructure crippled, Los Angeles became the new capital since California was the least affected state. However, Mexico's economy plunged into chaos, its worst in history, prompting millions of illegal immigrants to cross the border. Some states began abandoning the Union to become their own independent nations. Since San Antonio was also effectively eradicated, Aztlan, a Hispanic state, rose up to claim its sovereignty - claiming the Southwest, from southern Texas, northern Mexico, New Mexico, and Arizona. The coalition of Native tribes included the Navajo, Hopi, Apache, and the Pueblo. These areas, irate because of their political and historical oppression, expelled the Anglos. Aztlan's main goal was to recapture California, an area formerly belonging to Mexico.

Aztlan was recognized by many nations, including by Japan. In this fictional account, the Japanese play a pivotal role. Strieber used current events while writing *Warday*, incorporating Japan-phobia into his novel. For one thing, Aztlan heavily relied on Japanese electronics[366] and the Japanese also provided medicine to this new rebellious nation. [367] Aztlan's currency is backed up by the Japanese yen, [368] and El Paso also has many Japanese-made Toyotas. [369] Reaching California, Strieber and Kutka find out that the Japanese were hired to service that state's railroad system, the magnetically operated bullet train. [370] They interview an economist who says Japan may be a superpower in the near future. [371] Lastly, the

[366] Ibid., p. 74-5.
[367] Ibid., p. 85.
[368] Ibid, p. 88.
[369] Ibid, p. 100.
[370] Ibid, p. 172-4.
[371] Ibid, p. 191.

Japanese are the wealthiest of all Californians. [372] The theme of Japan-phobia should be clear. Although it has elements of racism, there is a trace of white guilt. The Greys, for that reason, serve as haunting reminders.

The survivors of the atomic bomb dropped on Hiroshima, says Lifton, lived the rest of their lives with guilt. Immediately after the dropping of the Bomb, there were women and children dying in the city's streets. Radiation exposure made the survivors' hair fall out, bleed from the rectum or mouth, and odd marks in their bodies appeared. The dying victims' bodies became skeletal. For those who had already died, after days and weeks, their rotting corpses reached a mature stage of decomposition. The infected environment, the perception went, was a deathtrap, a city that was slowing dying. In a blink of an eye though, Hiroshima turned itself around. Still in all, casualties surviving the Bomb were stigmatized; they were cut off from their own society. The odd bodily and burn marks reminded other Japanese citizens of the ghastly, not exactly subconscious fear of death. Lifton's extensive psychiatric study of Japanese atomic bomb survivors led him to conclude they were suffering from "death guilt" and "death anxiety." In order to emotionally deal with the trauma, they did so through "psychic numbing." Lifton stresses we are all survivors of Hiroshima, including survivors of an imagined future nuclear holocaust. [373]

Part of that survivor's guilt, Lifton continues, is haunting from the supernatural. The "Homeless Dead" are spirits or ghosts who died suddenly and may be phantoms, wandering far from

---

[372] Ibid, p. 194.

[373] Robert J. Lifton, *Death in Life: Survivors of Hiroshima*. Random House, New York, 1967.

home. They are dangerous to the living and they can cause terror or physical harm. "Hungry Ghosts" from the Far East are like Eastern European vampires; they suck the blood of their victims in order to live and perform the proper rituals calm the hostile ghosts. Conversely, ancestor souls can be elevated to god status thereafter. [374]

Meehan says, "Strieber's (*Communion*) read like a modern-day ghost story, and was compelling enough to become # 1 New York Times best-seller by May of 1987." [375] The 1950s flying saucer films, also says Meehan, are horror movies, the invasive aliens have supernatural characteristics, including the fear of Communism as well as the fear of nuclear annihilation. Hollywood took the notion of "brainwashing" from the Korean War to convey hostile aliens taking over people's minds (a 1950s version of demon possession). Although many of these invaders came from Mars (formerly the Roman god of war), they are brittle and weak (very similar to the Greys, features of which resemble Jewish Holocaust survivors and survivors from Hiroshima). These films portray the aliens' planet as dying from warfare and ecological disaster, with the intent to enslave humanity. The Greys also take on vampire characteristics. Rather than sucking blood, they steal eggs and semen. They can make their captives act like zombies and are also capable of stealth invasion. Some of these aliens operate like spirits; they can resurrect the dead to attack the living in order to achieve world conquest. [376]

Vallée looked to Japanese culture where he suggests there might be a connection. He mentions

[374] Ibid, p. 492-3.
[375] Meehan, *Saucer Movies*, p. 229.
[376] Ibid, p. 33-104.

small statues of human beings that were carved in a prior Japanese era. He said they have short hands and large horizontal eyes, closely resembling the Greys of today. [377] Vallée is referring to what are called Dogu clay figurines, exclusive to the Jomon era (10,000 BCE to 300 BCE). The Japanese of that period made small humanoids. Their eyes are large and have slits going across. They are not slanted. The arms and legs are short as well and these figurines were dressed in elaborate, majestic fashion, seemingly looking like ancient Samurai outfits. It is theorized they may have served for religious purposes, either for good health or for funeral rites. It is no accident these figurines look like the Greys, when, as we have been arguing, the Greys have exaggerated features of Japanese atomic bomb survivors. More importantly, the Dogu clay figurines are reminiscent of the Greys in relation to Ancient Astronaut Theorists since the Japanese of the Jomon period made these figures to resemble themselves. The meaning of such figurines, in the eyes of some Ancient Astronaut Theorists, is death by nuclear means. What is more acceptable is not the meaning of the Dogu figurines given by ancient alien enthusiasts. The proper recognition and context is acknowledging the postmodern day perception of some ancient alien theorists, not the Dogu figurines from Jomon Japan. Meaning given to the same religious objects may not have the same meaning for someone else.

---

[377] Jacques Vallée, *Dimensions: A Casebook of Alien Contact*. Souvenir Press, London, 1988, p. 10.

10

The New Millennium

The latter part of the twentieth century witnessed a frenzy of UFO, and alien-related encounters. It seems as the new millennium approached, the last decade of the twentieth century would outdo the 1950s. There were sightings everywhere. But more so, there were alien abductions. Many abductees, despite experiencing rape under hypnosis (even through conscious recall), saw the experience as a spiritually transcending one. The theme of the end-times remains the same. The fear of technology, most especially the Bomb, has been a feature of post-Hiroshima.

Contactees Await the New Millennium

By the 1970s, the contactee movement slowed down significantly. We recall the Ancient Astronaut Theory taking off in this decade. It is not so easy to determine whether the Ancient Astronaut Theory inspired contacteeism to decline. What was more noticeable was how UFO religiosity went through a respite. Many contactee groups folded while others had membership populations drop off. Renewed interest took place during the latter part the 1970s. As the new millennium approached, new UFO religions were started. It was believed that a new era would begin with the landing of a spaceship to take the chosen ones. Part of this millennial frenzy was, indeed, the Ancient Astronaut Theory. Belief in ancient aliens became very popular throughout the 1990s and even throughout the early 2000s.

The Aetherius Society, for example, is not a new UFO religion. The Aetherius Society's anticipation of the new millennium is one of ushering in the age of science. It will be inseparable with religion. They say evidence of ancient UFOs can found in the Bible and other religious texts. As stated earlier, George King claimed to have received communication from interplanetary masters and was given wisdom for the scientific age. He was also told that life on planet Earth is millions of years old. King backs up his claim by referencing sacred texts that suggest old civilizations ended due to atomic weapons.

Humankind has been getting help from aliens since ancient times. Nuclear explosions wiped out one of their planets. Out of sympathy, the aliens want to make sure that the same thing would not happen again. Nonetheless, the Aetherius Society believes in reincarnation. They also believe there is a spiritual energy crisis. Prayer sessions are conducted to gather energy. Other forms of preparations took place for the new millennium. [378]

The Unarius Academy of Science is another UFO religion that has been around since the 1950's. Founder Ernest Norman took an astral flight to the planet Venus where the planet is more advanced and spirituality developed. [379] Scientists, though, considered this planet a dangerous place. Clairvoyants Ernest and Ruth Norman found the Academy in 1954. Although Mr. Norman died in 1971, his wife continued the group until 1993 when she died. This

[378] George King and Richard Lawrence, *Contact With the Gods From Space: Pathway to the New Mellennium*. The Aetherius Society, 1996.
[379] Ernest L. Norman. *The Voice of Venus*. Unarius Academy of Science (1956) 1995.

UFO group is based out on El Cajon, a suburb of San Diego. Heaven-on-Earth will be built once a UFO lands in 2001. Members are taught to channel extraterrestrials. They also are encouraged to believe in past lives. Happiness would soon arrive. The New Age will be brought in when the spaceship lands, although a UFO never landed.

Since Ruth Norman thought highly of reincarnation, she believed her husband Ernest Norman was the reincarnation of Jesus. Ernest was the main channel, while the students were the sub-channels. Ruth became Uriel when she was crowned "Queen Uriel" after she received a transmission of a celebration taking place on planet Eros. Unarians had various mythologies explaining origins of Earth and relations with other planets. They believe God is the ultimate being and the aliens are the messengers. Group myths are borrowed by television and movies. Characters therein are identified with other details of past lives that are claimed by watching dramas.

There are various beliefs among the Unarians. They believe they are Aryan aliens, light-skinned aliens who enlighten indigenous populations in the universe. Elder brothers teach in celestial realms where seven planets reside. There is a higher spiritual frequency there. When out-of-body experiences occur, it is believed that it is possible to travel to other planets. To the Unarians, there are many levels in astral worlds; high planets are heavenly and lower planets are dark or hellish. Sometimes, dark entities come to Earth and possess Earthling bodies. The Unarians believe that extraterrestrials have done extensive traveling, such as Martians, who settled in Atlantis then migrated back to Mars. Given the different layers of this otherworldly experience, it has Dante written all over it. Of more significance, the Unarians believed in millennium change. They believed 9/11 was part of the prophecy of changes to come. 2001 had arrived but there were no alien landings. The Unarians were not disappointed. They believed violence kept the aliens away. Unarian Academy of Science is a UFO religion that continues to believe in aliens despite the elusiveness of their objective existence. Then again, giant leaps of faith has always been the hallmark of all religions.

The Ashtar Command is another long-surviving UFO religion. They are a channeling UFO group which was founded by contactee George Van Tassel in 1952 when he spoke with the alien Ashtar. Thousands would attend the Giant Rock Convention every Friday night to see Van Tassel speak with Ashtar. Another contactee, Robert Short, began getting messages as well, but Van Tassel believed they were phony messages, resulting in their friendship falling apart. Other individuals also began getting messages from Ashtar as well. They began combining spiritualism with extraterrestrial contact. By the 1970's, the Ashtar movement began dropping off, yet interest would rise in the 1990s with contactee "Tuella," or Thelma B. Terrill.[380]

Onc individual, a businessman, began receiving messages from Ashtar, commander of a big spaceship orbiting Earth. These transmissions supposedly took place in 1980. Ashtar gave warnings of things to come. The aliens had arrived to teach since we live in dangerous times. According to the channeled messages, there are underground cities on Earth where many races throughout the universe are keeping an eye on our violent planet. Part of Ashtar's spirituality education is to teach how to tap into psychic abilities so that the aliens can be spoken with.

---

[380] James R. Lewis, ed. *Encyclopedic Sourcebook of UFO Religions*. Prometheus Books. Anherst, New York, 2003. See "The Ashtar Command."

Since science and technology fouled up the world, a New World Order will take place. Evil will entrench itself as the new malignant empire. There are malevolent beings in the military and the government. There are also interplanetary pirates stealing minerals from Earth. Despite this UFOs are a symbol of hope, since world domination will be attempted. [381] This is one instance among many where the UFO Conspiracy Theory is intertwined with UFO spirituality.

Rather than seeing the dark side of things, Tuella herself believes that Ashtar is a loving being. When the space landings occur, they will take the chosen ones. She channeled these messages a few years before the year 2000. [382] Before the grand exodus from this planet, according to Tuella's channelings with Ashtar, Earth will undergo vast changes, politically, culturally, socially, and such. [383] For example, global warming, albeit a secular form of millennialism, was incorporated by some who promote alternative spirituality. [384]

---

[381] Timothy Green Beckley. *New World Order: Prophecies from Space: A Channeled by the Ashtar Command*. Innerlight Publications. New Brunswick, NJ, 1990.

[382] Tuella. *UFO's To Assist in the "Great Exodus" of Human Souls Off This Planet: Project World Evacuation*. Inner Light Publications. New Brunswick, NJ, 1993.

[383] Tuella. *Cosmic Prophecies For the Year 2,000: A Channeled Symposium of What We Can Expect For the Rest of the Decade*, Inner Light Publications New Brunswick, NJ, 1994.

[384] On this note, I remember seeing psychic Sylvia Brown on an episode on the *Oprah Winfrey Show* some years ago, sometime before 2012. Brown told Oprah's audience how she expected drastic changes to come, for example weather related, as omens just in time for a new golden era. And as the camera focused on some audience members, it was noticeable how some were spooked out of their wits. Brown assured the audience it will be nothing like the movie. If only they hear me watching TV that Brown's speculations are nothing short of horse shit.

For this reason, channeling has become very popular. [385] Ethnographer Diana Tumminia shares her knowledge of the Unarius Academy of Science. Members are encouraged to channel the Space Brothers for awareness and wisdom. Whether through dreams, channelings, past-life therapy, visualizations, and other forms of mental activities, these contactee members can gain infinite consciousness by contacting higher beings, higher dimensions, and higher frequencies. As Tumminia puts it, it does not matter if these activities do not fall under the scope of empiricism, because the Unarians go by their own "science." [386] What is striking, unlike the contactees of the 1950s and unlike the Raëlians, as the new millennium approached was the insular forms of alien spirituality and UFO religions.

Conforming to the beat of its own drum is the bizarre UFO religion/cult, Heaven's Gate, was based in a suburb of San Diego. The neighborhood was filled with stench. Authorities responded to a call and found 39 bodies of young men inside a million-dollar home. They had committed suicide. They were wearing dark pants and tennis shoes. They appeared no older than 24 years of age. Officials speculated the dead members belonged to a doomsday/cultist sect. [387] Since

---

[385] I remember meeting two channelers, one of which is a co-member of a writer's group that I belong to in New York City. After I told her I was UFO skeptic, as she nicely put it, "I belong on the other side." Before I met her, however, it was about the winter of 2011 while drinking coffee at a Starbuck's I met a self-proclaimed channeler who told me she channeled John Mack, the alien abduction researcher/hypnotherapist who died by getting hit by a car (or, perhaps a truck). The channeler told me how she expected foul play regarding Mack's untimely death.

[386] Diana G. Tumminia, "In the Dreamtime of the Saucer People: Sense-Making and Interpretive Boundaries in a Contactee Group." In Diana G. Tumminia, ed., *Alien Worlds: Social and Religious Dimensions of Extraterrestrial Contact*. Syracuse University Press, Syracuse, 2007, Ch. 5.

[387] Todd S. Purdum. *New York Times*, "39 Men Found at San Diego Estate in Apparent Suicide." March 27, 1997, p. A1.

members all had short hair, it was believed they were all men. Later, it was found that women were among the dead as well.

Explanations of all kinds rushed in. The suicide had come after the first day of spring, a comparison to other suicides. Right after the fall equinox, 53 of the Solar Temple committed suicide. Sixteen more committed suicide right after the winter solstice. However, there was no link with the Heaven's Gate cult. [388] It would become clear the cult was not motivated by seasonal change. Rather, the impending arrival of a comet passing over Earth was the inspiration.

Upon further investigation, the UFO cult started in 1975 in Houston by a platonic couple, Marshall Herff Applewhite and Bonnie Lu Nettles. Mr. Applewhite referred to himself on the group's Internet site as Do, the musical tone, while Ms. Nettles, who already died more than a decade before, was referred to as Ti. The cult isolated itself since they thought the world was corrupt and evil. The only way to salvation was to rid oneself of the body, traveling by the soul and arriving on board the spaceship flying behind the Hale-Bopp comet. Documents left behind indicated that Applewhite and Nettles were representatives of an extraterrestrial realm called the Kingdom of Heaven. Heaven's Gate believed one must be detached from money, sex, and family life. Economics, politics, and religious institutions were under control of evil forces. Applewhite and Nettles believed they were extraterrestrials that came to Earth to teach the proper laws of the universe. [389]

---

[388] Gustav Niehbuhr. *New York Times*, "Deaths at Season's Change Echo Suicides." March 28, 1997, p. B15.
[389] Gustav Niehbuhr. *New York Times*, "On the Furthest Fringes of Millennium." March 28, 1997.

Heaven's Gate members said farewell in videotapes as they were "shedding their containers." Their souls were being transported to the spaceship. Investigating authorities believed swallowing toxins induced the mass suicide. The different levels of decomposition indicated that the suicides took place in waves. [390] The 24 dead members were found lying down on their beds with sheets covering them. The last two to go tucked in their fellow members, but there was no one to tuck in the last two. As the two lay dead on their beds, they were not as tucked as the previous 22 were. Thus, all suicidal members of this cult were going home to be one with the cosmos, a belief extracted from Judeo-Christian roots; the soul ascends to heaven when one dies.

Heaven's Gate was started by Marshall Herf Applewhite. He was a music teacher at an Episcopal church in Houston. That changed about 1972. He was fired because of his homosexuality from the University of St. Thomas and checked himself into a psychiatric hospital to cure himself of what he believed was a sexual disease. He met a nurse, Bonnie Lu Nettles, who dabbled in astrology. They had a platonic relationship and went off together to find new converts. It was sometime afterwards that Mr. Applewhite, who preached androgyny, castrated himself. At least five others in the cult did the same. [391]

Applewhite instilled the belief that gods, who created the Kingdom of Heaven, planted souls. At the end of an epoch, they are to return to heaven in outer space lead by a representative.

---

[390] Todd S. Purdum, New York Times, "Videotapes left by 39 Who Died Described Cult's Suicide Goal.", March 28, 1997.
[391] Howard Chua-Eoan. Time, "Imprisoned By His Own Passions", New York: Apr. 7, 1997.

Applewhite convinced himself and others he was the right person. As far as Applewhite's religious background, he was brought up in church. His father was a minister. But as it turns out, Heaven's Gate was a modern-day Gnostic, first-century Christian cult. Like the Gnostics, Heaven's Gate believed in the dualism between soul and body. The soul originated from a celestial place and took on a body on Earth. Applewhite did say he felt trapped in his body. Since physicality was evil, sexuality had to be repressed, including acts of reproduction. Androgyny was also emphasized. Members dressed alike with short haircuts. Lastly, Applewhite had apocalyptical visions about the Earth being recycled. [392]

In fairness to UFO buffs, many are repulsed by the beliefs held by Heaven's Gate. UFOlogy, rather than UFO religiosity and spirituality, is preferred by believers. In clarification, UFO believers such as abductees, do not appear to worship aliens. A UFO group such as Heaven's Gate, do worship aliens as postmodern gods. The survival of death was promised with the belief in a soul. Also, Heaven's Gate provided the hope of a better life. They found life on Earth incorrigible. Inspired by science fiction, Heaven's Gate could not distinguish reality from fantasy since it was influenced by pop culture, such as *Star Trek* and *The X-Files*. [393]

While the majority of UFO religion members are White Americans, there have been a few Afrocentric oriented UFO groups. The Nation of Islam has always preached that the White man is the Devil for inflicting historical oppression, including slavery. Included in their beliefs is the Biblical prophet

---

[392] Kenneth L. Woodward and Brad Stone. *Newsweek*, "Christ and Comets", March 7, 1997, p.40.
[393] Richard Corliss. *Time*, "A Star Trek into the X-Files." New York, April 7, 1997, pg.42.

Ezekiel, who was whisked away into the heavens; they considered this encounter to be a UFO. This was thought to have been a message from God as an omen of the impending arrival of the end-time. Modern UFOs are indeed considered doomsday omens, including the destruction of Christianity, the religion of the slave masters who oppressed the black race. Therefore, the only salvation of blacks was conversion to Islam.[394]

The United Nuwaubian Nation of Moors was a full-fledged Afrocentric UFO cult. Originally based in Brooklyn, they moved to the small town of Eatonton, Georgia where they ran into trouble with the locals over illegal use of the land. The Nuwaubians preached a spaceship would land on May 5, 2003 and take the chosen ones, the colored people of planet Earth since their descendants are believed to be Egyptians and Native Americans and are believed to be superior over whites. Founder Malachi Z. York would be arrested as the result of numerous child sexual molestation charges. The end of the Nuwaubians came when their compound was raided.[395]

The theme of sex has been pervasive in the history of many religions. Heaven's Gate insisted celibacy, while the leader of the Nuwabians abused his charismatic powers. Raël, leader of the Raëlians, is also a charismatic leader who preached the freedom of having sex.

The Raëlian movement was founded by the French racecar driver Claude Vorilhon. Calling himself as Raël, Vorilhon claimed he was the half-brother of

---

[394] Michael Lieb. *Children Of Ezekiel: Aliens, UFO's, the Crises of Race, and the Advent of End of Time*. Duke University Press. Durham, N.C., 1998.

[395] Julius H. Bailey, *Journal of the American Academy of Religion*, "The Final Frointier: Secrecy, Identity, and the Media in the rise and Fall of the United Nuwaubian Nation of Moors." June, 2006, pp.302-323.

Jesus and Muhammad. His God is Yahweh while the aliens, the Elohim, are super-scientists. They chose Raël so that he can spread the religion of science and technology. Headquartered in Quebec, Canada, the Raëlian movement challenges the status quo. This UFO religion believes that there are global stressors, such as overpopulation, racism, sexism, and the atomic bomb, all of which must be challenged. The Raëlians have a liberal philosophy towards sex. They practice sex freely with other members of the organization, including multiple partners. Members even proclaim to have sex with aliens. On the practical level, the Raëlians pass out condoms to school kids to prevent teen pregnancy. In perspective, though, the Raëlians are a millenarian religion. They believe a new calendar began right after the dropping of the atomic bomb on Hiroshima. If there is a nuclear holocaust, they believe Raël's group will be saved. The arrival of the Elohim is expected to be in 2035. As materialists, however, Raëliens want to cheat death through cloning, by which eternal life is achieved. Life after death is attained by physical means since Raëlian philosophy rejects the notion of the soul. [396]

As fundamentalists, the Raëlians believe in literal interpretations of Abrahamic texts, using old-time religion in the context of postmodern fears. As many Christians await the return of Christ, the Elohim are expected to return, according to Raël's telepathic messages. As a religion that strictly adheres to materialism, Yahweh – the leader-God of the Elohim – is not supernatural. Only through science and technology can the world be saved. Globalization is only possible through the

---

[396] Susan J. Palmer. *Aliens Adored: Raël's UFO Religion*, Rutgers University Press, New Brunswick, NJ, 2004.

revolutionary abilities of material science by which an Earthly paradise will be forthcoming. [397]

Alien Abduction: Symbol of Moral Regression

We end with a strange trip to another realm, alien abductions. They are interpreted differently by different researchers. Their relation as a religious experience is the most relevant. Whether seeing a UFO or being abducted, the search for cosmic transcendence is part of the UFO myth. We will see in a moment how alien abduction provides a spiritual answer, despite abductees describing their abduction experiences as some form of rape, although we determined earlier they are fantasy role-playing under hypnosis. As a spiritual experience it fits perfectly in a scientific age.

The alien abduction experience became prominent in the 1980s, but even more so by the 1990s. It developed slowly since the 1960s with Barney and Betty Hill, and then exploded right before the millennium. Betty and Barney Hill's alien abduction, which was deemed as nothing more than a dream by their hypnotist, was not a religious experience. It had invasive overtones, the Hills victimized by a sexual-medical experience, an important aspect of the narrative. The Hills' alien abduction account was the first American encounter with purported aliens. It influenced others to have the same experience, eventually becoming an experience with religious properties.

---

[397] Bryan Sentes and Susan Palmer, "Presumed Immanent: The Raëlians, UFO Religions, and the Postmodern Condition." In Diana G. Tumminia, *Alien Worlds*, Ch. 4.

This occurred as abductees influenced each other's experience by reading books by prior abductees. Betty Andreasson, who claimed to have been flown to a magical place, saw her abduction as a religious experience. She was a religious woman who believed in aliens and obviously sought spiritual transcendence, which she found in the context of the UFO myth. Alien abduction researcher Raymond Fowler was not skeptical of Andreasson's fantastical narrative. The creatures and the spiritual beings she encountered were not dismissed as fantasy. Instead, it became common to see the alien abduction narrative as a mystical/spiritual event as more and more individuals, suspecting they were kidnapped, went to see hypnotists and thereby became convinced that they were kidnapped by invaders from outer space.[398] At the threshold of a new era, one could expect – in whatever form of mundane stirrings of one's choosing – drastic changes. One needs to admit how our current postmodern times reflect an unprecedented era in human history. It should be clear that, although UFOs and alien abductions are expressions of myth making, they are products of new forms of consciousness.

Alien abductions provide a sense of wholeness to many who experience them. Researcher John E. Mack took a keen interest in this subject. He disagreed with other researchers, such as Budd Hopkins and David Jacobs, both arguing the alien abduction experience was a physical event. According to Mack, alien abductions do not take place within the traditional framework of the West. To understand John Mack's perspective, we shall explore his perception of reality with his essay "Blowing the Western Mind."

---

[398] Raymond E. Fowler. *The Andreasson Affair*, Prentice-Hall, Inc. Englewood Cliffs, New Jersey, 1978.

John Mack asserts the materialist view arose in the West, which was used to promote dominion over nature and peoples. However, a new paradigm emerged in contrast to materialism; according to Mack, there are realities beyond the physical. This realization emerged in conjunction with the physical stress caused by the Western/materialist view. Besides the material world, consciousness takes place in other realities as well. What takes place in one realm affects the other. Mack believes we can experience other realities without using the traditional empirical method. A change of consciousness is needed, other than the materialist view.[399]

Mack's metaphysical philosophy has quasi-spiritual/fourth dimensional overtones. He seems to be saying that if we adopt the indigenous worldview where spirituality is central, we can live in a more harmonious environment, not to mention having a spiritual connection with other realities. It is not entirely clear whether suspending disbelief of the material world could benefit society as a whole. Still, there are creative individuals who do just that, momentarily suspending disbelief in order to achieve their goals. One, however, cannot expcot to live in a fantasy world. Even if doing so, most are aware stepping back into reality is the safest way to survive.

Since Mack's extraterrestrials are not physical, the alien abduction experience takes place in another dimension and consciousness. Mack is fond of non-Western consciousness and also believes the Earth will go through an alteration of consciousness. This is conveyed telepathically to abductees. The aliens tell their captives there will be cataclysms before consciousness is altered during which the

---

[399] John E. Mack M.D., "Blowing the Western Mind" found in www.johnemackinstitute.org/ejournal/article?id=25.

change would take place during the actual takeover of Earth. To many abductees, aliens are the intermediaries between humans and God, the new angels. When these angels capture abductees, they feel joyous during the trip to the spaceship, for it is as though they are going home. Then the sentiment changes; when the abductees return to Earth, they are sad. [400]

Mack thought the aliens were from another realm although he knew his beliefs were incredible. The abductees came to believe the aliens were spirit guides, such as emissaries from the divine. A sense of love developed between the abductees and the wise and protective aliens. This love becomes impassioned during sexual encounters between aliens and humans. One could equate this with having sex with God, the ultimate passion and awareness as a result. Yet the aliens understood the possibility of the destruction of the Earth since their world was destroyed by science and technology. Therefore, they bring compassion, love, and guidance. Mack believes the union of aliens and humans is an act of religious love, [401] all of which is experienced in the minds of the abductees.

There are different ways to deal with the disenchantment brought on by postmodernism. John Mack's aliens are one way of exploring space age spirituality. Alien abductions provide the experience of the awesome since old-time religion had been a disappointment in the West. This is a liberal spiritual approach among many in the current market. Yet, the rise of materialism in the context of the space age has called for a different kind of cosmic

[400] John E. Mack. *Abduction: Human Encounters With Aliens*, Macmillan Publishing, Co., New York, NY, 1994.
[401] John E. Mack, M.D. *Passport to the Cosmos: Human Transformation and Aliens Encounters*, Crown Publishers, New York, 1999.

transcendence. The need to tap into alternative consciousness is apparent as well as the accompanying beings. These sexual-spiritual experiences fill the void of aloneness. (At least, that is the goal.) However, from the conservative perspective, as we will detail further, fundamentalism has made great strides since the beginning of the post-war period. We cannot assume this is cause and effect, but we can ascertain that as science has shown its propensity for destruction – as demonstrated in Hiroshima and in conjunction with global destruction – life after death, as promised by the Christian script, must be assured.

UFO spirituality, according to Richard Landes, falls into the millennial category. Ever-changing technology makes this so, because the future will likely be improved compared to the present. That is why Landes calls space-alien religiosity millennial. The concern of alien worshippers has everything to do with technological destruction, technology belonging to advanced civilization, not Third World societies. When it comes to far superior alien technology, humans are no match. However, these advanced beings are friendly. And as the new divine order, belief in God may not be the answer. [402]

Millennialism in Perspective

We end our intellectual journey with a brief look at the UFO craze from a global perspective, not just in the West. We will make a brief comparison with the alien abduction phenomenon and the spread of Pentecostalism around the world in order to demonstrate how paranormal experiences are cultural bound, not otherworldly.

---

[402] Richard Landes, *Heaven on Earth: The Varieties of the Millennial Experience*. Oxford University Press, Oxford & New York, 2011, p. 393-5.

The modern age of UFOs began in Europe in 1946, one year before Kenneth Arnold's sighting. The Condon Committee reported, "There were 997 UFO reports that reached the Swedish government from private citizens in that country during 1946." [403] Initially, the Swedish government did not know the origins of these aerial phenomena. Certainly, though, Swedes were seeing things in their sky during that time. They were under stress, the political climate not helping either. It was the beginning of the Cold War, and thus, it was speculated that these "ghost rockets" were confiscated German V-2 missiles from World War II that the Soviets were launching as practice shots. When considering that Sweden distrusted Russia for quite some time, this explanation makes sense. When officials investigated, Swedish authorities concluded that their citizens were witnessing meteor showers under unusual atmospheric conditions. [404] Of course, there was also the social-psychological condition, where apparitions are "seen" as signs of great stress. The literal objects in flight when not at first recognized might be interpreted to fit the current situation. As such, unidentified flying sightings cannot fall under the *Jungian* archetype, since such meteor showers may be interpreted differently to conform to different situations. It was June of 1947 when Kenneth Arnold saw the so-called flying saucer over the skies of the state of Washington. The media influence, a reflection of globalization, placed the flying saucer craze at the fore all over the world, coupled with the stressful fact that relations with the Soviet

---

[403] Daniel S. Gilmor, ed. *Final Report of the Scientific Study of Unidentified Flying Objects: Conducted By the University of Colorado Under Contract to the United States Air Force*. E.P. Dutton & Co., Inc. New York, 1969.

[404] Robert E. Bartholomew and George S. Howard. *UFOs & Alien Contact: Two Centuries of Mystery*. Prometheus Books. Amherst, NY, 1998, see index for "ghost rockets."

Union had continued to dwindle. Thus, the secret-weapon explanation was the most popular one until Donald Keyhoe blamed the Air Force of covering up alien visitations two and a half years later.

It is common to consider UFOs a religious event. This is no exception to the Fátima miracle in Portugal. After the series of sightings of the Virgin Mary from 1916-1917 by three Portuguese children, a crowd was hoping to catch a sighting of the Virgin. On October 13 1917, they witnessed a "dancing sun" after a rainstorm. It appeared to drop from the heavens and back and forth from its original position as it changed colors. Back then, the event was interpreted as a sign from God. After 1947, some believed it to be a UFO, a sign of some unknown divine order who may or may not be God's messenger. According to some Christian fundamentalists, however, these aliens are not benign. Therefore, these evil beings and their reasons for abducting people have everything to do with the current Apocalypse. There is no doubt that Wells' Martians invading London was his parody of the *fin de siècle*.[405] H.G.'s *War of the Worlds* contained blood-sucking Martians, while evil abducting aliens steal human sperm and eggs.

Supernatural sightings can increase exponentially in anticipation of the abrupt change of times. Jesus was very busy exorcising demons in the New Testament, where many during his day believed the end was near. A collective crisis can turn into an epidemic of bizarre behavior. The Fátima miracle took place during World War I, a time of stress. Catholic scholarship has recognized there has been an

---

[405] H.G. Wells, *War of the Worlds*, 1898; *Fin de siècle* was dubbed by the French as the end of the nineteenth century drew near, in anticipation of the dawn of the twentieth century. For a discussion of the *fin de siècle*, see Damian Thompson, *The End of Time: Faith and Fear in the Shadow of the Millennium*. University Press of New England, Hanover & London, 1996, pgs., 103, 104, 107, 110, 117, 118, 120, 126, and 318.

explosion of sightings of the Virgin Mary. Social stress and religious anxiety is rightly recognized as the culprit. [406] Mary speaking to the children, as the crowd gathered, relaying messages of prophecies. (Interestingly, the children served as mouthpieces were engaged in pre-UFO contacteeism). Repent, or face the angry God. It was 1917, the year when Communism was a major threat to the Catholic world. [407] Post-1947 attributes UFOs and alien abductions as expressions that a New Age and a drastic change, is just around the corner.

While we cannot make a definitive connection between supernatural intervention and millennial fears, the connection is hard to ignore. There may be unconscious origins to this, but not exactly in the Jungian sense. There is a level of awareness when interpreting paranormal activities as signs of great change. Damian Thompson makes a good case in his *The End of Time: Faith and Fear in the Shadow of the Millennium.* Since the early days of the Bible, millennialism has been inspired by numbers (i.e. the numbers of the Trinity). Most specifically, is the notion that the Bible was divided by a 1,000 years. Martin Luther, more than any other radical, was the most influential when it came to independent scriptural interpretation. The Reformation started in Germany, then spread to England. English Protestants would take their form of Christianity across the Atlantic. There were millennial movements in the late nineteenth century that died down later. It picked up again in the 1990s with all kinds of charismatic movements that came and went. Some observers

---

[406] John Whelan, "What's Mary trying to Tell Us?", *U.S. Catholic*, August 1991, p.30-36.
[407] Damian Thompson, *The End of Time,* p. 174.

attribute such hysteria to anticipation of the arrival of the third millennium. [408]

While UFO sightings were not as prominent as in years past, the 1980s witnessed the emergence of alien abductions, surging in the 1990s. The concern of environmental disaster was pushed by abductees. Even if one does not believe in alien abductions, it was hard to ignore the millennial frenzy as the 1990s came to a close. Y2K, for example, was a secular form of millennialism. If one is a fan of the *Terminator* films, the scenario of nuclear destruction caused by the worldwide computer networks that became aware was still inviting.

When it comes to the most well-known Space age mythology, the 1970s in general, but more so 1973, was pivotal in leading to the explosive activities of the 1990s. The very last national wave came in 1973, starting in the summer and petering out by October. It started in the American southwest where there were rumors of crashed UFOs. Interestingly, the UFO wave of 1973 inspired Steven Spielberg to direct *Close Encounters of the Third Kind*, where the short and skinny aliens inspired the development of the Greys. As far as skeptics were concerned, the stress of stagnation and most especially the oil embargo were very worrying for many Americans. [409] When it came to reports of UFO crashes, news reports of these accounts were ammunition for some to resurrect the Roswell Incident, which was forgotten in 1947. Since the accusation of the government hiding aliens was dying (Keyhoe's last hurrah), a new twist was needed

[408] Damian Thomas, *The End of Time: Faith and Fear in the Shadow of the Millennium*. University Press of New England, Hanover and London, 1996.
[409] Andreas Killen, *1973 Nervous Breakdown: Watergate, Warhol, and the Birth of Post-Sixties America*. Bloomsbury Publishing, London & New York, 2006, p. 133-6.

to spice up the UFO Conspiracy Theory. This theme took off in the 1980s.

As it turns out, the trend against the U.S. government was on the rise in the 1970s. UFO theorists tied the government's knowledge of extraterrestrials, when the alien abduction narrative and The UFO Conspiracy theory were tied together as overlapping themes. [410] The "invisible government" and its nefarious, secret activities (not just UFOs) were divulged by the government to the public during the 1970s. The government's reasoning for secretly experimenting on humans was a form of Cold War strategy against the Soviets. It was one thing to learn about the covert operation called The Manhattan Project and the devastating effects of atomic radioactivity during the 1950s and 1960s, but it is another to carry out MK Ultra, a secret military project that administered LSD to unsuspecting soldiers to see if they will spill the beans if captured, as a brainwashing experiment. The push through the Freedom of Information Act, has compelled the government to declassify previous secret information. In what could be called, "the Cosmic Watergate," several UFO investigative bodies, from the 1970s through the 1990s, emerged to compel the government to release what it knows. Out of this, the Majestic-12 emerged as documents that purport twelve elitists were part of a secret government within the government – were assembled to study the recovered technology of the alleged UFO that crashed in the summer of 1947. Even if the UFO community called Majestic-12 a hoax, it did not stop many from visiting Roswell and publish their books. The flood of publications led to the percolation of the UFO Conspiracy Theory. As influential author and most famous abductee, Whitley Strieber alludes to the U.S. government having full knowledge of alien abductions

---

[410] Bridget Brown, *They Know Us Better Than We Know Ourselves*, Ch. 6.

and allowing aliens to kidnap humans. Throughout the 1990s, government officials (like President Clinton) publically apologized to the families' victims for government wrongdoings. For example, for four decades ending in 1972, African Americans from Alabama were denied treatment of syphilis (The Tuskegee Experiment), a study done to see its long-term effects. Even public apologies were not enough to the most fanatical UFO conspiracy theorists. (Other type of conspiracy theorists would hold these experiments against the government).

It is our argument that the UFO Conspiracy Theory is a millennial movement. By demonizing the government as an evil bureaucracy, believing that it hides occult-like knowledge, it takes on the role of Antichrist. What the UFO Conspiracy Theory suggests is that the government is deceitful and is not steering society in the right direction. This sentiment has precedents in history. For example, the loudest Protestant critics against the Catholic Church in the sixteenth century were during a time when many believed history will end. [411]

As for those writers going to Roswell to conduct research on the Roswell Incident, these actions have strong overtones of pilgrimage. Going to Roswell is not religious, but visiting this historical site does have meaning, meaning that could be tied to the self-definition of Americanism. The UFO and its dead occupants are reminiscent of the pioneering spirit and pride of the frontier. These aliens trekked from far away, seemingly for particular purposes, but died upon arriving here. As far as the Majestic-12 documents, the number twelve should be significant, indicating the twelve lost tribes of Israel. The hoaxer(s) who pulled the prank may have deliberately selected the number twelve. To

---

[411] Damian, *The End of Time*, p. 74.

the most hardened believers of the 12, elitists mentioned in these documents are evil.

This leads to the Dark Side Hypothesis. As a major strain of the UFO Conspiracy Theory, the hypothesis stresses the government has allowed aliens to abduct people in order to experiment on them, no less unethical procedures. According to the Dark Side Hypothesis, 35 UFOs crashed in the southwestern U.S. and over 100 alien bodies were carted away by the government. High-ranking government officials made a deal with the aliens; in exchange for alien technology, aliens were allowed to abduct humans and experiment on them. These experiments are said to take place in underground bases, such as Area 51. Abductees, though, say the Dulce Facility in New Mexico is the most prominent. It is a multilayered underground research facility. The idea of underground military bases (like Area 51) reasonably exists. But then again, what goes on in these facilities sounds more like folklore than real events. What it appears to be is the dire need to believe in the fantastic, as part of narcissist grand illusions, may be related to mental illness. [412]

As far as we know, no one has come forward to admit Majestic-12 is a hoax, unlike crop circles artists Doug and Dave. These British misfits created intricate designs on farmer's crops and thus the name. Crop circles came into the spotlight when drinking buddies Doug and Dave deliberately and secretly created crop circles in the middle of the night. They started in the 1970s and continued throughout the 1990s. After public arousal by way of

---

[412] Although we don't want to be reductionists, there is a connection between the mentally ill and the belief the government is after them. This I learned from a social worker who works at a psychiatric unit. I also met a chronic mental patient who was so sure the government secretly experimented on him. Nonetheless, we cite Bridget Brown's, *They Know Us Better Than We Know Ourselves*, p. 124-33.

media, they finally admitted to the pranks. [413] The appearance of crop circles dwindled, but never disappeared altogether. Believers in the mystical, attributed crop circles to aliens without the intervention of humans. The weird thing though was how crop circles were being reported all over the world. Skeptics pointed out that there were copycats imitating Doug and Dave. As expected, albeit a minority, swore some crop circles could not have been designed by humans. Rather, there must have been some kind of occult force responsible. Some new-agers tied crop circles to their spirituality.

Hysteria related to alien encounters was occurring in different parts of the world. In Russia, right after the fall of Communism, there was an increase of crop circle reports. Sightings of UFOs and alien abductions also increased. These alien encounters of the Russian kind came right in time for the new millennium. These sightings were not given religious significance by the atheistic Russians. [414] Once Communism fell, this may have unnerved some Russians and Eastern Europeans in general. Mexico was undergoing its own anxiety with the spark of rumors of UFOs. Mexico had their share of sightings, particularly during the 1990s. Besides being influenced by the United States UFO millennial frenzy, Mexico was itself at a time of transition, "As the twenty-first century dawned, Mexicans, like other peoples around the globe, were adjusting to a relatively uncertain and insecure existence in a world of rapid change." [415] Although UFOlogy arrived in

---

[413] Jim Schnabel. *Round In Cirlces: Physicists, Poltergeists, Pranksters and the Secret History of the Cropwatchers*. Hamish Hamilton. London, U.K., 1993.

[414] Sabrina P. Ramet. "UFOs Over Russia and Eastern Europe", *Journal of Popular Culture*. Winter 1998, pg. 81.

[415] Alicia Hernández Chávez. *Mexico: A Brief History*. Translated by Andy Katt. University of California Press, Los Angeles, 2006, pg. 295-296.

late-1970s China,[416] just before the new millennium there were many sightings of weird things in the Chinese sky. It's possible the Gregorian calendar may have been an influence. Some say aliens are interested in China's development. The Chinese have taken the study of UFOlogy seriously. They do not consider it superstition; rather, they call it science.[417] It wouldn't be surprising that the transformation of China has led some to seek the skies for answers. This is common when societies go through stressful and uncertain times. Apparitions are a way to project fears and desires. China's economic boom may have stirred anxiety within its own country. What is suspect is military activity by the Chinese, just like in the early days of the Cold War in the United States. China has also developed a space program. Objects in flight may be secretive and may have mystified aerial observers. The Chinese are not culturally related to Westerners, yet have industrialized their society. They consider mysterious aerial sightings to be interplanetary. Clearly, they borrowed this from the West. The Chinese, like other civilizations, are in debt to the rash of sightings in 1973.

1973 was a major turning point in the history of UFOs and alien abductions. There were several abduction reports; one of them comes from Budd Hopkins; Hopkins reveals how one experiencer one night in 1973 while driving on a particular road in Maryland could not account for the missing time without any UFO sighting.[418] Also in 1973, David Jacobs wrote his dissertation, *"The UFO Controversy in*

---

[416] *UFO Folklore.* See "UFOs in China!" in
www.ufoevidence.org/topics/china.htm July, 2007.
[417] *The Associated Press*, "China Sees UFOs and Calls it Science, Not Superstition." Jan.2, 2000,
www.ufoevidence.org/documents/doc431.htm.
[418] Bridget Brown, p. 41.

America." [419] Because of Hopkins and Jacobs, the alien abduction narrative took off a decade later, including a sinister plot, where fringe minds grabbed the opportunity to blend in their version of the UFO Conspiracy Theory.

The mythical creatures known as chupacabras landed in Puerto Rico as a form of diabolical importance. Extraterrestrial humanoids are distinctive to their country of origin. While the U.S. does have blond-haired, blue-eyed, robotic aliens, the Greys are the most popular type of alien reported. In the island of Puerto Rico, it is no different; known as the "chupacabras," the goatsucker, this creature/humanoid was known to suck the blood of farm animals. During the early 1990s, there were UFO sightings that were later linked to the chupacabras. Sheep were found with puncture wounds on their chests and were drained of blood. People claimed to have seen the creature that was described as demon-like with claws, hairless, and a tail. It also had two legs, was no more than four feet tall, with slanted eyes. Other sightings of dead animals were no longer just sheep, but other animals as well, such as birds, chickens, cows, horses, dogs, and cats. Sightings then spread to other parts of the world – Florida, Texas, and Mexico. Several theories surfaced. The chupacabras was thought to be the result of genetic manipulation. Some speculated that it was a mutation of aliens, yet others thought they were primates who escaped a research center. The chupacabras may have been wild dogs or some unknown creature. And, there is of course, the idea that it may be nothing more than an urban legend. [420]

---

[419] Ibid., p. 43, 65.

[420] James R. Lewis. *UFOs and Popular Culture: An Encyclopedia of a Contemporary Myth.* ABC-CLIO. Denver, Co., 2000, pg. 71-73.

Chupacabras is similar to cattle mutilations, where sightings spread from one Midwestern American state to another during the 1970s. According to speculation, aliens were abducting cattle and taking samples by surgically removing parts of their bodies for scientific study. The hysteria spread to other rural areas, staying in the American scene. If the cattle mutilations were universal, there would have been sightings in other parts of the world. In this same way, the next of kin factor, the connection of ethnic identity, played a role like it did with chupacabras.

Benjamin Radford's investigation into the chupacabra (he prefers chupacabra without the "s") is the best one to date. [421] After five years of investigating the chupacabra, Radford concludes it is completely mythical and hysterical. Despite the lack of physical evidence of this blood-sucking animal, it has folkloric value. This is the heart of our thesis when exploring the meaning of UFOs and alien abduction. The chupacabra was blamed by peasant farmers for killing and sucking their animals dry, as though they were not financially struggling to begin with. Radford asserts this blood-sucking creature represents anti-American imperialism among Puerto Ricans and Latin Americans. Puerto Ricans accepted the theory that the U.S. government made the chupacabra in its laboratory, an experiment gone wrong. Radford traces this Puerto Rican folklore back to Europe's vampire myth. European vampirism, according to Radford, mixed with native cultures outside of Europe. In East Africa, fear of local natives being abducted by blood-sucking creatures reflected Western colonialism. [422] In the Andes of South

---

[421] Benjamin Radford, *Tracking the Chupacabra: The Vampire Beast in Fact, Fiction, and Folklore*. University Press of New Mexico Press, Albuquerque, 2011.
[422] Ibid, p. 26-7.

America, foreigners and Americans can be accused of being disguised *likichiri*, nocturnal "fat stealers," creatures who come to take the fat by surgical precision from the sides of the sleeper. These stolen fats are believed to circulate on the international market. Although the *likichiri* is not supernatural, it does have paranormal abilities[423], similar to the chupacabra. In the end, the chupacabra is nothing more than wild dogs who bite down their fangs on the neck of farm animals, mostly but not always for sport. Among the animals being attacked, not only does death come quickly, the blood settles and in some areas the blood coagulates. When the carcasses were cut open, the farmers could not find blood since they were looking in the wrong place.

The chupacabra emerged as a satanic agent, dubbed as such since farmers were already struggling to make ends meet. Therefore, chupacabras was ominous, a gloomy sign of the Apocalypse. Rumors were spread by the tightly-knit Pentecostal community in Puerto Rico. These were similar to the circumstances surrounding stories of satanic ritual abuse in the late 1980s.[424] Following this pattern, there has been millennialism on a global level. The intensity of the missionary effort in the Third World, the obligation to save souls (collect souls like aliens abduct people), is not coincidental to millennial fears of the late twentieth century,[425] let alone the early twentieth. As per UFO enthusiasts in Puerto Rico, chupacabras were an evil and a serious threat.[426] Likewise, after a chupacabra made its appearance in Nicaragua, a Pentecostal minister interpreted it as a sign of the end.[427]

---

[423] Ibid, p. 29-33.
[424] Ibid, p. 36.
[425] Damian, *The End of Time*, p. 151-2.
[426] Radford, *Tracking the Chupacabra*, p. 42.
[427] Ibid, p. 54.

In perspective, the rash of sightings from all over the world, as is the alien abduction narrative, is millennial. That Chupacabras look hideous and ferocious, its demonic behavior was drawn from the tradition of the Western motif of evil spirits and vampires. The Greys has taken on characteristics of evil beings.

British UFOlogist Jenny Randles considers the state of consciousness while leaving another in the UFO experience as the "Oz factor" referring to Dorothy from the movie *The Wizard of OZ* who found herself in the Land of Oz after being knocked in the head by debris from a tornado. Randles writes, "…creates the impression of temporarily having left our material world and entered another dreamlike place with magical rules." [428] Randles struggles with the idea of otherworldly experiences as inner reality; fairies, apparitions, and tribal states of consciousness are psychological experiences and interpreted as otherworldly. While Randles notes African and Asian abductions are rare compared to the West, she realizes that alien abductions are predominantly Caucasian experiences. They are either deluded or some kind of intelligence prefers white people. [429]

No, this evidence points to a more prosaic explanation – namely that the content of altered states of consciousness, psychological expressions – have everything to do with sociological conditions. In 1973, Sister Agnes Katsuko of Akita, Japan was contacted by the Virgin and told her humanity must repent. If this warning is not heeded, the Father in heaven would make it rain fire and punish the

---

[428] Jenny Randles. *Alien Abductions: The Mystery Solved: Over 200 Documented UFO Kidnappings Investigated.* Inner Light Publications. New Brunswick, N.J., 1998, p. 22.
[429] Ibid, p. 158.

wicked.[430] This nun's mystical event took place during the UFO flap of 1973. This does not mean Sister Agnes was necessarily influenced by the multitude of UFOs in that year, but it is a possibility. One cannot, however, forget how anxiety abounded because of the oil embargo. It is also important to note the general upward trend of mediums onwards from the 1970s.[431]

Comparing UFOs to a manifestation of societal crisis, the twentieth century has also recorded apparitions of the Virgin. Her "witnesses" tend to be peasant children in Catholic countries. A remarkable study was done by a Canadian social scientist, compiling hundreds of reports of Mary. After computer analysis, Mary made her appearances to girls at puberty. Also of interest, many of these girls had lost their mothers or important maternal figures within the last two months.[432] Sex is an important component of paranormal experiences.

Millennium movements, like say that of Damian Thomas, are accompanied by odd behavior. Sex, for example, is practiced in one extreme or another; it is either celibacy or promiscuity.[433] It is certainly not a moot point to once again mention that the alien abduction narrative is full of sex. In fact, John Mack notes how his abductees tend to have psychosexual dysfunctions.[434] The alien abduction narrative is sex crazed, as sex crazed as the Raëliens we saw earlier. Their exact opposite would be the celibate Heaven's Gate. This very odd cult committed suicide, believing their souls were escaping their bodily prisons and ascending to the UFO traveling behind Hale-Bopp Comet in 1997.

---

[430] Thomas, *The End of Time*, p. 179.

[431] Ibid, p. 203.

[432] Ibid, p. 177-83.

[433] Ibid, p. Xii – Xiii.

[434] John E. Mack, *Abduction*, 1994, p. 398.

There are conservative evangelicals who believe they will meet Jesus in the sky once tribulations begin. The ultimate incentive is to preach the word of God to the whole world, known as the Great Commission. Because of such missionary zeal, Pentecostalism spread like wildfire to West Africa, the Far East, and Catholic-dominated Latin America.[435] Recall that alien abductions are Western bound. Thus, we prove its cultural, Earthly origins.

The flip side to alien abductions seems to be possession by the Holy Spirit. The Toronto Blessing, for example, occurred in 1994 at the Airport Vineyard Church near Toronto Airport. This was a sect that taught the forces of the Holy Spirit and evil forces will culminate by the end of the twentieth century. During nightly sermons, numerous worshippers fell and laughed uncontrollably. Since this movement spread to other English-speaking societies, hundreds of thousands were ensnared by spiritual fervor. These altered states were attributed to millennial frenzy.[436] In the 1980s (just as alien abductions were soaring), there were elderly Christian fundamentalists, spreading by books and radio chatter, the expectation of the rapture to occur within the decade.[437] As Pentecostalism spread, it incorporated traditions of shamanism. In the confusion brought on by developing societies within the fast-paced movement of late-twentieth-century modernization, conversion is an overwhelming experience.[438] What needs to be understood is that the conversion experience entails religious warfare against evil spirits and demons.[439] Alien abductees have been having otherworldly experiences of their own as a form of converting to global

---

[435] Thomas, *The End of Time*, p. 152-55.
[436] Ibid, p. 139-41.
[437] Ibid, p. 145.
[438] Ibid, p. 155.
[439] Ibid, p. 159.

consciousness, whether it is mixed with New Age or some other kind of spirituality, let alone the spiritual dimensions of the Ancient Astronaut Theory. Biblical angels transformed from supernatural beings into quasi-physical matter aliens, some benign, others ruthless.

There is a sociopolitical angle in alien abductions. Even in Western countries where the alien narrative is pervasive, despite the fact that there are non-Caucasian populations, abductees have been disproportionally white. The message is to submit to a higher order of things, to a higher civilization. Since populations outside of the West are either developing or undeveloped, the white abductees (even non-white abductees who identify with Western ways), are turning to super-advanced aliens in the current spiritual crisis. In our unprecedented era, on the very heals of globalization, abductees reject materialism in favor of shamanism, albeit in space age form. In some circles, namely those who adhere to Mack's New Age perspective, the incorporation of different religions is welcomed. Liberal abductees tend to fall in this category. However, right-wing Christians do not perceive abducting aliens as benevolent whatsoever. Crusaders against alien abductions put a satanic spin on the narrative as a sign of the end of the world.

In parallel, the missionary zeal of Christians going to non-white and economically impoverished countries is the very opposite of alien abduction because converting to Christianity deals with battling with demons and evil spirits, not with aliens. Alien abductions are rituals, and as such, are cosmic rites of passages. The Christian conversion experience is also a cosmic rite of passage. Both acknowledge there is a universe, but understand it with different lenses. As many people

have claimed to be abducted, the Pentecostal movement
has been far more impressive.

In effect, the spread of global Pentecostalism
is a Eurocentric battle against non-white, non-
Western heathen forces. The conversion experience
involves possession (or abduction) of the Holy
Spirit, often accompanied by speaking in tongues. The
spiritual battle is against evil forces. Thus, the
conversion experience – since it incorporates native
shamanism – is actually a *deconversion* event. No
longer does the shaman experience consist of
interacting with benevolent spirits, since
Pentecostal authorities treat it as demonic activity.
Conversion – as warfare against diabolical forces –
requires exorcism. As a signature occasion,
conversion is a purgatorial act – a charismatic
experience that breaks the ties of native
religiosity.

Earlier we alluded to the regression of the
West. Some have said the West has declined. The West
has decolonized, but in a sense it has not. NATO and
the United Nations revolve around Western ideals. The
obsession of the U.S. is to spread democracy; some
have said it is the political expression of manifest
destiny and there are multitudes of military bases
around the globe. Some have even accused the U.S.
government of being an international dictator, using
whatever resource necessary to police the world. The
most influential form of psychological influence has
historically been the rigorous persuasion of the
missionary. Convert or go to hell. Whenever normalcy
drastically changes or even if the threat of
extinction is perceived, odd behavior can result.
Both ways, abduction and conversion experiences are
rooted in confusion and guilt.

This inner reality is fascinating. As a role
reversal, white guilt in the abduction storyline

places manifest destiny on its head – and those converting to Pentecostal Christianity, through the experience of demonic possession – seem to fend off deep-rooted doubts. It seems plausible such invading demons attacking the bodies of humans may represent unwanted, mundane desires. They could also represent unconscious resentment of religious authority.

Yet it does seem the Left and the Right are warring with each other. The Right's obsession with satanic forces can be traced back to satanic ritual abuse in the early 1980s, a hysteria that spread across American towns. Keep in mind, the abduction craze was beginning to take off. Also keep in mind, both abductions and ritual abuse accusations were done and fostered in therapeutic environments. Indeed, Satanic Ritual Abuse took off because it was the response to the influential wave of New Age spirituality in the 1980s. The channeling of spirits, including space aliens, was associated with satanic worship. *This Present Darkness*, by Frank Peretti sold over a million copies. The fictional story is staged in small-town America, where a very conservative minister leads a campaign against New Age believers and its associative spirits as invasive demons. *Present Darkness*, even to the alarm of moderate conservative evangelicals, has sparked rage and suspicion towards New Age and Leftists Christians. "Regaining lost territory" became a rallying cry against any form of what was viewed as false spirituality and fake Christians, all agents of the Devil. [440]

When it comes to allegations of sexual abuse, Dr. Elizabeth Loftus and her colleague, Katherine Ketcham, were so exact and eloquent about this matter:

---

[440] Thompson, *The End of Time*, p. 159-66.

Rumors and fears are often a thin cover for common prejudices. Satanists, witches, Gypsies, Jews, homosexuals, Communists - really it didn't matter who the "demon" was as long as he encapsulated the most grotesque and tarrying images of evil. All prejudice begins with this process of stereotyping and then projecting outward onto an individual, a non-conforming group, an imagined entity, a political party, or an entire race...the sense, the feeling, or the fear of diabolical malevolence.[441]

The global zeal of Pentecostalism' s mission to convert heathens is their form of manifest destiny. Damian Thompson compares apocalyptic beliefs to orthodox Christianity, where end-time believers have deliberately concentrated their missionary efforts to places where hardcore, Christian conservatism is the religion of the outsider. [442]

Aliens who abduct humans are not necessarily alien forces. Rather they are divine agents who have come to Earth to save humanity from its own peril. At the same time, if they do not hybridize with humans, their extinction is guaranteed. The Space age has brought about a new awareness. According to the alien abduction narrative, humanity ought to humble itself to the grandiosity of the universe. Indeed, materialism did bring progress, but simultaneously damaged different facets of life, including the environment, the break with old-time religion, and the human psyche. The sense of sophisticated civilization; the perception that the right religion, the perception of superior ideology, and the perception of election brought on by world hegemony is not the answer.

But what is the answer? We should suspect humanity will find a way as it usually does.

---

[441] Dr. Elizabeth Loftus and Katherine Ketcham, *The Myth of Repressed Memory: False Memories and Allegations of Sexual Abuse*. St. Martin's Press, New York, 1994, p. 258.

[442] Thompson, *The End of Time*, p. 210.

The alien abduction narrative takes place in a dream state that is riddled with guilt.[443] This is also millennial. As discussed previously, the Greys look like children. These extraterrestrials are sickly and are dying, hence their dire need to hybridize with the human race. Children in impoverished countries are born with a great disadvantage, many suffering from diseases and hunger. The sickly child is reminiscent of the medieval changeling, an ugly child, who might have been mentally retarded, parents at that time believing the unwanted child belonged to the kidnapping-prone fairies. They whipped and shook the child violently with the hopes that the fairies return their actual child. In today's era, unwanted children are aborted. Guilt can still manifest through miscarriages. Self-loathing can result of being a bad mother. As most abductees are women, there is a role reversal, where the alien's oversized eyes is looking down on the abductee who is laying down while she is paralyzed. Such large eyes may have religious overtones, the face of the big-headed alien acting out the Beatific Vision, the holy experience of looking into God's eyes.

The alien abduction motif, once represented by the Greys, has been giving way to the Reptilians (or Reptoids) or lizard-looking aliens since the late 1990s. Christopher Partridge gave a fascinating lecture in 2004 at the University of Chester in the U.K. He discussed how the Greys, drawn from theosophy, have been bumped by the more sinister aliens, having been drawn from the Bible and pop culture sources, namely books and movies. The Bible has been used by Ancient Astronaut Theorists to cite the Watcher angels to claim they had love affairs with human women. The Greek daemons also had sexual

---

[443] David Silvier, "Paradises of Greys Oriental Elements in the Abduction Experience." http://greyfalcon.us/alien%20abduction.htm. Retrieved 4/13/15. You must scroll down.

encounters with human women, only to be classified as strictly evil beings once Christianity became the dominant religion in the Hellenistic Greco-Roman Empire. Both the Watcher angels and the daemons became fallen angels. The present conspiracy theory of David Icke promotes covert secret societies, like the Illuminati. Individuals who hold high-powered positions in government and financial institutions are the hybrid offspring of fallen angels. According to Icke, the fallen angels are not evil entities; they are extraterrestrials who copulated with the women of Earth. Generations later, in our present day, these reptilian hybrids kidnap babies so they could sacrifice them to Satan. As such, the Greys were dethroned. [444]

The Reptilian motif still coincides with the idea of the West and the rest. David Icke's conspiracy theory, albeit dressed up in millennial garb, promotes utter hatred against the power holders. Conspiracy expert Michael Barkun succinctly states, "A main characteristic is a deep suspicion of authority – religious, political, academic, etc." [445] Elaine Pagels hit the nail on the head when stated that just because many in our day and age do not believe in Satan, the evidence shows how conspiracism promotes a cosmic war between good and evil. [446] Just like the days of the New Testament, it is millennial frenzy all over again. Jesus was not only a radical, he lived his life as a peasant who

---

[444] Christopher Partidge, *Understanding the Dark Side: Western Demonology, Satanic Panics, and Alien Abduction.* Chester Academy Press, Chester, U.K., 2006.

[445] Carol Faulkner, "A Culture of Conspiracy: An Interview with Michael Barkun." Usreligion.blogspot.com/2013/04a-culture-of-conspiracy-interview-with.html. Retrieved on 4/08/2015.

[446] Chip Berbet, "Dances with Devils: How Apocalyptic and Millennial Themes Influence Right Wing Scapegoating and Conspiracism." www.publiceye.org/apocalyptic/dances_with_Devils_1.html. Retrieved on 04/08/2015.

physically combatted the greed of the Rabbinic order in Jerusalem during Rome's reign. This was a period filled with many accounts of demonic possession. To the current framework of the conservative Christian, all alien abductions are satanic to begin with, no matter if the aliens are the Greys, Nordic, or Reptilian.

According Partridge's lecture, satanic panics and alien abduction can thank Christian demonology, starting with the apocalyptic theme during the early days of the Bible, culminating during the witch craze in early modern Europe. After centuries of recession, satanic evil made a comeback with pop culture. One can pin point H. G. Wells' *War of the Worlds,* vampire aliens that they are. Wells' invading aliens had a major impact in UFOlore. Repackaged in the 1950s through Hollywood, the alien abduction storyline emerged in the second part of the twentieth century, because of movies and books. [447]

In short, societies, seemingly those who reached post-industrialism, experienced their level of happiness plummet. It is not safe to assume that there is no room for joy, only to recognize the UFO and alien abduction myth represent a pervasive atmosphere of spiritual emptiness. For that matter, believing in UFOs and alien abduction may not be the answer either. Be that as it may, what UFOs and alien abduction teach is that the so-called progress of modernity is actually degradation, and it is alienating!

---

[447] Partridge, *Understanding the Dark Side.*

About the Author

Albert Ramos resides in Manhattan, New York City. He acquired his Bachelor of Arts in sociology from Brooklyn College (CUNY), in 1994.

Ramos is not only a UFO skeptic; he is also a social theorist. He is an opinionated writer and blogger. His blog address is aramosakaprofessorcolumbia.blogspot.com. He is affectionately called "Professor Columbia" since Ramos conducts research at the Columbia University Libraries. Ramos wrote *Why Modern Society Invented UFOs*, is an updated version to *How Modern Society Invented UFO's*, Ramos' very first publication.

Ramos, a fan of religion, does not limit his writing to skepticism. His second publication, *A History of Traditional Eastern Religions from India to Japan*, Ramos discusses religions from the East and how they shaped the cultures and philosophies of those regions.

Ramos is currently working on a colossal project entailing the war between Good and Evil and how they relate to Western notions of progress in religious and secular expressions. *Opposing Forces* traces the history of the Devil and the beginning of apocalyptical fervor and how the saved will go to Heaven. The belief that history is destined to a reach a goal has also been expressed secularly, such as in Marxism. Despite its secular expressions, Ramos shows that satanic evil never dies. The second part of the twentieth century saw the rise of the obsession with evil and how to defeat it. That is why Hollywood's good guy versus bad guy is so alluring.

As a secular expression of Good versus Evil, Ramos' "The Epic Moch Winter Warfare: Why is the

259

Super Bowl a Big Deal?" ties Christmas, a favorite
commercial holiday, with the Super Bowl and its zany
commercials as a festive and capitalist event. This
fascinating   read   can   be   found   at
aramosakaprofessorcolumbia. blogspot. com.

One   can   find   books   by   Albert   Ramos   at
Amazon. com.

Bibliography

Allit, Patrick. 2003. *Religion in America Since 1945: A History.* New York: Columbia University Press.

Andrews, Tamra. 1998. *Legends of the Earth, Sea, and Sky: An Encyclopedia of Nature Myths.* Santa Barbara and Denver: ABC-CLIO.

Appelle, Stuart, Steven Jay Lynn, Leonard Newman, and Amme Malaktaris, Eds. 2014. ""Alien Abduction Experiences." In *Varieties of Anomalous Experience: Examining the Scientific Evidence,* by Etzel, Steven Jay Lynn, and Stanley Krippner, Eds. Cardena, Ch. 8. Washington, D.C.: American Psychological Association.

Arlès, Phillip. 2008. *The Hour of Our Death: The Classic History of Western Attitudes Toward Death Over the Last One Thousand Years.* Vintage Books.

Arndt, Jamie and Jeff Greenberg. 1996. "Fantastic Accounts can Take Many Forms: False Memory Construction? Yes. Escape From Self? We Don't Think So." *Psychological Inquiry* 127.

Aveni, Anthony F. n.d. *Between the Lines: The Mystery of the Giant Ground Drawings of Ancient Nazca, Peru.* Austin: University of Texas Press.

Bailey, Julius H. June 2006. "The Final Frontier: Secrecy, Identity, and the Media in the Rise and Fall of the United Nuwaubian Nation of Moors." *Journal of the Academy of Religion* 302-323.

Barker, Gray. 1956. *They Knew Too Much About Flying Saucers.* New York: University Books.

Barkun, Michael. 2003. *A Culture of Conspiracy: Apocalyptic Vision in Contemporary America.* Berkeley: University of California Press.

Barrett, Deidre. 2010. *Hypnosis and Popular Media.* Santa Barbara: ABC-CLIO.

Bartholomew, E. Robert and George S. Howard. 1998. *UFOs and Alien Contact: Two Centuries of Mystery.* Amherst, NY: Prometheus Books.

Bartholomew, Robert. 2001. *Little Green Men, Meowing Nuns, and Head-Hunting Panics: a Study of Mass Psychogenic Illness and Social Delusion.* Jefferson, NC: McFarland & Company.

Beardslee, David C. and Donald D.O' Dowd. 1961. "The College Student Image of the Scientist." *Science* 997-1001.

Beckley, Timothy Green. 1990. *New World Order: Prophecies from Space: A Channeled by the Ashtar Command.* New Brunswick, NJ: Innerlight Publications.

Beloff, John. 1993. *Parapsychology: A Concise History.* New York: St. Martin's Press.

Benjamin, Noys. 2005. *The Culture of Death.* New York: Berg.

Berlitz, Charles and William L. Moore. (1980) 1988. *The Roswell Incident: The Classic Study of UFO Contact.* New York: Berkeley Books.

Bethurum, Truman. 1964. *Aboard A Flying Saucer.* Los Angeles: Devors & Co.

Billing, Otto. 1982. *Flying Saucers: Magic in the Skies: A Psychohistory.* Cambridge, M.A.: Schenkman Publishing.

Blackmore, Susan. n.d. "Abduction by Aliens or Sleep Paralysis?" *Committe for the Scientific Investigation of Claims of the Paranormal.*

Bleir, Everett F., Ed. 1990. *Science Fiction: The Early Years.* Kent, OH and London: The Kent State University Press.

Bold, Janet. 1997. *Fairies: Real Encounters with Little People.* New York: Carroll and Graf Publishers.

Bowers, Kenneth S. and John D. Eastwood. 1996. "On the Edge of Science: Coping with UFOlogy Scientifically." *Psychological Inquiry* 136.

Boylan, Richard and Lee K. Boylan. n.d. *Close Extraterrestrials Encounters: Positive Expriences With Mysterious Visitors.*

Brandon, Ruth. 1983. *The Spiritualists: The Passion for the Occult in the Nineteenth and Twentieth Centuries.* New York: Alfred A. Knopf, Inc.

Briggs, Katherine. (1978) 2003. *The Vanishing People: Study of Traditional Fairy Beliefs.* London & New York: Routledge.

Broad, William J. 1997. "CIA Admits Goverment Lied About U.F.O. Sightings." *New York Times*, August 3: 1.12.

Brock, J. Erland, General Editor. 1988. *Swedenborg and His Influence.* Bryn Anthen, P.A.: The Academy of New Church.

Brown, Bridget. 2007. *They Know Us Better Than We know Ourselves: The History and Politics of Alien Abductions.* New York and London: New York University Press.

Bruce, Steve. 2002. *God is Dead: Secularization in the West.* Malden, MA: Blackwell Publishing.

Bryan, C.D.B. 1995. *Close Encounters of the Fourth Kind: Alien Abduction, UFO's and the Conference at M.I.T.* New York: Alfred A. Knopf.

Bullard, Thomas. 1989. "UFO Abduction Reports: The Supernatural Kidnap Narrative Returns in Technological Guise." *Journal of American Folklore* 147.

Burton, Dan and David Grandy. 2004. *Magic, Mystery, and Science: The Occcult in Western Civilization.* Bloomington, IN: Indiana University Press.

C., Sherwood John. May/June 2002. "Gray Barker's Book of Bunk: Moth, Saucers, and MIB." *The Skeptical Inquirer.*

Carr, Cynthia. 2006. *Our Town: A Heartland of Lynching, a Haunted Town, and the Hidden History of White America.* New York: Crown Publishers.

Chavez, Alicia Hernandez. 2006. *Mexico: A Brief History.* Los Angeles: University of California Press.

Chernus, Iran. 1986. *Dr. Strangegod: on the Symbolic Meaning of Nuclear Weapons.* Columbia: University of South Carolina Press.

263

Clancy, Susan A. 2005. *Abducted: How People Come to Believe They Were Kidnapped by Aliens.* Cambridge, MA and London: Harvard University Press.

Clark, Jerome. 1998. *The UFO Encyclopedia: The Phenonmenon from the Beginning: Volume 1: A-K, second edition.* Detroit: Omnigraphics.

Clark, Lynn Schofield. 2003. *From Angels to Aliens: Teenagers, the Media, and the Supernatural.* New York & London: Oxford University Press.

Clark, Steven E. and Elizabeth F. Loftus. 1996. "The Construction of Space Alien Abduction Memories." *Psychological Inquiry* 140.

Clute, John and Peter Nicholis, Eds. 1993. *The Encyclopedia of Science Fiction.* London: Orbit, Inc. A division of Little and Company, Ltd.

Colavito, Jason. 2004. "Charioteer of the God." *Skeptic Magazine* 36.

—. 2005. *The Cult of Alien Gods: H.P. Lovecraft and Extraterrestrial Pop Culture.* Amherst, NY: Prometheus Books.

Colorado, University of. 1969. *Final Report of the Scientific Study of Unidentified Flying Objects.* New York: E.P. Dutton and Colorado University Press.

Cooper, Milton William. 1991. *Behold a Pale Horse.* Flagstaff, AZ: Light Technology Publishing.

Corliss, Richard. 1997. "A Star Trek into the X-Files." *Time* 42.

Cowley, Robert. 2005. *The Cold War: A Military History.* New York: Random House.

Crowe, J. Michael. 1986. *The Extraterrestrial Life Debate: 1750-1900: The Idea of Plurality of Worlds from Kant to Lowell.* New York: Cambridge University Press.

Cuoghi, Diego. 2004. "The Art of Imagining UFO's." *Skeptic Magazine.*

Däniken, Erich Von, (1981) 1982. *According to the Evidence: My Proof of Man's Extraterrestrial Origins.* New York: Michael Heron and Souvenir Press.

—. (1968) 1969. *Chariots of the Gods? Memories of the Future_Unsolved Mysteries of the Past.* New York: G.P. Putnam's Sons.

—. (1968) 1970. *Gods from Outerspace: Return to the Stars or Evidence for the Impossible.* New York: G.P. Putnam's Sons.

—. (1972) 1973. *Gold of the Gods.* London: Souvenir Press.

—. 1973. *In Search of Ancient Gods: My Pictorial Evidence for the Impossible.* Toronto: Michael Heron and Souvenir Press.

—. (1974) 1975. *Miracles of the Gods: A Hard Look at the Supernatural.* London: Souvenir Press.

—. 2000. *Odyssey of the Gods: An Alien History of Ancient Greece.* Boston: Element Books.

—. (1981) 1982. *Pathways to the Gods: The Stones of Kiribati.* New York: Michael Heron and Souvenir Press.

—. 1996. *The Eyes of the Sphinx.* New York: Berkeley Books.

—. (1982) 1984. *The Gods and their Design.* London: Michael Heron and Souvenir Press.

—. (1995) 1997. *The Return of the Gods: Evidence of Extraterrestrial Visitations.* Rockport, MA: Element Books.

Dean, John W. 1953. *Flying Saucers and the Scriptures.* New York: The Britisn Book Centre.

Denzler, Brenda. 2003. "Attitudes Toward Religion and Science in the UFO Movement in the United States." In *UFO Religions*, by Christopher, Ed. Partridge, 301-13. New York and London: Routledge.

Derry, Charles. 1977. *Dark Dreams: A Psychological History of the Modern Horror Film.* South Brunswick & New York: A.S. Barnes & Company.

Derry, T.K. and Trevor I. Wiliams. (1960) 1993. *A Short History of Technology: From the Earliest Times to A.D. 1900.* New York: Dover Publications.

Downing, Barry H. 1968. *The Bible and Flying Saucers.* Philadelphia and New York: J.B. Lippincott & Co.

Dr. Dodzik, Peter. 2003. *Is Sleep Paralysis the Cause of Alien Abductions?* April. www.sleepandhealth.com.

Dr. Hynek, J. Allen. (1977) 1998. *The Hynek UFO Report.* New York: Souvenir Press.

Dr. Loftus, Elizabeth and Katherine Ketchman. 1994. *The Myth of Repressed Memory: False Memories and Allegations of Sexual Abuse.* New York: St. Martin's Press.

Dyk, Gregory van. 1997. *The Alien Files: The Secrets of Extraterrestrial Encounters and Abductions.* Rockport, MA: Element.

Egmond, Ton Van. 2007. *Understanding Western Tourists in Developing Countries.* Netherlands: NHTV Breda University of Applied Sciences.

Ellwood, Robert S. 1997. *The Fifties Spiritual Marketplace: American Religion in a Decade of Conflict.* New Brusnwick: Rutgers University Press.

—. 1994. *The Sixties Spiritual Awakening: American Religion Moving from Modern to Postmodernism.* New Brunswick: Rutgers University Press.

Emmott, Bill. 1992. *Japanphobia: The Myth of the Invincible Japanese.* New York: Time Books.

Englehardt, Tom, Second Edition. 2007. *The End of Victory Culture: Cold War America and the Disillusioning of a Generation.* Amherst, MA: University of Massachusetts Press.

Evans-Wentz, W.Y. 1966. *The Fairy in Celtic Countries.* New York: Citadel Press.

Faulkner, Carol, 2013, *U.S. Religion.* April. Accessed April 8, 2015. usreligion.blogspot.com/2013/04a-culture-of-conspiracy-interview-with.html.

Feder, Kenneth L. 1996. *Frauds, Myths, and Mysteries: Science and Pseudoscience in Archaeology, Second Edition.* Mountain View, CA.: Mayfield Publishing Company.

Festinger, Leon, Henry W. Reicken, and Stanley Schacter. 1992. *When Prophecy Fails.* Minneapolis: University of Minnesota Press.

Finucane, Ronald C. 1982. *Appearances of the Dead: A Cultural History of Ghosts.* London: Junction Books.

—. 1996. *Ghosts: Appearances of the Dead and Cultural Transformation.* Amherst, NY: Prometheus Books.

Fiore, Edith. 1989. *Encounters: A Psychologist Reveals Case Studies of Abductions by Extraterrestrials.* Doule Day.

Force, Headquarters of the United States Aif. 1995. *The Roswell Report: Fact vs. Fiction in the New Mexico Dessert.* Washington, D.C.

Fowler, Raymond E. 1978. *The Andreasson Affair.* Englewood Cliffs, NJ: Prentice-Hall, Inc.

Frazer, Kendred. Barry Karr, and Joe Nickell. 1997. *The UFO Invasion: The Roswell Incident, Alien Abductions, and Government Cover ups.* Amherst, NY: Prometheus Books.

Frazer, Kendrick. 1992. "Science is Still Well Regarding in U.S., NSB Report Says." *Skeptical Inquirer* 8-11.

Friedman, Stanton T. and Don Berliner. 1992. *Crash at Corona: The U.S. Military Retrieval and Cover-up of a UFO.* New York: Paragon House.

Friedman, Stanton T. 1996. *Top Secre/Majic.* New York: Manlowe & Company.

Fry, Daniel W. 1952. *The White Sands Incident.* NA: publisher unknown.

Fuller, John G. 1966. *The Interrupted Journey: Two Lost Hours "Aboard a Flying Saucer".* New York: The Dial Press.

267

Gaddis, John Lewis. 1968. *The U.S. and the Origins of the Cold War: 1943-1946.* Ann Arbor: The University of Texas at Austin.

Gilbert, Sandra M. 2006. *Death's Door: Modern Dying and the Ways we Grieve.* New York and London: W.W. Norton & Company.

Gildenberg, B.D. n.d. Accessed June 2007. www.csicop.org/si/2004-05/skyhook.html.

—. 2004. *www.csiop.org/si/2004-05/skyhook.html.* www.csicop.org.

Gilmor, Daniel S. Ed. 1969. *Final Report of the Scientific Study of Unidentfied Flying Objects: Conducted by the University of Colorado Under Contract to the United States Air Force.* New York: E.P. Dutton & Co.

Guiley, Ellen Rosemary. 1994. *The Complete Vampire Companion: Legend and Lore of the Living Dead.* New York: Macmillan.

Hamilton, J. Calvin. n.d. *www.solarviews.com/eng/cometancient.hptl.* Accessed July 2007. www.solarviews.com.

Hancock, Graham, Robert Bauval and John Grisby. 1998. *The Mars Mystery: A Tale of the End of Two Worlds.* London: Michael Joseph.

Henriksen, Margot A. 1997. *Dr. Strangelove's America: Society and Culture in the Atomic Age.* Berkeley: University of California Press.

Henriksen, Margot A. 1997. "The Berlin Crisis, the Bomb Shelter Craze and Bizarre Television: Expressions of an Atomic Bomb Age Counterculture"." In *The Writing on the Cloud: America Confronts the Atomic Bomb*, by Alison M. and Christopher D. Geist, Eds. Scott, 151-173. New York & London: University Press of America.

Holdsworth, Robert D. 1989. *Let Your Life Speak: A Study of Politics, Religion, and Antinuclear Weapons Activism.* Madison: The University of Wisconsin Press.

Holton, Gerald, 1994. "The Antiscience Problem." *Skeptical Inquirer* 264.

Hopkins, Budd and Carol Rainey. 2003. *Sight Unseen: Science, UFO Invisibility and Transgenic Beings.* New York: Pocket Books, division of Simon & Schuster.

Hopkins, Budd. n.d. *Intruder Foundation.* Accessed October 2005. www.intruderfoundation.com.

—. 1981. *Missing Time: A Documented Study of UFO Abductions.* Prentice Hall.

Imbrogno, Phillip J. 2010. *Ultraterrestrial Contact: A Paranormal Investigator's Exploration into the Hidden Experience.* Woodbury, MN: Llewelyn Publications.

Jacobs, David M. 1992. *Secret Life: First Hand Accounts of UFO Abductions.*

—. 1998. *The Threat: Secret Agenda: What the Aliens Really Want and How They Plan to Get It.* New York: Simon & Shuster.

James, King. n.d. "Genesis." In *The Holy Bible: Old and New Testaments* , 19:24-26. NA: Thomas Nelson Bibles.

Jenkins, Phillip. 2004. *Dream Catchers: How Mainstream America Discovered Native Spirituality.* Oxford & New York: Oxford University Press.

Jung, Carl Gustav. (1958) 1978. *Flying Saucers: A Modern Myth of Things Seen in the Skies.* Princeton: Princeton University Press.

Kaku, Michio. 1994. *Hyperspace: A Scientific Odessey through Parallel Universes, Time Warps, and the Tenth Dimension.* New York: Oxford University Press.

Kastenbaum, Robert. 2004. *On Our Way: The Final Passage Through Life and Death.* Los Angeles and Berkely: University of California Press.

Katz, Michael S. 1986. *Ban the Bomb: A History of SANE, the Committee for a Sane Nuclear Policy, 1957-1985.* New York & London: Greenwood Press.

Keel, A. John. n.d. *greyfalcon.us/The%20Man%20who%20Invented%20Flying%20saucers.htm.* Accessed September 11, 2014. www.greyfalcon.us.

Keith, Jim. 1997. *Casebook on the Men in Black.* Lilburn, GA: Illuminati Press.

—. 1999. *Saucers of the Illuminati.* Lilburn, GA: Illuminet Press.

Kellehear, Allan. 2007. *A Social History of Dying.* Cambridge and New York: Cambridge University Press.

Keyhoe, Donald E. 1973. *Aliens From Space: The Real Story of Unidentifed Flying Planets.* Garden City: Doubleday & Co. Inc.

—. 1953. *Flying Saucer From Outer Space.* New York: Henry and Holt Company.

—. 1955. *The Flying Saucer Conspiracy.* New York: Henry Holt and Company.

—. 1960. *The Flying Saucers: Top Secret.* New York: G.P. Putnam's and Sons.

Keyhoe, E. Donald. 1950. *The Flying Saucers Are Real.* New York: Fawcett Publications.

Killen, Andreas. 2006. *1973 Nervous Breakdown: Watergate, Warhol, and the Birth of Post-Sixties America.* London & New York: Bloomsbury Publishing.

King, George and Richard Lawrence. (1956) 1995. *Contact With the Gods From Space: Pathway to the New Millennium.* The Aetherius Society.

Klass, Phillip. 1989. *UFO Abductions: A Dangerous Game.* Buffalo: Prometheus Books.

Kottmeyer, Martin. n.d. *CSiCop.* Accessed September 15, 2012. www.CSiCop.org/sb/show/eyes_that_spoke.

Kunzendorf, Robert G., Nicolas P. Spanos, and Benjamin Wallace, Eds. 1996. *Hypnosis and Imagination.* Amittyville: Baywood Publishing Company, Inc.

Kurtc, Paul. 1992. "The Growth of AntiScience." *Skeptical Inquirer* 8-11.

Landes, Richard. 2011. *Heaven on Earth: The Varieties of the Millennial Experience.* Oxford and New York: Oxford University Press.

Lawler, Andrew. 1996. "Support for Science Stays Strong." *Science* 1256.

Lenski, Noel, Ed. 2006. *The Cambridge Companion to the Age of Constantine.* New York: Cambridge University Press.

Lerro, Bruce. 2000. *From Earth Spirits to Sky Gods: The Socioecological Origins of Monotheism, Individualism, and Hyperabstract Reasoning from the Stone Age to the Axial Iron Age.* New York and Oxford: Lexington Books.

Leslie, Desmond and George Adamski. 1953. *Flying Saucers Have Landed.* New York: The British Book Centre.

Lewis, James R. 2003. *Encycopedia Sourcebook of UFO Religions.* Amherst, NY: Prometheus Books.

—. 2000. *UFOs and Popular Culture: An Encyclopedia of a Contemporary Myth.* Denver: ABC-CLIO.

Lieb, Michael. 1998. *Children of Ezekiel: Aliens, UFO's, the Crisis of Race, and the Advent of End of Time.* Durham, NC: Duke University Press.

Lifton, Robert J. 1967. *Death in Life: Survivors of Hiroshima.* New York: Random House.

Mack, John E. 1994. *Abduction: Human Encounters with Aliens.* New York: Macmillan Publishing.

—. 1999. *Passport to Cosmos: Human Transformation and Alien Encounters.* New York: Crown Publishers.

Marchetti, Gina. 1993. *Romance and the "Yellow Peril:" Race, Sex, and Discursive Stratergies in Hollywood Fiction.* Los Angeles and London: University of California Press.

McAndrew, James. 1997. *The Roswell Report: Case Closed.* Washington, D.C.: U.S. Government Printing Office.

McConkey, Kevin and Peter W. Sheehan. 1995. *Hypnosis, Memory, and Behavior in Criminal Investigation.* New York: The Guilford Press.

McCulley, Dale. Fall 1994. "Satanic Ritual Abuse: A Question of Memory." *Journal of Psychology and Theology* 167-172.

Mcdaid, Liam. 2004. "Legends of the Dogon." *Skeptic Magazine* 40.

McGowan, Don. 1994. *What is Wrong with Jung.* Buffalo: Prometheus Books.

Meehan, Paul. 1998. *Saucer Movies: A Ufological History of the Cinema.* Lanham, M.D.: Cambridge and Malden.

Meeks, Dimitri and Christian Favard-Meeks. 1996. *Daily Life of the Egyptian Gods.* Ithaca, N.Y.: Cornell University Press.

Menzel, Donald H. and Lyle G. Boyd. 1963. *The World of Flying Saucers: A Scientific Examination of a Major Myth of the Space age.* Garden City, NY: Double Day & Co.

Moller, David Wendell. 2000. *Life's End: Technocratic Dying in an Age of Spiritual Yearning.* Amityville, NY: Baywood Publishing Company.

Morris, Narelle. 2011. *Japan-Bashing: Anti-Japanese SInce the 1980s.* New York: Routledge.

Nagel, Robert. 2005. *Space Exploration: Almanac: Volume I.* FarmIngton Hills: Thompson Gale.

Newitz, Annalee. 1993. *Bad Subjects.* May. Accessed September 2007. www.bad.eserver.org/issues/1993/06/newitz.html.

Newman, Leonard S. and Roy F. Baumeister. 1996. "Toward an Explaination of the UFO Abduction Phenomenon: Hypnotic Elaboration, Extraterrestrial Sadomasochism, and Spurious Memories." *Psychological Inquiry* 99.

Nieves-Rivers, Angel. November/December 2003. "The Fellowship of the Rings: UFO RIngs versus Fairy Rings." *Skeptical Inquirer.*

Norman, Ernest L. (1956) 1995. *The Voice of Venus.* Unarius Academy of Science.

Ofshe, Richard and Ethan Waters. 1994. *Making Monsters: False Memories, Psychotherapy, and Sexual Behavior.* New York and London: Charles Scribner Sons.

Palmer, Susan J. 2004. *Aliens Adored: Rael's UFO Religion.* New Brunswick, NJ: Rutgers University Press.

Partridge, Christopher. 2006. "Understanding the Dark Side: Western Demonology, Satanic Panics and Alien Abduction." *Inaugural and Professorial Lectures.* Chester, UK: Chester Academic Press. 1-68.

Partridge, Christopher. 2003. "Understanding UFO Religions and Abduction Spiritualities." In *UFO Religions*, by Christopher, Ed. Partridge, 21-6. London & New York: Routledge.

Passantino, Robert and Gretchen Passantino. Fall 1992. "Satanic Ritual Abuse in Popular Christian Literature: Why Christians fall for a lie searching for the truth." *Journal of Psychology and Theology* 299-305.

Pauwels, Louis and Jacques Bergier. 1960. *The Morning of the Magicians.* London: Souvenir Press.

Pavaski, Ronald E. n.d. *Return to Armageddon: The United States and the Nuclear Arms Race, 1981-1999.* New York: Oxford University Press.

Peterson, Christian. 2003. *Ronald Reagan and Antinuclear Movements in the United States and Western Europe, 1981-1987.* Lewiston, NY and Queens, Ontario: The Edwin Mellen Press.

Pope, Nick. 1997. *The Uninvited: An Expose of the Alien Abduction Phenomenon.* Woodstock & New York: The Overlook Press.

Purkiss, Diane. (2000) 2001. *At the Bottom of the Garden: A Dark History of Fairyland, Hobglobins, and Other Troublesome Things.* New York: New York University Press.

Quigley, Christine. 1996. *The Corpse: a History.* Jefferson, NC: McFarland and Company.

Radford, Benjamin. 2011. *Tracking the Chupacabra: The Vampire Beast in Fact, Fiction, and Folklore.* Albuquerque: University Press of New Mexico.

Ramet, Sabrina P. Winter 1998. "UFOs Over Russia and Eastern Europe." *Journal of Popular Culture* 81.

Randle, Kevin D. 1994. *The Truth About the UFO Crash at Roswell.* New York: M. Evans and Company.

Randle, Kevin. 2007. *Kevin Randle Blogspot.* August. Accessed September 14, 2012. http:kevinrandle.blogspot.com/2007/08/abduction-enigma.html.

Randles, Jenny. 1988. *Alien Abductions: The Mystery Solved: Over 200 Documented UFO Kidnappings Investigated.* New Brunswick: Inner Light Publications.

Randles, Jenny and Peter Warrington. 1985. *Science and UFOs.* New York & Oxford: Basil Blackwell.

Restall, Mathew. 2011. *2012 and the End of the World: The Western Roots of the Mayan Apocalypse.* New York and Toronto: Rowan and Littlefield Publishers.

Rev. Faulkner, John, Ed. 1951. *Arcana Coelitica, The Heavenly Arcana: Contained in the Holy Scriptures or Word of the Lord Unfolded Here Those Which Are In Exodus Together With Wonderful Things Seen in the World of Spirits and in the Heaven of Angels. Vol X.* New York: Swedenborg Foundation, Inc.

Riley, Glenda. 2004. *Confronting Race: Women and Indians on the Frontier.* Albuquerque: University of Albuquerque.

Rojcewicz, Peter M. April/June 1987. "The Men in Black Experience and Tradition: Analogues with Traditional Devil Hypothesis." *Journal of American Folklore* 148-60.

Rojecki, Andrew. 1999. *Silencing the Opposition: Antinuclear Movements and the Media in the Cold War.* Chicago: University of Illonois Press.

Russell, Jeffrey Burton. 1984. *Lucifer: The Devil in the Middle Ages.* Ithaca and London: Cornell University Press.

Ruy, Bruce. 1997. *Hollywood v. the Allens: The Motion Picture Industry's Participation in UFO Disinformation.* Berkeley, CA.

Sagan, Carl and Thorton Pages, Eds. 1972. *UFO's - A Scientific Debate.* Ithaca: Cornell University Press.

Salmi, Hannu. 2008. *Nineteenth-Century Europe: A Cultural History.* Cambridge and Malden, M.A.: Polity Press.

Schlager, Neil. 2000. *Science and Its Times: Understanding the Social Significance of Scientific Discovery.* Farmington Mills, MI: The Gale Group.

Schnabel, Jim. 2004. *Round in Circles: Poltergeists, Pranksters, and the Secret History of the Cropwatchers.* Amherst, NY: Prometheus Books.

Scully, Frank. 1950. *Behind the Flying Saucers.* New York: Henry Holt and Company.

Seed, David. 2004. *Brainwashing: The Fictions of Mind Control: A Study of Novels and Films.* Kent: The Kent State University Press.

Seife, Charles. 2004. "Physics Enters the Twilight Zone." *Science.*

Sentes, Bryan and Susan Palmer. n.d. "Presumed Immanent: The Raelians, UFO Religions, and the Postmodern Condition." In *Aliens Worlds:*, by Diana G. Tumminia.

Sentes, Bryan and Susan Palmer. 2007. "Presumed Immanent: The Raelians, UFO Religions, and the Postmodern Condition." In *Alien Worlds: Social and Religious Dimensions of Extraterrestrial Contact*, by Diana G. Tummni, Ch. 4. Syracuse: Syracuse University Press.

Shaver, Phillip R. and Mario Mikuliner. 2012. "A Body of Terror: Denial of Death and the Creaturely Body." In *Meaning, Morality, and Choice: The Social Psychology of Existential Concerns*, by Phillip R. and Mario Mikuliner, Eds. Shaver, Ch. 5. Washington, D.C.: American Psychological Association.

Shaver, Phillip R. and Mario Mikuliner, Eds. 2012. "Helplesness: A Hidden Liability Associated with Failed Defenses Against

Awareness of Death." In *Meaning, Morality, and Choice: The Social Psychology of Existential Concerns*, by Phillip R. and Mario Mikuliner Shaver, Ch. 2. Washington D.C.: American Psychological Association.

Sherwood, John C. May/Jun 1998. "Gray Barker: My Friend, the Myth Maker." *The Skeptical Inquirer.*

Silver, David. n.d. *Grey Falcon.* Accessed April 13, 2004. http://greyfalcon.us/alien%20abduction.htm. .

Sitchin, Zecharia. 1976. *The 12th Planet.* New York: Stein and Publishers.

Slotkin, Richard. 1973. *Regeneration Through Violence: The Mythology of the American Frontier, 1600-1800.* Middletown, CT: Wesleyan University Press.

Springhall, John. 2001. *Decolonization since 1945.* New York: Palgrave.

Steele, Shelby. 2006. *White Guilt: How Blacks and Whites Together Destroyed the Promise of the Civil Rights Era.* New York: HarperCollins Publishers.

Stephens, Walter. 2002. *Demon Lovers: Witchcraft, Sex, and the Crisis of Belief.* Chicago: University of Chicago Press.

Strieber, Whitley and James W. Kunetka. 1986. *Nature's End: The Consequences of the Twentieth Century.* New York: Warner Books.

Strieber, Whitley. 1987. *Communion: A True Story.* New York: HarperCollins.

—. 1984. *Warday and the Journey Onward.* New York: Holt, Rienehart and Winston.

—. 1985. *Wolf of Shadows.* New York: Alfred A. Knopf.

Temple, Robert K.G. 1976. *The Sirius Mystery.* New York: St. Martin's Press.

Thomas, David E. Sep/Oct. 1998. "The Aztec UFO Symposium: How the Story Started as a Con Game." *Skeptical Inquirer.*

Thomas, Paul. (1962) 1965. *Flying Saucers Through the Ages.* London: Neville Spearman.

Thompson, Damian. 1996. *The End of Time: Faith and Fear in the Shadow of the Millennium.* Hanover & London: University Press of New England.

Thompson, Keith. 1991. *Angels and Aliens: UFOs and the Mythic Imagination.* Reading, MA: Addison-Wesley.

Tucker, Frank H. 1968. *The White Conscience.* New York: Federick Unger Publishing.

Tuella. 1994. *Cosmic Prophecies for the Year 2,000: A Channeled Symposium of What We Can Expect For the Rest of the Decade.* New Brunswick, NJ: Inner Light Publications.

—. 1993. *UFO's To Assist in the Great "Exodus" of Human Souls Off This Planet: Project World Evacuation.* New Brunswick, NJ: Inner Light Publications.

Tumminia, Diana G. 2007. "In the Dreatime of the Saucer People: Sense-Making and Interpretive Boundaries in a Contactee Group." In *Alien Wordls: Social and Religious Dimensions of Extraterrestrial Contact*, by Diane G. Tumminia, Ch. 5. Syracuse: Syracuse University Press.

Turner Ph.D., Karla. 1994. *Taken: Inside the Alien-human Abduction Agenda.* Tallahassee: Rose Printing.

Turner, Alice K. 1993. *History of Hell.* New York: Harcourt Brace & Co.

Upchurch, Thomas Adams. 2008. *Race Relations in the United States, 1960-1980.* Westport, CT & London: Greenwood Press.

Vallée, Jacques. 1965. *Anatomy of Phenomenon: Unidentifed Flying Objects: a Scientific Appraisal.* Chicago: Henry Regnery.

Vallée, Jacques. 2007. "Consciousness, Culture, and UFOs." In *Alien Worlds: Social and Religious Dimensions of Extraterretrial Contact*, by Diana, Ed. Tumnia, 193-209. Syracuse: Syracuse University Press.

—. 1988. *Dimensions: A Casebook of Alien Contact.* London: Souvenir Press.

—. 1969. *Passport to Magonia: On UFO's, Folklore, and Parallel Worlds.* Chicago: Contemporary Books.

Van Dusen, Wilson. (1974) 2004. *The Presence of Other Worlds: The Psychological/Spiritual Findings of Emmanuel Swedenborg.* West Chester, P.A.: Chrysalis Books.

Vorilhon, Claude "Rael". (1986) 1988. *The Message Given to me by Extraterrestrials: They Took Me to their Planet.* Tokyo: AOM Corp.

Walker, Jesse. 2013. *The United States of Paranoia: A Conspiracy Theory.* New York: HarperCollins.

Walter, Barbara, Ed. 1995. *Out of the Ordinary: Folklore and the Supernatural.* Logan: Utah University Press.

Weart, Spencer R. 1988. *Nuclear Fear: A History of Images.* Cambridge, MA and London: Harvard University Press.

Wells, H.G. 1898. *War of the Worlds.*

Wendling, E. Amy. 2009. *Karl Marx and Technology.* New York: Palgrave Macmillan.

White, Carolyn. (1976) 2005. *A History of Irish Fairy Beliefs.* New York: Caroll & Graf Publishers.

Williamson, George Hunt. 1953. *"Other Tongues-Other Flesh".* Amherst, WI: Amherst Press.

Williamson, George Hunt and John McCoy. 1955. *UFO's Confidential! The Meaning Behind the Most Closely Guarded Secret of All Time.* NA: Publisher unknown.

Wright, Lawrence. 1994. *Remembering Satan.* New York: Alfred A. Knopf.

Index